THE PSYCHOLOGY OF

SPINE

SURGERY

THE PSYCHOLOGY OF

SPINE

SURGERY

Andrew R. Block

Robert J. Gatchel

William W. Deardorff

Richard D. Guyer

AMERICAN PSYCHOLOGICAL ASSOCIATION • Washington, DC

BS

First printing March 2003
Second printing January 2004

Published by
American Psychological Association
750 First Street, NE
Washington, DC 20002
www.apa.org

To order
APA Order Department
P.O. Box 92984
Washington, DC 20090-2984
Tel: (800) 374-2721; Direct: (202) 336-5510
Fax: (202) 336-5502; TDD/TTY: (202) 336-6123
On-line: www.apa.org/books/
E-mail: order@apa.org

In the U.K., Europe, Africa, and the Middle East, copies may be ordered from
American Psychological Association
3 Henrietta Street
Covent Garden, London
WC2E 8LU England

Typeset in Goudy by Stephen McDougal, Mechanicsville, MD

Printer: United Book Press, Inc., Baltimore, MD
Cover Designer: Naylor Design, Washington, DC
Technical/Production Editor: Casey Ann Reever

Library of Congress Cataloging-in-Publication Data

The psychology of spine surgery / by Andrew Block ... [et al.].
   p. cm.
   Includes bibliographical references and index.
   ISBN 1-55798-997-4
     1. Spine—Surgery—Psychological aspects. 2. Chronic pain—Treatment.
3. Cognitive therapy. I. Block, Andrew.
   RD768 .P79 2003
   617.5'6059'019—dc21
                                    2002153088

British Library Cataloguing-in-Publication Data
A CIP record is available from the British Library.

Printed in the United States of America

2/27/07

To the spine surgeons of the Texas Back Institute: Stephen Hochschuler, Ralph Rashbaum, Richard D. Guyer, Scott Blumenthal, Jack Zigler, Mike Hisey, Bart Sachs, and Renato Bosita. Thanks for your support and encouragement. To Debbie, for all she is and does.
—*Andrew R. Block*

To my three beautiful granddaughters:
Ellie, Emma, and Iris.
—*Robert J. Gatchel*

To my dear friend, Dr. Ted Goldstein, a unique spine surgeon who truly understands the psychology of spine surgery and a physician who practices the art of healing. To my family, who have supported me through yet another project.
—*William W. Deardorff*

To Leon L. Wiltse, MD, for introducing me to the interplay of mind and body in the treatment of spine injuries. To my father, Samuel Guyer, MD, for inspiring my love for medicine. To my wife, Shelly, and my children Kim, Jeff, and Lindsay for their love and support.
—*Richard D. Guyer*

CONTENTS

PREFACE

The authors of this text include three psychologists (Block, Gatchel, and Deardorff) and one orthopedic spine surgeon (Guyer). We have focused our entire professional careers on the evaluation and treatment of chronic pain patients, especially those with back and neck injuries. In many ways we have changed and evolved our individual and collective foci as the field of spine surgery has grown and evolved. This text represents another step in that evolution.

Each of us began by studying with mentors at once brilliant, forceful, and energetic. For Block these mentors were Rogers Elliott, John Corson, Ed Kremer, and Frank Keefe. Gatchel's interest in health psychology was inspired by Peter Lang, his mentor while in graduate school at the University of Wisconsin. For Deardorff, internship training was provided by one of the undisputed fathers of pain management, William Fordyce. Guyer completed his spine training under two of the major pioneers in spine surgery—Henry Bohlman at Case Western Reserve and Leon Wiltse, Long Beach, California. In fact, it was Leon Wiltse who was among the first to extend his vision beyond the operating room to conduct research on the psychosocial influences on spine surgery outcome.

As the field of pain management has grown, many disciplines have come under its umbrella. So it was natural that spine surgeons and psychologists came together in the 1980s and 1990s. Surgeons have long recognized both the limits of their effectiveness and the fact that emotions and personality can strongly affect the patient's recovery from and rehabilitation after spine surgery. Psychologists, however, recognize that pain almost always has a physiological basis and that patients cannot overcome pain problems without medical treatment. Thus, despite disparate training and perspectives, the psychologist authors of this text joined up with a spine surgeon to extend a biopsychosocial perspective to the understanding and treatment of spine surgery patients.

Each of us has published extensively in the psychology of spine pain and spine surgery. Our publications include academic works (e.g., *Psychosocial Approaches to Pain Management*, Turk & Gatchel, 2002), large compendia (e.g., *Rehabilitation of the Spine*, Hochschuler, Cotler, & Guyer, 1992), clinical guides (e.g., *Presurgical Psychological Screening in Chronic Pain Syndromes*, Block, 1996), and even a mass market book (*Back Pain Remedies for Dummies*, Sinel & Deardorff, 1999). In this book we provide information and guidance on the evaluation and treatment of spine surgery patients that is both academically sound and clinically useful.

In 1999 the psychologist authors of this book, along with Ted Goldstein, MD, presented a series of symposia at annual meetings of the North American Spine Society and the American Academy of Orthopedic Surgeons. This book grew out of these symposia. We express our deep appreciation to Dr. Goldstein for contributing to these symposia and for his support and encouragement, both professionally and personally. We also are extremely grateful to Dr. Donna Ohnmeiss, DSc, for her contributions throughout this book, especially to chapter 1. Vanessa Downing at APA also provided invaluable assistance through the revision and editing process.

The authors would like to make the following acknowledgments: Andrew R. Block thanks his dedicated assistant, Sam Signoretta, for her help in compiling the manuscript and for bearing with him through the preparation of another book. Robert J. Gatchel again expresses his appreciation to Carol Gentry for all of her work during the preparation of this manuscript. William W. Deardorff specially acknowledges his close friend, Dr. John Reeves, for his important contributions to the surgery preparation chapters; much of the material in these chapters was based on their previous book together, *Preparing for Surgery* (Deardorff & Reeves, 1997). Richard D. Guyer thanks Stephen Hochschuler and Ralph Rashbaum for their encouragement.

THE PSYCHOLOGY OF

S P I N E

SURGERY

INTRODUCTION
SPINE SURGERY: THE ELUSIVE
NATURE OF PAIN RELIEF

For the patient with chronic intractable back pain, surgery offers the prospect of dramatic improvement. The hope is that one relatively brief, technologically sophisticated surgical intervention can alter the patient's condition from one of protracted dysfunction, discomfort, and dependency to one of productivity, ease of movement, and emotional stability. Such results, however, are not easily, quickly, or uniformly achieved. Relief, even when it comes, does so slowly and with great effort. Although spine surgery is most often successful in ameliorating painful conditions, on average it leads to only about a 50% reduction in pain level and moderate increases in functional ability—results that may take many months to accomplish. More significantly, about 25% of patients do not experience relief at all.

Patients who have undergone unsuccessful spine surgery may continue along a path marked by increasingly invasive and unsuccessful interventions, leading ultimately to total disability and despair. On the way to this physical and emotional nadir, huge financial, medical, and personal resources are wasted. As one unsuccessful spine surgery leads to another, the direct medical costs can easily mount to six figures. And as time without relief becomes more protracted, the patient's financial resources dwindle—disability benefits are terminated or decreased, medical bills mount, and the possibility of returning to work diminishes. The surgery that once appeared the answer to a desperate prayer becomes a cause of ruin.

Spine surgery's ultimate effectiveness, as we will demonstrate in this book, depends on much more than the surgeons' diagnostic acumen and technical skill. Psychological factors exert very strong influences—ones can that improve, or inhibit, the patient's ultimate recovery. This book examines research demonstrating that surgical results can be greatly augmented by the inclusion of psychological components in the assessment and preparation of patients for spine surgery, as well as in post-operative rehabilitation. We tie this research to information, practical techniques, and suggestions that health psychologists can use in work with spine surgery patients. Health psychologists can be important allies in helping spine surgery patients (and their surgeons) both achieve the improvements they seek and avoid the devastation of failed spine surgery.

LIFE WITH CHRONIC BACK PAIN

The patient with chronic back pain is challenged in many areas. Facing pain on a daily basis can make life depressing, oppressive, and monotonous, and it can force a kind of tunnel vision in which "finding a cure" becomes one's sole focus. In addition, pain inhibits the ability to work, strains financial resources, decreases emotional control, and alters family relationships. Patients vary considerably in their ability to confront life's difficulties, and many have inadequate resources for dealing with the overwhelming effects of chronic pain. Finally, the landscape of treatment for back problems is ever-changing; it is little wonder that the popular press, close friends, or relatives may give charlatans and hucksters credibility equal to that of fellowship-trained spine surgeons.

Low back pain is a nearly ubiquitous medical problem. At least 70% of Americans experience at least one episode of back pain during their lifetimes (Frymoyer et al., 1983; Taylor & Curren, 1985). Back pain is the most common cause of pain-related hospitalizations and was responsible for 2.8% of all hospital discharges in 1976–1980 (Deyo & Tsui-Wu, 1987). Fortunately, 80% to 90% of individuals recover from their back pain, whether they receive treatment or not (Spengler et al., 1986; Waddell, 1987). However, the small percentage of people who do not recover quickly present a costly problem to society and a great challenge to health care providers.

Back pain is the most common reason for filing workers' compensation claims (Guo, Tanaka, Halperis, & Cameron, 1999); 25% of industrial claims are for low back pain, and these claimants consume 87% of the country's total back-related medical costs (Levitt, Johnston, & Beyer, 1971). Other studies have found an even greater disproportion, with 6% to 10% of claimants consuming between 50% and 86% of the total costs related to back pain (Hashemi, Webster, Clancy, & Volinn, 1997; Linton, 1997; Spitzer et al.,

1987). One author estimated that the average annual cost of lost productivity in the United States due to back pain was $28 billion in 1996 (Rizzo, Abbott, & Berger, 1998).

The unfortunate patient who does not recover quickly from back pain faces many perplexing questions: How can I best overcome the difficulties pain causes, while avoiding treatments that will be ineffective? Whom can I trust to heal rather than harm me further? How can I identify the basis of my pain? How do I hold onto realistic hope, when a chorus of voices offer conflicting advice? Finding answers to these questions requires persistence, research, faith, insight, and financial resources—elements that may be elusive when pain is one's constant companion.

The challenges faced by the chronic back pain patient mirror those faced by the patient's physician. The physician is armed with an increasingly sophisticated set of diagnostic procedures and equipment, able to detect even microscopic plausible causes for the pain. Yet these tools often do not provide definitive answers. For example, many tests detect tissue damage in the absence of pain; magnetic resonance imaging identifies disc abnormalities in up to 40% of pain-free individuals (Barron & Zazandijan, 1993; see also chapter 1 for a more thorough discussion). Before undertaking surgery, the surgeon must clearly link any identified physical pathology to the patient's pain experience.

Unfortunately, the intense emotions chronic pain patients experience complicate the medical diagnostic process. It is difficult, if not impossible, for the physician to strip away the depression, stress, and anxiety associated with chronic pain sufficiently to "accurately" assess the patient's pain sensations. Further, the desperate search for a cure may lead the patient to consciously or unconsciously overstate symptoms. The physician must take care not to ignore conflicting, ambiguous, or contradictory medical evidence in the genuine desire to provide such a cure.

The physician faces further obstacles in dealing with insurers and employers, who may have become so (understandably) skeptical of treatment for chronic back pain that they refuse authorization for critical diagnostic procedures and treatments. Underlying the entire process is a medico-legal system that simultaneously penalizes both medical care that could be considered excessive and care that is withheld.

Thus, evaluation and treatment of the chronic pain patient occur in a context of conflicting and sometimes incompatible needs. The patient enters the physician's office with a desperate need for relief of pain and improvement in abilities. The physician must balance a scientific approach to diagnosis and treatment with judgment about the patient's ability to respond to intervention and must beware of responding precipitously to the patient's desperate cries for relief. The employer and insurer, reacting to requests for intervention, need to balance financial concerns with quality of treatment, expediency with measured recovery.

ENTER THE HEALTH PSYCHOLOGIST

Within this conflictual, emotionally charged context of chronic back pain, psychologists and other mental health professionals are increasingly being consulted. Training and experience in behavioral medicine or health psychology enable the psychologist to bring additional clarity and direction to the enigmas of assessing and treating patients with chronic back pain. Their training provides health psychologists with a plethora of information demonstrating the inextricable binding of body and mind. Emotions, for example, can have profound effects on healing, as demonstrated by a study of students who volunteered to be given mucosal wounds (Marucha, Kiecolt-Glaser, & Favagehi, 1998). These students healed more slowly and had less production of proinflammatory cytokines during academic examination periods than during vacations.

Personality also can strongly influence physical factors. Research on the effects of marital conflict in men who scored high for "cynical hostility" found that during conflict these men had greater increases in cardiovascular parameters and suppression of immunologic function than did noncynical men (G. E. Miller, Dopp, Myers, Stevens, & Fahey, 1999). From research demonstrating psychosocial influences on health behaviors, such as smoking cessation, diet or, exercise (Oman & King, 2000), to studies showing the effect of interpersonal factors on adherence to medication and treatment regimens (O'Brien, 1980), the evidence is clear that the relationship between body and mind can be symbiotic—or mutually destructive.

There is no area in which the interdependence of mind and body is better recognized, or perhaps more thoroughly studied, than the relationship of psychosocial factors to chronic pain. Nearly every text on chronic pain acknowledges this relationship in large sections examining emotional and behavioral components of the pain experience (e.g., Loeser, Butler, Chapman, & Turk, 2001). Many texts used in health psychology training programs specifically address the interface of physical and mental factors (Block, Kremer, & Fernandez, 1999; Gatchel & Turk, 1999). Spine surgeons, despite their rigorous training in diagnostic acumen and surgical techniques, are increasingly acknowledging the importance of psychological assessment of spine surgery candidates. Leon Wiltse, one of the most respected spine surgeons in the United States, observed that

> A given patient's response to pain is very much a psychological phenomenon. . . . Even if the patient has objective findings which justify surgery, arrangements should be made for psychological counseling before and after surgery. . . . If the patient has unfavorable findings by psychological testing, and few objective findings, the surgeon should be very slow to resort to surgical treatment, since the symptoms are not likely to be relieved. (Wiltse & Rocchio, 1975, p. 482).

GENERAL PLAN OF THE BOOK

This book is designed to provide health psychologists with information and techniques that can help them (a) identify patients for whom psychosocial factors make it unlikely that spine surgery will be effective; (b) prepare patients to undergo spine surgery; and (c) improve rehabilitation outcomes for chronic back pain patients who undergo spine surgery. The book opens with a part (chapter 1) on the physiologic bases of spine pain and the surgical techniques used to correct underlying pathology. Part 1 also introduces failed back surgery syndrome, for which surgical procedures are designed to ameliorate pain rather than to remove or correct the source of the pain.

Part 2 of the book (chapters 2 through 6) discusses presurgical psychological screening, a method for identifying patients at high risk for poor surgery results. This part reviews all available literature that has examined factors negatively influencing outcome. A model and procedures for determining surgical prognosis are described.

Part 3 (chapters 7 through 10) examines treatment procedures used to prepare the patient for spine surgery. In more than 200 research studies conducted over the past 30 years, psychological interventions that help prepare the patient for surgery interventions have been shown to produce the following benefits: decreased patient distress before and after surgery, reduced need for pain medications, fewer postoperative complications, quicker return to health, enhanced patient satisfaction, reduced health care demands and utilization, and potential savings of thousands of dollars per surgery. This part provides many practical suggestions psychologists can use in preparing patients for surgery.

The final part of this book (chapters 11 and 12) examines the influence of psychosocial factors on the postoperative rehabilitation process. Part 4 reviews a widely used rehabilitation model, functional restoration, and demonstrates how it has been successfully applied in recent years following spine surgery. Again, the emphasis is on practical suggestions, particularly for health psychologists. Finally, a Glossary at the end of the book provides definitions for the terms used throughout the text.

I

SPINE INJURIES

1

THE HUMAN SPINE: BASIC ANATOMY AND SURGICAL PROCEDURES

Spine surgery is science and art, intuition and expertise. The protracted pain experiences that bring patients to the office of a spine surgeon have causes that range from frustratingly subtle to screamingly obvious. The success of spine surgery depends not only on careful identification of the basis of pain, but also on the experience and technical skill of the surgeon in correcting underlying pathological conditions. In this chapter we begin with a brief overview of spine anatomy and then review the types of injuries and conditions that surgeons may identify as the cause of protracted back pain. We also discuss the types of surgeries available to correct or ameliorate these conditions.

It is critical that the health psychologist involved in presurgical psychological screening (PPS) understand both the pathological conditions and the surgeries designed to overcome them. Armed with such knowledge, the psychologist is in a much better position to understand the stamina, patience, and energy required for recovery. Further, knowledge of spine anatomy and interventions allows the psychologist to better assist in preparing the patient to undergo surgery.

With contributions by Dr. Donna Ohnmeiss.

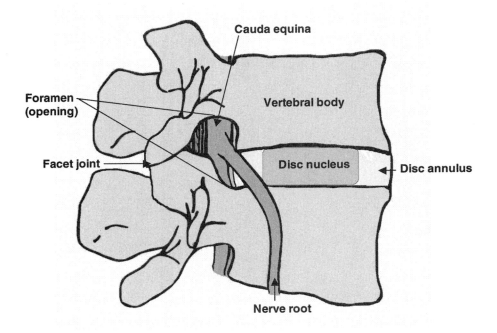

Cauda equina

Foramen
(opening)

Vertebral body

Facet joint

Disc nucleus

Disc annulus

Nerve root

Figure 1.1. A spinal segment, composed of two vertebrae and an interposed disc.

BASIC SPINE ANATOMY

The lumbosacral spine comprises five vertebral bodies in the lumbar spine and the sacrum. Each vertebra is made up of the body and the posterior elements (Figure 1.1). The vertebral body provides support to the trunk. The posterior elements are load bearing, play a role in trunk motion, and create protected passageways for neural structures. The spinal cord ends at the upper end of the lumbar spine. Below the spinal cord is the cauda equina, which is formed by the nerve roots that exit at each vertebral level through a passageway called the foramen. The facets of adjacent vertebral bodies meet to form the facet joints. These joints have a role in load bearing and in motion of the spinal segment.

A spinal motion segment is made up of two vertebrae and the intervening intervertebral disc. The center of the disc is the disc nucleus, which is surrounded by multiple layers of a stiffer cartilage called the disc annulus (see Figures 1.1 and 1.2). The disc endplate is the interface with the vertebral bodies. The disc is avascular and receives nutrients only through diffusion from the vertebral body through the endplates. A normal disc nucleus has a high water content and assists in load bearing. A spinal motion segment is sometimes referred to as a "three-joint complex," formed by the disc and the related two facet joints at each spinal level. Pain may arise from compression

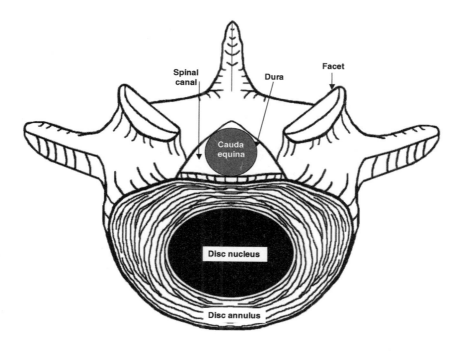

Figure 1.2. Axial view of a lumbar vertebra and disc, also showing the cauda equina.

of the neural tissue by either disc or bone, from the disc itself, or from the facet joints, ligaments, or boney fracture of a vertebra.

SPINE CONDITIONS FOR WHICH SURGERY IS CONSIDERED

Except in emergency cases, back pain patients should undergo a comprehensive program of nonoperative treatment before considering spine surgery. This nonoperative care should incorporate medication, education, stretching, strengthening, and possibly other efforts such as weight reduction, smoking cessation, relaxation or stress management, and coping skills. Fortunately, fewer than 1% of individuals with back pain eventually undergo surgery; these patient have failed to gain adequate pain relief from nonoperative management. The following sections of this chapter discuss several of the most common conditions for which surgery may be considered.

Disc Bulge, Herniation, and Disruption

There is much controversy in the literature of radiologists, as well as of spine surgeons (both orthopedic and neurosurgical), as to when a disc bulge is significant. It is part of the normal aging process for a disc to bulge. As a disc degenerates and its height decreases, the diameter of the disc increases. This is similar to a tire losing air, resulting in the bulging of its sidewalls. The structure of the disc remains intact. A disc bulge is not necessarily pathologic. However, a disc bulge in the presence of a congenitally small spinal canal may cause pain by compressing the nerve roots.

A disc herniation can be thought of as the next progression of a disc bulge. The nucleus continues to degenerate and the annular fibers begin to tear, allowing the nuclear material to protrude against the annulus wall, which then bulges and compresses the nerve root. There are different types of disc herniation. One is a contained herniation, in which the outer wall of the annulus remains intact, but tissue from the nucleus passes through tears in the annular layers. The outer layers of the annulus are innervated by nociceptors (damage-sensing nerve fibers), and thus a tear in the disc may be painful. Also, the nucleus contains neurotoxic agents that may cause chemical irritation of the nociceptors in the outer annulus (see Figure 1.3).

A more severe herniation results in a piece of the nucleus passing all the way through the outer wall of the annulus. In this situation, the fragment may cause nerve root compression, and the nucleus's neurotoxic agents may cause chemical irritation of the nerve roots. In some cases, this fragment becomes completely separated from the disc and travels into the spinal canal. Some patients perceive that this fragment floats around; however, it does not float, but rather stays where it has been extruded.

The next condition, which is more controversial, is called *disc disruption*. Disc disruption represents the earliest phases of disc degeneration, in which one may see only a tear of the annulus of the disc. Often magnetic resonance imaging (MRI) will show dehydration of the disc (the disc appears dark on the MRI scan). Symptomatic disc disruption is diagnosed by discography showing a tear of the ring of the disc with the patient's symptoms being reproduced during the disc injection. Some practitioners feel that discography is not reliable, but nonetheless it remains the only test available to determine the sensitivity of the annular fibers.

Spinal Stenosis

Stenosis is a narrowing of a passageway. There are two primary locations of spinal stenosis: the spinal canal may narrow where the spinal cord or cauda equina passes, and the foraminal openings may narrow where the nerve roots exit from the central spinal canal. Spinal stenosis is a very common problem that becomes more prevalent with aging. Stenosis may be congenital or acquired in nature. In individuals born with a small spinal canal, problems can occur through bulging of the disc or thickening of the ligaments (that is, the ligamentum flavum) around the nerve sac. Acquired spinal stenosis occurs usually in older adults from the sixth decade on; the ligaments shorten and thicken as the disc narrows. The facet joints hypertrophy (i.e.,

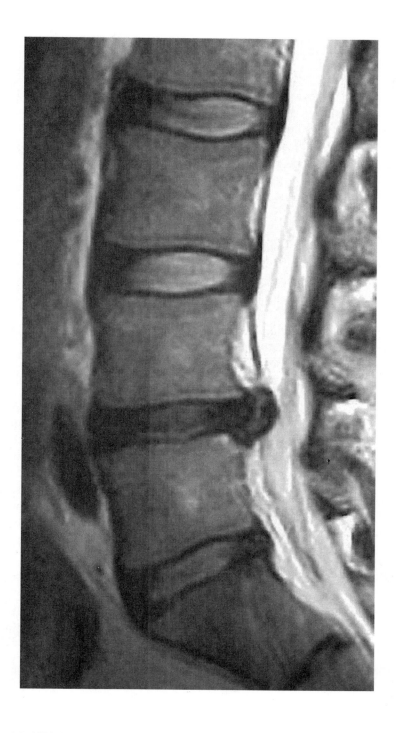

Figure 1.3. MRI demonstrating disc degeneration and a large disc herniation at the L4-5 level. Note the degeneration of the disc, indicated by its dark appearance compared to the other discs.

enlarge), and all these factors result in a narrowing of the spinal canal or foramen, or both. This creates problems consistent with spinal stenosis, or even pain with progressive ambulation. Typically, patients have less pain when they bend forward and have more pain when they extend. They feel worse when walking down a hill and better walking up a hill. When bending forward in walking up a hill, the foramina, the openings where the nerve roots exit from the cauda equina, open up, decompressing (relieving pressure from) the nerve roots. When walking down a hill, one tends to lean backwards to maintain the center of gravity. Bending backward causes these spaces to become even smaller, further compressing the nerve roots.

Spondylosis

Spondylosis is related to disc degeneration and results in a narrowing of the spinal canal, which may cause compression of the cauda equina or nerve roots. Radiographically, spondylosis can be manifest by a narrowing of the disc or by the presence of bone spurs (osteophytes) on the periphery of the vertebral body. Spondylosis is not necessarily a source of pain, but it reflects the age-related degeneration of the spine. The condition may occur in conjunction with acquired stenosis.

Spondylolisthesis

Spondylolisthesis is a condition in which the pars interarticularis (the bony structure that joins the upper and lower facet joint of a vertebrae) develops a stress fracture and then heals with fibrous tissue. If it is unilateral, it is called spondylolysis (not to be confused with spondylosis); if it is bilateral, the vertebral body can slip out of alignment, producing spondylolisthesis. Spondylolisthesis is graded into four categories based on the extent to which the upper vertebral body has slipped across the lower vertebral body. Grades I through IV are defined as follows: 0% to 25%, 26% to 50%, 51% to 75%, and 76% to 100%. Usually the stress fractures occur between the ages of 5 and 20 years. In the United States the prevalence among men is 7.5%, with a lower prevalence in women of 5.5%. There is some variation based on ethnicity; for example, American Eskimos have a much higher incidence of approximately 50% (Kettelkamp & Wright, 1971).

Spondylolisthesis can also be related to activities. For example, the incidence is greater in gymnasts and interior football linemen due to the progressive trauma of hyperextension that they repeatedly demand from their spines. The fracture of the pars may be painful; however, pain may be produced by compression of the nerve roots as the superior vertebral body moves forward relative to the inferior body. Also, the disc at the involved level may become painful if it is injured or torn due to the slippage of the superior vertebral body.

Failed Back Surgery Syndrome

Failed back surgery syndrome is a vague term often applied when an individual has undergone a previous surgery and has had a poor outcome. Failed back surgery syndrome can arise from multiple etiologies. The most common etiology is poor selection—that is, surgery for back pain in an individual with a poor psychological profile and borderline pathologic indications (Oaklander & North, 2001). Also, poor selection may stem from an inadequate diagnostic workup that did not fully or correctly identify the origins of the patient's pain.

Other etiologies of failed back surgery syndrome arise from the procedure itself. This syndrome can follow from a procedure that is performed at the wrong level of the spine, that is inappropriate for the patient's problems, or that is poorly performed technically. Also, the procedure may damage the nerve roots, causing short- or long-term problems. In some cases, significant scarring from the surgery may cause compression of the nerve roots or may tether the nerve root, making it less mobile and more likely to be affected by a small disc herniation.

Other definable causes of failed back surgery syndrome are recurrent disc herniation and symptomatic pseudoarthrosis (failure to achieve bony union in an attempted spinal fusion). In the typical course of recurrent disc herniation, a patient does well for a period of time following discectomy and then has a new onset of radicular pain.

Scar tissue resulting from a discectomy procedure may also be a cause of renewed pain after surgery. In some cases, this is difficult to distinguish from recurrent disc herniation, but clinical evaluation, careful history taking, and MRI scanning with and without contrast can be very helpful in making this differential diagnosis.

The most frustrating group of failed back surgery patients are those with no identified behavioral problems, a clear diagnosis with correlating physical examination and imaging studies, and a technically correct procedure with no complications, but who fail to achieve a good result and who have no clearly identifiable cause for ongoing symptoms.

DIAGNOSTIC PROCEDURES

Certainly, trauma can lead to spinal fractures. However, most back injuries are soft tissue injuries of the muscles, ligaments, and discs. A great challenge in treating patients with back pain is the difficulty in accurately diagnosing the structure, or structures, that have been injured and are responsible for producing the pain. This challenge has two primary components. First, one must be able to identify a tissue abnormality. Second, and more difficult, one must determine if the tissue abnormality is related to the patient's symptoms. The physician must use a comprehensive physical examination and history combined with the results of imaging and other evaluations to arrive at a diagnosis. A number of diagnostic procedures can be used to help determine the etiology of the patient's pain, including plain radiographs, computed tomography (CT), magnetic resonance imaging, myelography, bone scanning, electromyography (EMG), discography, facet joint injections, differential spinal, and sacroiliac joint injections.

Plain Radiographs

The first and most basic imaging study is the plain radiograph. Radiography is important because it gives an overall view of the alignment of the spine. Perhaps the most important plain radiographs are those made with the patient in flexion and extension while standing. These often demonstrate instability of the lumbar spine that is not easily seen in a supine anterior/posterior or lateral radiograph. Disc space narrowing, which is related to severe disc degeneration, can be assessed from lateral radiographs. Plain radiographs can also identify evidence of spondylolisthesis and other deformities of the spine, such as scoliosis.

Computed Tomography

Computed tomography (CT) scanning is performed with the patient lying on a table with a large cylinder around it. Like a plain radiograph, CT uses radiation to generate images. Unlike radiography, it creates cross-sectional views of the body. CT is helpful in visualizing bony structures in great detail and shows arthritic changes of the spine, spinal stenosis, and evidence of stress fractures, as well as disc herniations. CT has been largely supplanted by the newer technology magnetic resonance imaging. CT scanning is still very useful when performed after the injection of contrast in procedures such as myelography and discography (see below). Postinjection CT studies provide an axial view through the spine, allowing one to better determine the location and extent of abnormalities.

Magnetic Resonance Imaging

MRI (Figure 1.1) is probably the best diagnostic tool after radiographs. During the scanning procedure, the patient is positioned in a tube housing a large, strong magnet. The magnetism interacts with the cells of the patient's body. Based primarily on the water content of various tissues, an image is produced that helps identify soft-tissue abnormalities. Approximately 10% of patients are claustrophobic and cannot tolerate being placed inside the tube-like structure. Such patients can be given a mild sedative to keep them relaxed during the scanning.

Open MRI scanners have been developed; in some cases the image quality is not as good as that achieved using traditional scanners, but this technology is continually improving. Upright scanners are also being developed that will allow the patient to be scanned while standing and in flexion and extension. These may prove to be very helpful; back pain can be mechanical and affected by load and position, factors that cannot be investigated with the patient in the supine position in traditional scanners. In addition, the quality of any MRI is compromised if the patient moves while the image in being generated, presenting a difficulty with patients trying to maintain a fixed standing posture.

Although MRI is a very good tool for spinal imaging, there are difficulties with clinical application of its results in identifying the source of the patient's pain. Several studies reporting the results of MRI in persons with no back pain have found abnormalities in 28% to 76% of participants (Boden, Davis, Dina, Patronas, & Wiesel, 1990; Boos et al., 1995; M. C. Jensen et al., 1994) The greatest percentage of abnormal MRI results in asymptomatic participants was identified in a group matched by age, gender, and occupation to a group of back pain patients (Boos et al., 1995). The authors of the study followed a group of 46 asymptomatic participants for an average of 5 years and found that physical job characteristics and psychological aspects of work were stronger predictors of the development of back pain than were abnormalities seen on the initial MRI (Boos et al., 2000). These results emphasize the importance of correlating the abnormalities visualized using imaging with a detailed analysis of the patient's complaints.

Myelography

Myelography, which has been used for several decades, has been the mainstay of spinal evaluation but lacks the ability of the MRI scan to clearly delineate spinal tumors or to scan and screen the lower thoracic and lumbar spine. Myelography is performed by injecting a water-soluble contrast into the dural sac. If there is compression on the sac, a filling defect or a compression of a nerve will appear, indicating a defect. Myelography combined with CT scanning leads to a very accurate diagnosis for spinal stenosis. The axial CT views obtained with the contrast in the dural sac allow good delineation of the location and extent of nerve compression.

Myelography has an advantage over MRI in that one can obtain radiographic views with the patient in the upright position and in flexion and extension, enabling one to truly see the effects of the bulging disc and signs of instability. In many cases the combination of CT and myelogram with flexion and extension films can render visible a spondylolisthesis that is not visualized by MRI. Although MRI is a valuable diagnostic tool, many radiologists and clinicians think that the CT with myelogram remains the gold standard for patients with stenosis, particularly in the cervical spine.

Bone Scanning

In bone scanning, radioactive technetium is injected into the patient's vein. Calcium is tagged with the radioactive technetium, which is then taken up in areas of active bone repair. The patient is scanned 3 hours later with a Geiger counter-type machine that shows "hot" spots associated with areas of high activity related to repair of a stress fracture, tumor, or infection. (MRI is much more sensitive for the diagnosis of spinal tumors.)

Electromyography

The electromyogram, a nerve conduction study, is helpful for patients who have leg complaints with weakness, numbness, or pain, but in whom the clinician cannot find any objective abnormality by examination. A negative EMG is a strong indication that the patient is not having any significant nerve compression or irritation.

Discography

Discography is a unique evaluation in that it is a radiographic evaluation as well as a pain modulation test. Radiographic contrast material is injected into the nucleus of intervertebral discs suspected of being degenerated or disrupted. A postdiscogram CT scan allows determination of damage to the disc. The discogram procedure is unique because injection of a damaged disc frequently provokes the patient's normally occurring pain (in 93% of cases), whereas injection of a normal disc is not pain provocative (Vanharanta et al., 1987).

Discography has been available since the late 1940s and has been the source of much controversy. Today, however, it is generally accepted, although there are still opponents who feel that it lacks sensitivity. The most recent criticism of discography stems from studies performed by Carragee et al. (Carragee et al., 1999, 2000), who performed discography in patients with no current low back pain who had undergone cervical spine surgery (Carragee et al., 2000). They found that among patients with a good result from cervical spine surgery, only 10% reported pain during discography, whereas 40% of those with a poor outcome and 83% of those with a somatization disorder reported pain during discography. This study suffers from the same primary shortcoming as others of its type. For a discogram to be considered as having a clinically positive finding, pain similar to the patient's presenting symptoms must be produced. By definition, this cannot happen in an asymptomatic participant. In patients undergoing discography, some do experience pain that is dissimilar to their typical symptoms, a finding that excludes the disc as the source of the patient's pain. Dissimilar pain is more frequently provoked in older participants with degenerated discs than in younger participants (Vanharanta et al., 1989).

The Carragee et al. (2000) study confirmed the results of two previous studies finding that there is a behavioral component to discographic pain provocation. One study found that elevated scores on the Hysteria and Hypochondriasis scales of the Minnesota Multiphasic Personality Inventory–2 (MMPI-2) were related to an increased incidence of patients reporting pain during the injection of a nondisrupted disc (Block, Vanharanta, Ohnmeiss, & Guyer, 1996; see chapter 4 for further discussion). Similarly, patients with abnormal pain drawings were found to be more likely to report pain during the injection of a nondisrupted disc (Ohnmeiss, Vanharanta, & Guyer, 1995).

Although the results of discography can be questioned, it is the only test that allows a true diagnosis of internal anatomic abnormalities of the disc (Figure 1.2). Furthermore, it provides a pain provocation test; if the contrast injection reproduces the patient's pain exactly, the clinician has more information on which to base a diagnosis of the source of the pain. Conversely, in some cases a xylocaine discogram may be performed; instead of provoking pain, the physician injects an anesthetic agent into the disc to determine if this provides temporary relief of the patient's pain. If so, it provides support that the disc is related to their clinical symptoms.

Facet Joint Injections

Facet joint injections involve the instillation of a local anesthetic along with steroids into the facet joints to determine if the pain is coming from the joints. If the patient experiences immediate relief of pain, one can surmise that some of the pain is coming from the facet joints. It must be kept in mind that 25% of body weight is borne by the facet joints and the other 75% by the discs. In a review of the literature on low back pain and facet joints, it was reported that 15% to 40% of chronic low back pain is attributable to the facet joints (Dreyer & Dreyfuss, 1996). However, although there is a mechanical relationship between the facets and the disc, facet joint pain is rarely associated with discogenic pain (Schwarzer et al., 1994). It may be that discogenic pain and facet joint pain occur at different phases of the deterioration of the spinal segment.

Differential Spinal

The differential spinal is a study that is sometimes used with the goal of determining whether the patient has "central pain" (modified by the patient's psychological makeup) versus "peripheral pain" (arising from local structures within the lumbar spine or leg). The patient is injected with an anesthetic that will produce a block first of the sympathetic nerves, then of the sensory nerves, and finally of the motor nerves. Some consider this test to constitute a chemical transection of the spinal cord, because once the block is complete, no nerve input can ascend beyond the level of the block. If indeed the patient still complains of pain after having a block, the pain may be more centrally mediated, that is, may have a psychological basis.

Sacroiliac Joint Injections

The sacroiliac joint should not be overlooked as a possible origin of pain in the low back, buttocks, and possibly thighs. Sacroiliac joint injections are similar to facet joint injections in that an anesthetic agent is injected into the joint. If the patient experiences a significant reduction in pain, the sacroiliac joint may have a role in the patient's pain complaints. In 43 chronic pain patients with pain centered below the L5-S1 level who were referred for other diagnostic procedures, sacroiliac joint anesthetic injections were also performed (Schwarzer, Aprill, & Bogduk, 1995); 63% of the patients reported similar or exact reproduction of their pain. Gratifying or total pain relief was achieved in 30% of the 43 patients on injection of a local anesthetic into the sacroiliac joint. This study, along with others, supports the assertion that the sacroiliac joint is a source of symptoms in an appreciable percentage of patients and is likely often overlooked.

SURGICAL PROCEDURES

Surgery for back pain is a last resort. Except in emergency situations, many treatment options can and should be attempted before considering invasive interventions. The first regimen consists of reduced or modified activities and medications. Although reduced activities may help give injured tissue an opportunity to heal, bedrest for longer than 2 days should be avoided (Deyo, Diehl, & Rosenthal, 1986). The next phase of treatment should incorporate stretching and exercise undertaken progressively, beginning with light activities and progressing to more demanding activities. Treatment under the supervision of a physiatrist, chiropractor, or physical therapist is generally helpful at this point. Patients should understand that this phase may not result in immediate relief; in fact, they may experience flare-ups of their symptoms before getting significant relief.

One group of investigators compared the results of three treatments for acute back pain: bed rest of 2 days duration, mobilization exercises, or continuation of normal activities as tolerated (Malmivaara et al., 1995). They found that the group assigned to normal activities had better results than either of the other two groups. Indahl, Velund, & Reikeraas (1995) compared the results of back pain treatment using conventional methods with treatment using patient education with a particular focus on reducing fear of increased pain and encouraging engagement in appropriate activities. They found that the group with the educational intervention had better results.

If the patient's pain does not improve with nonoperative treatment, however, then consultation with a surgeon may be beneficial. The following are descriptions of some of the surgical procedures available for the correction of back pain.

Laminectomy/Discectomy

In a laminectomy/discectomy (often incorrectly called a "laminectomy"), a patient with a herniated disc first has a small amount of bone removed from the lamina. This is followed by a discectomy, involving the decompression of the nerve root by removing the disc tissue that is pressing on it. There is a variation called microdiscectomy, which uses small incisions and intraoperative magnification to accomplish the same result. The whole disc is not removed, and only a portion of the nucleus (i.e., the center of the disc) is removed. The nucleus constitutes approximately 50% of the surface area and the annular fibers of the ring the remaining 50%. The expected result from such a surgery is 85% to 95% relief of buttock and leg pain, provided the patient has a primary complaint of leg pain, a positive physical finding consistent with nerve root compression (i.e., motor, sensory, or reflex abnormalities) and a correlating diagnostic study such as an MRI scan.

Intradiscal Electrothermal Therapy

Intradiscal electrothermal therapy (IDET) is a relatively new treatment that involves the passage of a catheter into the ring of the disc to treat either annular tears or the very early stages of degenerative disc disease. The catheter has a heating element toward the end of its tip. It is hypothesized that IDET produces pain relief by neuroablation (destruction of nerve tissue) of the nociceptive fibers in the disc annulus or by changing the structure of the collagen tissue in the disc, which results in healing of tears in the disc annulus. The reported results of this treatment are variable, ranging from 30% to 80% improvement (Blumenthal et al., 2001; Carragee, Khurana, Alamin, & Chen, 2001; Derby, Eek, & Ryan, 1999; Karasek & Bogduk, 2000; J. A. Saal & Saal, 2000; J. S. Saal & Saal, 2000). Use of this treatment is still in its early stages, and indications are being determined. In studies at the Texas Back Institute, we found that approximately 70% of patients with a normal anterior disc height and an annular tear have a good result. The results were worse among patients with disc degeneration or previous spine surgery.

Facet Rhizotomy

Facet rhizotomy involves ablation of the nerve that innervates the facet joints (the medial branch of the posterior primary ramus). Patients with facet-mediated pain are usually diagnosed by having a good response to facet joint injection, which is then followed by an anesthetic block of this nerve. If a good response is obtained, then the patient is a candidate for the facet rhizotomy.

Foraminotomy

Foraminal stenosis is a form of spinal stenosis in which there is compression of the nerve root. Often the compression is caused by degenerative conditions resulting in bony overgrowth of the facet joints or osteophytes on the vertebral bodies. A foraminotomy involves increasing the opening of a narrowed foramen, thus relieving the pressure on the exiting nerve root by removing a portion of bone and increasing the space available for the exiting nerve root.

Spinal Fusion

Spinal fusion has many variations. In essence, a fusion is carried out to eliminate motion of a painful motion segment (unit formed by two adjacent vertebral bodies and the intervening disc). One approach to this procedure is an interbody fusion, in which the disc is totally removed and an implant is placed in the void. The implant can be bone from the patient (autogenous bone graft), donor bone (from a cadaver), or a variety of carbon and metal cages that act as spacers or that screw into the disc space. These spacers are filled with bone that eventually "fuses" to the adjacent vertebrae. Fusions can be performed along the posterior lateral aspects of the spine—that is, the facet joints and the transverse processes—using autogenous bone, donor bone, or the various bone substitutes.

Internal fixation also comes in a variety of forms, including pedicle screws, which are placed through the pedicles into the vertebral body and then connected by either plates or rods, and facet screws, which are placed across the facet joints and to wires and cables. Sometimes a fusion is carried out anteriorly if the pathology is felt to be anterior alone. Sometimes an anterior fusion is combined with a posterior fusion (called a circumferential or 360° fusion), which gives the most reliable results in terms of a solid fusion. Anterior or posterior fusions alone of one and two levels provide a solid fusion in an estimated 60% to 90% of patients. With a circumferential fusion, the fusion rates are extremely high, above 90% (Agazzi, Reverdin, & May, 1999; Fritzell, Hagg, Wessberg, & Nordwall, 2002; Penta & Fraser, 1997; Slosar, Reynolds, Schofferman, Goldthwaite, White, & Keaney, 2000; Thalgott et al., 2000; Wetzel, Brustein, Phillips, & Trott, 1999; Whitecloud, Castro, Brinker, Hartzog, Ricciardi, & Hill, 1998).

Disc Replacement

The most recent surgical technology available to the back pain patient is the artificial disc. Currently, a Food and Drug Administration IDE (Investigational Device Exemption) study is under way in the United States with the Link SB Charité III prosthesis (Link Spine Group, Inc.). This device had been implanted in Europe in over 2500 patients since the mid-1980s. Another IDE study has been initiated evaluating the ProDisc (Spinal Solutions), which is another total disc replacement device that has been used in Europe since the early 1990s. The short-term results of disc replacement procedures are similar to those of fusions. The artificial disc has the advantage of maintaining motion and, hopefully, reducing the incidence of degeneration at the level above the procedure. Several other devices are on the horizon, and others that have been used in other parts of the world may soon be undergoing studies in the United States.

Procedures to Alleviate Failed Back Surgery Syndrome

Because failed back surgery syndrome is a catchall diagnosis, possible treatments vary greatly and are dependent on the results of the diagnostic evaluations. If there is clear pseudoarthrosis, a repeated attempt to obtain a solid fusion may be warranted. If the symptoms are related to recurrent disc herniation, then a repeat discectomy or fusion may be indicated. In some patients with persistent pain following laminectomy/discectomy or decompression who may have iatrogenic instability, spinal fusion may be indicated. Other possible pain origins in this group of patients are a painful disrupted disc under a spinal segment that has been fused posteriorly and changes in spinal structures after spinal fusion.

Spinal fusion results in changes in the load distribution of the lumbar spine and other nearby structures. In a patient with pain following fusion, the clinician should first consider whether the spine is solidly fused, which is very difficult to determine from imaging studies. If there is no clear indication of a failure to achieve bony fusion, then the clinician should consider the facet joints, discs at the levels adjacent to the fused segment, and the sacroiliac joints.

If there is no evidence of any residual neural compression and no evidence of a pseudarthrosis and the patient complains of significant back and leg pain, spinal cord stimulation may be considered. Spinal cord stimulation involves implanting one or two multielectrode leads over the dura in the thoracic spine and delivering electrical impulses whose location and intensity are controlled by an external programming unit. It is theorized that the leads stimulate A-delta nerve fibers, overriding pain signals traveling on the slower C fibers. The device does not actually eliminate the pain but rather produces paresthesia sensations in the areas where the patient usually experiences pain. (It works on a totally different basis than transcutaneous electrical nerve stimulation and should not be confused with this therapy.)

In extreme cases of failure to respond to treatment, a morphine pump may be installed as a treatment of last resort to try to provide pain relief. The catheter is placed epidurally to minimize systemic effects.

DISCUSSION

Almost everyone experiences back pain during their lifetimes. Fortunately, the vast majority recover with no or minimal care. However, the small percentage of people who do not have an uneventful recovery experience significant disruption in their lives and consume a large amount of resources in the form of both medical costs and expenses related to lost workdays.

Public education can be a powerful tool for assisting in recovery from back pain as well as reducing medical costs and avoiding surgery. The power of a large-scale public education campaign was recently reported by Buchbinder, Jolley, & Wyatt (2001). They conducted a mass media campaign targeted to the general public to encourage a quick return to activities after the onset of back pain, emphasizing that rest for extended periods of time was not necessary. The campaign was successful at reducing visits to physicians, lost workdays, and the overall cost of back pain.

The treatment of patients with back pain is a rapidly changing arena. There are continual improvements in diagnostic imaging and in clinicians' understanding of the complexity of back pain and the many factors related to it. Further, there are new minimally invasive procedures and new implants available. Unfortunately, clinicians are still far from being able to correctly and totally diagnose the causes of back pain in a short period of time or with only one test in any individual patient. The challenge still remains in deriving a working diagnosis from which to generate a treatment plan and monitor treatment effectiveness. However, this process can be enhanced by an awareness that back pain, particularly chronic pain, is influenced by many physical and psychological factors. As evaluation tools continue to evolve, along with the field's understanding of the causes and effects of back pain, the number of people who become chronic pain sufferers will decrease, and our ability to provide optimal treatment for those who do become afflicted with chronic back pain will improve.

II

PSYCHOLOGICAL SCREENING OF SPINE SURGERY CANDIDATES

2

PRESURGICAL PSYCHOLOGICAL SCREENING: RATIONALE AND PROCESS

Why should a surgeon want a health psychologist to assess a patient before surgery? Shouldn't the surgeon's training have prepared him or her to be not only a proficient technician but also an astute judge of the patient's personality and emotional makeup? And why would any doctor risk losing income because a psychologist recommends not proceeding with surgery? This chapter describes the rationale for presurgical psychological screening (PPS) and outlines a systematic, empirically driven approach to PPS. In doing so, the chapter reviews the large body of research identifying psychosocial factors that may have a negative impact on the outcome of spine surgery. The chapter will demonstrate that although certain personality and behavioral factors can individually exert a strong influence on surgical recovery, assessment of combinations of risk factors and strengths can lead to powerful surgical outcome prediction.

RATIONALE FOR PRESURGICAL PSYCHOLOGICAL SCREENING

Improved Spine Surgery Outcome

An experienced spine surgeon has seen many successes. Certainly, the majority of patients improve as a result of spine surgery. Statistical analyses have demonstrated that spine surgery both is cost effective and leads to significant improvements in lifestyle. Atlas, Keller, Robson, Deyo, and Singer (2000), for example, conducted a 4-year follow-up in patients with lumbar spinal stenosis and found that those treated surgically (primarily with a decompression) had significantly less back and leg pain, and had greater satisfaction, than did those treated nonsurgically. In a similar vein, Malter, Larson, Urban, and Deyo (1996) found that quality of life for patients with herniated lumbar discs who underwent discectomy was significantly greater than that of patients treated conservatively, for up to 5 years. In addition, the study found that the cost-effectiveness of discectomy was significantly greater than that of such procedures as coronary artery bypass grafting for single-artery disease and greater than medical therapy for moderate hypertension.

Surgeons are aware that their many successes are counterbalanced by some notable failures. Spine surgery is certainly not a panacea. In a review of all lumbar discectomies conducted up to the time of publication, Hoffman, Wheeler, and Deyo (1993) found a mean success rate of 67%. Similarly, Turner et al. (1992), reviewing all published research on spinal fusion, found that successful clinical outcome was obtained in 65% to 75% of patients, with success rates lower the more levels fused and generally the more invasive the procedure. Franklin, Haug, Heyer, McKeefrey, and Picciano (1994) found that 68% of workers' compensation patients who underwent lumbar fusion were work disabled and 23% required further lumbar spine surgery 2 years postfusion. These results, and many others, emphasize the elusive nature of chronic pain. Even though the physical underpinnings of chronic pain may be identified and corrected, the subjective experience of and limitations caused by pain may continue unabated.

Surgeons' inclusion of PPS within the preoperative assessment of the spine surgery candidate rests on the recognition both that psychosocial factors can lead to reduced clinical results and that PPS can provide a systematic, scientifically sound means of predicting whether a given patient will benefit from surgery. PPS provides many additional benefits that the spine surgeon should be aware of; PPS can

- improve overall treatment outcome by screening out patients with a strong potential to experience poor outcome;
- provide a strong, empirically validated rationale for avoiding invasive procedures in cases where the surgeon feels uncomfortable about operating;
- reduce average treatment duration and cost by helping avoid ineffective procedures;
- improve outcome in patients undergoing surgery by identifying and, when necessary, treating emotional and behavioral problems;

- identify patients who are likely to develop medication or compliance problems; and
- reduce the number of problem patients in the surgeon's practice.

Avoidance of Failed Back Surgery Syndrome

Every spine surgeon, no matter how proficient, has had his or her share of surgical failures. Uppermost in the surgeon's mind is the desire to avoid the consequences of such failures, referred to in general as "failed back surgery syndrome" (see Exhibit 2.1). Such patients may need ever-increasing medication dosages to obtain relief and may call on the surgeon for refills, sometimes most inconveniently and insistently. The failed surgical patient's emotional distress almost inevitably increases, and often the surgeon becomes the target of this distress. The surgeon may undertake an escalating and increasingly frustrating quest to provide the patient with relief. Interventions often become more invasive and their outcomes less satisfactory. A failed simple laminectomy/discectomy may be followed by a much more extensive fusion, perhaps with instrumentation, leading to greater opportunity for failure. Many studies validate Waddell's (1987) suggestion that the probability of obtaining successful spine surgery outcome decreases significantly with each successive procedure. For example, Pheasant, Gelbert, Goldfarb, and Herron (1979) found that multiply operated patients had a lower probability of obtaining good outcome than did single-surgery patients. Results of a study by North et al. (1993) suggest that the long-term success rate in reoperated patients is one-third. The frustration and futility involved in trying to provide relief to the failed back surgery patient thus can consume tremendous energy and resources.

The thoughtful surgeon is searching to understand why some patients fail and how to avoid this outcome. Oaklander and North (2001) discussed several medical explanations for inadequate results. Sometimes patients come to the surgery with permanent, irreversible nerve damage, so that pain cannot completely resolve no matter how effective the intervention. Sometimes pain persists after surgery due to iatrogenic factors—the surgery can produce its own nerve damage, or a "segmental instability" can be created after "a generous laminectomy" (Oaklander & North, 2001, p. 1541). Nonsurgical complications, such as arachnoiditis (scarring and inflammation of the meninges), can also generate pain sensations. Such causes only the physician can correct by improving diagnostic acumen and technical expertise.

In addition to medical explanations for the failure of spine surgery, spine surgeons are typically aware that even perfect surgical correction of underlying pathology may not bring about successful clinical outcome. They do acknowledge, at some level, that psychosocial factors can negatively affect re-

EXHIBIT 2.1
Some Consequences of Failed Spine Surgery

1. The patient makes increasing demands on the physician for relief. The physician feels a strong sense of responsibility to provide relief when surgery has been ineffective.
2. The patient may become increasingly angry with the physician and perhaps litigious.
3. Medication use often escalates, increasing the chances of dependence or addiction. The patient overusing medication may call for refills after office hours.
4. In an attempt to provide relief, the physician may order conservative treatments with little chance of success, increasing the length and cost of care.
5. The patient may undergo increasingly invasive surgery, with subsequent opportunities for infection, instrumentation failure, and other iatrogenic complications.
6. The likelihood of successful outcome decreases with each spine surgery.
7. The chances that pain reduction and return to work will occur decrease as length of disability increases. Because failed back surgery lengthens the period of disability, patients are less likely to ever recover.
8. Financial incentives to remain disabled may outweigh incentives for recovery.
9. Failed spine surgery dramatically increases the total cost of the injury due to both direct treatment and surgeries and disability income benefits.

sults, and they may consider some of the more obvious emotional problems when making the decision whether to operate. They may be very reluctant to operate on patients with blatant psychopathology or documented drug addiction or those whom they perceive as exaggerating symptoms for financial or "secondary" gain. They certainly recognize when patients are severely depressed.

Physicians are perhaps less aware, however, of more subtle psychosocial problems and the influences of such problems on surgical outcome. In fact, a recent study by Grevitt, Pande, O'Dowd, and Webb (1998) suggested that surgeons may have limited ability to recognize patients' psychological problems, at least during the initial evaluation. In this study, 125 orthopedic patients were given two psychological questionnaires, the Modified Somatic Perception Questionnaire (MSPQ, Main, 1983) and the Zung Depression Inventory (Zung, 1965). Orthopedic surgeons independently evaluated the patients and categorized them as normal, at risk, distressed-depressive, or distressed-somatic. The testing revealed that 35 of the 125 patients were distressed and an additional 54 were at risk. The surgeons' impressions had only a 26% sensitivity in identifying distressed patients. Thus, surgeons' abilities to perceive subtle emotional disturbance may be limited.

Research has demonstrated that psychosocial evaluation can identify potential surgical nonresponders in a powerful and systematic fashion. The role of the health psychologist involved with back surgery patients includes helping surgeons become aware of and understand this body of research and its importance in ensuring surgical success and avoiding failed back surgery syndrome.

EXHIBIT 2.2
Referral Criteria for Presurgical Psychology Screening

❏ Symptoms are inconsistent with identified pathology.
❏ High levels of depression or anxiety are present.
❏ Sleep disturbance—insomnia or hypersomnia—is present.
❏ The patient has excessively high or low expectations about treatment outcome.
❏ Marital distress or sexual difficulties are present.
❏ The patient has negative attitudes toward his or her work or employer.
❏ Emotional lability or mood swings are evident.
❏ The patient has been unable to work or has had greatly decreased functional ability for 3 months or longer.
❏ The patient uses escalating or large doses of narcotics or anxiolytics.
❏ Litigation or continuing disability benefits have resulted from a spine injury.
❏ The patient has a history of noncompliance with medical treatment.
❏ The patient has a history of psychiatric or psychological treatment.

Necessity of referral for PPS:

0 or 1 criterion: It is not necessary to refer unless the patient desires screening.
2 or 3 criteria: The surgeon should consider referral.
4 or more criteria: The surgeon should strongly consider referral.

IDENTIFYING APPROPRIATE PPS CANDIDATES

Although it may be clear that psychosocial factors can influence surgery results, it is certainly also clear that surgery is often effective without consideration of such emotional or behavioral issues. After all, as noted previously, the success rates of fusions and laminectomy/discectomy procedures have ranged from 60% to 80%, and the majority of these patients never were evaluated by a health psychologist. How, then, can a surgeon recognize when PPS might be helpful in the diagnostic process? Exhibit 2.2 lists a number of referral criteria that a physician can easily identify during his or her initial evaluation of the patient. Psychosocial disturbance can cut a wide swath in the life of the chronic pain patient and can include emotional difficulties, impairments in work and home life, and dependence on medications. The surgeon can easily ask patients about aspects of their psychosocial history, especially treatment for emotional disturbance. The physician can also readily note behavioral factors: Is the patient's pain behavior consistent with the diagnosis? Does the patient have a history of noncompliant behavior with medical staff? Are there incentives to remain disabled? When the surgeon recognizes the presence of a number of these risk factors, including PPS within the diagnostic workup can be of great assistance.

There has recently been an attempt to create brief paper-and-pencil screening tools to more systematically identify spine surgery candidates likely to benefit by referral for comprehensive PPS. The most well developed and researched of these screening tools is the Distress and Risk Assessment Method (DRAM; Main, Wood, Hollis, Spanswick, & Waddell, 1992). The DRAM comprises two previously developed brief instruments: a modified version of the Zung Depression Inventory and the MSPQ. The total DRAM involves 45 items and requires about 10 min to complete. The DRAM went through careful test development, drawing on a sample of 567 chronic pain patients from a number of practices in Scotland.

DRAM results place patients into one of four descriptive categories, similar to those described in the Grevitt et al. (1998) study: normal (no distress), at risk, distressed-depressive (patients with relatively high score on the Zung Depression Inventory), and distressed-somatic (patients with a high score on the MSPQ and a moderate score on the Zung Depression Inventory). Results showed that patients in the two distressed groups had a 5.3 relative risk of poor outcome compared to the normal group, with 69% of the distressed patients achieving poor results.

The DRAM has been applied to the screening of chronic pain spine surgery candidates. Trief, Grant, and Fredrickson (2000) gave the DRAM to 102 subjects, the majority of whom underwent lumbar fusion. Regression analyses showed that the DRAM (combined with duration of pain) predicted daily function and ability to sustain work-leisure activities, as well as change in back and leg pain. The distressed groups showed less improvement than the normal groups on all these measures, and the at-risk group results fell between the two.

Two studies using the DRAM failed to find that distressed patients had significantly poorer outcome following posterior lumbar interbody fusion (Hobby, Lutchman, Powell, & Sharp, 2001) or lumbar discectomy (Tandon, Campbell, & Ross, 1999). However, both studies involved relatively small numbers of participants (fewer than 60), and in both cases the improvements shown by the distressed groups were less than those shown by normal groups, but not significantly so. This is important because, as pointed out by Main et al. (1992), "The DRAM is designed as no more than a first-stage screening procedure, whether as a confirmation of clinical impression, or to alert the clinician that a more comprehensive psychological . . . assessment is indicated" (p. 50). Thus, we recommend use of the DRAM for physicians who want to rely on a more standardized means of identifying patients for whom PPS would be valuable.

REFERRING THE PATIENT FOR PPS

The chronic pain patient seeking spine surgery understands that there is physical pathology causing the pain, the solution to which, apparently, is to repair tissue damage (or in the case of salvage procedures like spinal cord stimulation, to physically block nociception). Referring a patient for PPS presents the surgeon with a dilemma that requires much sensitivity: The surgeon must inform the patient that he or she must see a health psychologist

EXHIBIT 2.3
Presurgical Psychological Screening: Suggested Points for Patient Handout

- PPS is a routine procedure for spine surgery candidates, like any other medical test.
- PPS assists the surgeon in developing the most effective treatment plan for each patient.
- The surgeon recognizes that the patient has a legitimate injury and that the pain is real.
- PPS involves an interview and psychological testing by a health psychologist.
- Pain and injury create many changes in a patient's life, and these may influence the effectiveness of the surgery.
- PPS will help determine if the patient is ready for surgery and what type of preparation may help improve the patient's results.
- PPS allows the patient the opportunity to discuss any concerns about the surgery.
- PPS allows the patient to discuss emotional, marital, vocational, or other issues related to the pain or injury.

while avoiding the appearance of suggesting that the pain is "all in the patient's head."

The information the surgeon gives the patient in making this referral is the key to avoiding misunderstanding. Perhaps the most important task of the surgeon is to "normalize" the referral by explaining to the patient that PPS is a routine procedure frequently used in similar cases. Prepared handouts can provide the patient with information about the value of PPS (Exhibit 2.3). The surgeon can also state that the PPS referral does not mean that the surgeon questions whether the patient's pain is real, as a physiological basis for the pain has been identified.

It is critical that the surgeon not present the PPS as a determinant of whether the patient will be approved for surgery. In other words, the patient should not form the impression that although surgery is necessary to correct the problem, the PPS results may block the surgery from occurring. This impression will likely make the patient defensive and angry, and he or she will likely be very guarded during the PPS. The surgeon should explain that PPS is just one component of a comprehensive diagnostic process and that the surgeon makes his or her own determination of the weight placed on each component.

The timing of the referral for PPS should be managed as carefully as possible. Ideally, the physician should refer the patient fairly early in the diagnostic process, before the physician has reached a decision about the necessity of surgery. Early referral allows sufficient time for the evaluation to be authorized by insurance companies and for the patient to have a feedback session on the PPS results.

In preparing a patient for PPS referral, the surgeon should build on the other information he or she must provide about spine surgery and its risks. It is most important for the patient to understand that surgery is not necessarily the best solution to the pain and that it carries risk. Although all physicians inform the patients of surgical risk, patients are often unaware that reoperation is not uncommon in spine surgery. The surgeon should inform the patient that PPS may help avoid reoperation and may uncover ways to prevent a continued slide into disability. The surgeon who explains the PPS referral to the patient in a way that makes its value and benefits apparent helps the patient be more motivated for the evaluation and is more likely to be perceived by the patient as demonstrating concern for his or her welfare.

PRESURGICAL PSYCHOLOGICAL SCREENING: OVERVIEW OF THE PROCESS

Underlying Concepts

Responding to a growing body of research, a number of health psychologists are now providing presurgical psychological screening to chronic back pain patients being considered for elective spine surgery. Although there are a number of different screening systems, in general PPS can be defined as a diagnostic "approach that identifies and quantifies risk factors associated with poor surgical outcome, in order to render a decision concerning surgical prognosis" (Block, 1996, p. 6). This definition relies on several points. First, to be effective, PPS must stand on a strong base of empirically validated risk factors. Second, any identified risk factors must be examined in the context of the patient's entire picture. Both strengths and weaknesses must be weighed—for example, good coping skills might mitigate problems in adapting to financial stress—and the psychologist must examine the combination of risk factors and strengths in a systematic, quantitative fashion. Third, the psychologist must clearly communicate his or her recommendations concerning surgery on the basis of the identified risk factors. Finally, the psychological determination of surgical prognosis must be considered only one part of the comprehensive, diagnostic evaluation of the spine surgery candidate. In deciding on the best course of action, the surgeon must weigh the psychologist's results against the physical findings to determine whether to proceed with surgery, delay it, or take another course.

Surgical outcome prognosis is not a simple matter to assess. In its most straightforward conceptualization, the surgery is successful if the identified pathology is corrected. However, the patient may fail to experience or report any symptomatic improvement despite excellent surgical correction. For this reason, determining surgical success requires assessment of the major areas in which the chronic pain patient's life is affected by the injury. Ideally, surgery would then lead to improvement in all these areas.

Recently, the majority of studies on spine surgery have used some variation of the Stauffer and Coventry (1972) criteria to examine outcomes. These criteria assess results in terms of relieved pain sensation, reduced job impair-

TABLE 2.1
Criteria for Spine Surgery Outcome

Outcome	Pain Relief	Employment	Activities	Analgesics Use
Good	Most (76%–100%)	No limits	No limits	Infrequent
Fair	Partial (26%–75%)	Lighter work	Limited	Occasional
Poor	Little to none (< 25%)	Disabled	Greatly limited	Frequent

Note. Adapted from Klekamp, J., McCarty, E., & Spengler, D. (1998). Results of elective lumbar discectomy for patients involved in the workers' compensation system. *Journal of Spinal Disorders, 11,* 277–282. Adapted with permission from *Journal of Spinal Disorders* © 1998.

ment, improvement in functional activity, and decreased use of narcotic medications. Trief et al. (2000), for example, assessed outcomes similar to those described by Stauffer and Coventry (improvement in back and leg pain, ability to work and functional disability in lumbar surgery patients) using the Dallas Pain Questionnaire (Lawlis, Cuencas, & Selby, 1989). Klekamp, McCarty, and Spengler (1998) suggested a restatement of the Stauffer and Coventry outcome criteria that is both deceptively simple and yet complex enough to capture the major life areas affected by chronic pain (Table 2.1).

PPS provides more than a surgical prognosis, however, for the health psychologist gains a great deal of information that can help the health care team tailor treatments to the needs, personality, and expectations of the individual patient. PPS can help the health psychologist offer suggestions for maximizing surgical outcome, including suggestions for preparing the patient for surgery (see chapters 7 to 10) and for postoperative rehabilitation (see chapters 11 and 12). In patients for whom the PPS indicates a fair outcome prognosis, the evaluation may suggest certain ways to test and improve the patient's motivation and compliance; the psychologist's recommendation to proceed with surgery would then depend on whether the patient responds to these suggestions.

Information Gathering

The process of PPS described in this chapter relies on information drawn from three domains. First, the health psychologist must carefully review the patient's medical chart. Within the chart resides information about specific risk factors and about the general interaction of the patient and medical staff. Overutilization of prescription medication can often be identified by examining records of phone calls and by determining whether refills were provided earlier than expected. Anger or noncompliance may be explicitly documented or may be seen in a pattern of failed appointments or excessive appointment cancellation. The psychologist should also review the initial physical exam; the physician may have documented a pattern of pain behaviors that are inconsistent with the patient's diagnosis—so called nonorganic signs (Waddell, McCulloch, Kummel, & Venner, 1980).

The psychologist should examine even medical diagnostic tests because they may give clues to the contribution of psychosocial factors to the patient's pain complaints. For example, the dermatomal distribution of the patient's pain may not correctly correspond to disc herniation as viewed on magnetic resonance imaging scans. Likewise, computed tomography with discography may reveal pain reproduction on injection of a nondisrupted lumbar disc. The richness of information potentially provided by the medical chart cannot be overemphasized. Health psychologists will increasingly recognize the importance of such critical information as he or she builds a knowledge base concerning spine diagnostic and surgical procedures and as experience provides feedback about the relationship between patients' emotional processes and their surgical responses.

After reviewing the medical chart, the health psychologist gives the patient a semistructured interview. This interview is designed to elicit both clearly identified risk factors and strengths that may help the patient overcome such risk factors. The semistructured format of the interview ensures that all critical information is assessed and that the patient has the opportunity to discuss and expand on his or her concerns about the surgery. In addition, the interview builds rapport and a therapeutic alliance between the patient and the psychologist, which is often the most critical feature in bringing about long-term behavior and emotional change (Barber, Connolly, Crits-Christoph, Gladis, & Siqueland, 2000).

Psychological testing is the third critical source of information in PPS. Our own research (Block et al., 2001), as well as that of others (e.g., Spengler, Ouelette, Battie, & Zeh, 1990; Trief et al., 2000; Wiltse and Rocchio, 1975) indicates that psychological test results often carry the greatest value in predicting surgical outcome, greater even than that of medical diagnostic tests. Further, the testing can bolster or contradict the clinical impression developed by the psychologist during the clinical interview. The tests used in PPS have gone through extensive test development and allow for clear, objective evaluation of critical risk factors.

Screening Scorecards

Once the information-gathering phase of PPS is completed, the risk factors and other features of the patient's case are combined according to rules described in chapter 6. Our approach builds on previous "scorecards" designed to predict spine surgery results. The first such scorecard, developed by Finneson and Cooper (1979), listed factors that they felt militated for and against sanguine surgery results. Finneson and Cooper's scorecard listed seven positive factors, including "neurologic examination demonstrates a single root syndrome indicating a specific interspace" and "patient's realistic self-appraisal of future life style," and six negative factors, including "poor psychological background," "back pain primarily," and "history of previous law suits for medico-legal problems." The surgeon entered on the score risk factors for the individual patient. Identification of some of these factors involved highly subjective judgments by the surgeon. The risk factors were then assigned a priori weights and combined to predict the patient as having a good, fair, marginal, or poor prognosis. They found that at 3.8-year follow-up the good prognosis patients had achieved by far the best results, with poor prognosis patients improving the least (statistical tests were not performed).

More effective and empirically tested scorecards were developed by Spengler et al. (1990), Manniche et al. (1994), Junge et al. (1996), and Dzioba and Doxey (1984). Each of these scorecards has the same general approach of listing potential risk factors, empirically assessing the predictive value of each individual risk factor, and combining them, most often through a regression equation, to provide the most effective outcome prediction. In some cases (e.g., Junge et al., 1996), rules for combining risk factors were developed by providing empirically derived risk factor weights. Results from all these studies demonstrate that the accuracy of scorecards in predicting surgical outcomes at 2 to 4 years after surgery ranges from 75% (Junge et al., 1996) to 82% (Dzioba & Doxey, 1984). Compared to good prognosis patients, those with a poor prognosis generally obtain far less pain relief and improvement in functional ability, consume greater quantities of pain medication, and are more likely to undergo additional spine surgery.

The approach to PPS we describe in this book further refines the scorecard technique. We use a much broader set of psychosocial factors than have been examined in previous scorecard approaches, for the current approach has had the benefit of drawing on an extant body of research. This research, reviewed in the chapters in section 2, documents psychosocial factors that can negatively influence surgical outcome. In almost all studies, surgical failure is strongly correlated (r^2 = approximately 0.5–0.7) with certain individual measures of psychosocial distress. For example, Spengler et al. (1990), examining patients who underwent laminectomy/discectomy, found poor clinical outcome in 6 out of 7 patients having a high level of identified psychosocial risk, whereas only 4 out of 41 patients having a low level of psychosocial risk achieved such poor results. Similarly, Wiltse and Rocchio (1975) found that high scores ($T > 75$) on the Hypochondriasis and Hysteria scales of the Minnesota Multiphasic Personality Inventory correlated .60 to .65 with clinical outcome in a study of patients undergoing chemical chemonucleolysis.

Sorenson (1992) followed lumbar discectomy patients for 5 years and found that patients who scored high on a psychological "symptom admission" scale had a 14.6 times greater risk of poor outcome than did patients scoring low on this scale. Schofferman, Anderson, Hinds, Smith, and White (1992) found that patients with a strong history of childhood abuse or aban-

TABLE 2.2
PPS Prognosis and Surgery Recommendations

Prognosis	Surgery Recommendation
Poor	Avoid surgery if pain relief is the major goal. Recommend discharge.
	Avoid surgery if pain relief is the major goal. Provide conservative care only.
Fair	Hold on surgery, pending the outcome of psychological treatment, compliance measures, or surgical preparation procedures.
Good	Clear for surgery. Recommend postoperative psychological treatment.
	Clear for surgery. No psychological treatment is necessary.

donment failed to achieve good surgery outcome. These and many other studies provide testimony to the influence of psychosocial factors on surgical outcome.

Formulations of Recommendations Concerning Surgery

The key element of the PPS approach described in this book is the refinement of the specific recommendations concerning surgery. These recommendations are based on extensive research in our laboratory (Block, Ohnmeiss, Guyer, Rashbaum, & Hochshuler, 2001, described in detail in chapter 4), as well as on the research of others. A brief overview of these recommendations is given in Table 2.2. Patients who have a low level of risk factors are recommended to undergo the planned surgery, perhaps along with postoperative psychotherapy. Most patients who have a high risk level are given the recommendations to avoid surgery and to be treated conservatively. A small number of these patients, under restricted conditions, are recommended for discharge. The most complicated patients are those whose PPS results indicate that they have a moderate risk level. For these patients, psychological treatment, or "motivation and compliance measures" (see chapter 6) are recommended to improve or test the patient's readiness for surgery. If these measures are successful, the patient is deemed an acceptable surgical candidate. If not, the patient is recommended for conservative care only.

CONCLUSION

Chronic pain is a complex phenomenon involving an interplay of physical, emotional, behavioral, and cognitive factors. Working together, the spine surgeon, the health psychologist, and the chronic pain patient can come to understand this complexity and consider all factors in determining the best treatment options. Surgery is not the only, and may not be the best, approach to improving the patient's lot. In fact, surgery may be only the first step on a path of successively more invasive treatments, increasing disability, and heightened dependence on the health care system. Psychosocial factors often determine whether the patient can achieve pain relief and lifestyle improvement. The surgeon who recognizes these facts is in the best position to provide treatment to those likely to respond well while living up to the Hippocratic oath to do no harm.

3

MEDICAL RISK FACTORS: THE CHART REVIEW

The medical chart: Often resembling a pile of jumbled jackstraws pressed within a fraying, dog-eared binder, the chart of a chronic pain patient may consist of multiple volumes weighing several pounds each. Its contents often give testimony to many therapeutic dead ends, many inconclusive diagnostic tests. And yet, the chart contains a wealth of information relevant to recovery from spine surgery. The astute psychologist learns to comb through this mixture of data and detritus and can gain a great deal of knowledge before the patient ever sets foot in the interview room.

Many aspects of the patient's injury, proposed treatment, and personal characteristics are contained in the chart. Much of this information may be impressionistic, depending as it does on health care providers' observations of the patient across time. However, the chart also contains specific, objective aspects of the case, both demographic and medical, that have been associated with surgery results. In this chapter we review medical risk factors regarding which the chart can provide much evidence.

DURATION OF INJURY

Duration of injury is among the most important medical risk factors associated with reduced surgery results. Patients experiencing protracted pain

43

accumulate a series of experiences that may militate against improvement. As Mayer et al. (1987) noted, with increasing chronicity patients' physical abilities significantly decline. This phenomenon, termed deconditioning syndrome, occurs because patients naturally avoid activities that might cause an increase in pain (see chapter 11 for a more complete discussion). With back pain, almost any activity, even getting out of bed or walking, can provoke noxious sensations. As they seek to avoid pain, patients' muscle strength declines, tendons and ligaments shorten, and swelling may occur. Weight gain often accompanies decreased activity. Thus, a vicious circle may be established wherein any movement that might cause an improvement in strength, conditioning, or flexibility is increasingly avoided, further reinforcing the pain and disability.

The persistence of pain creates a number of other problems for recovery. The pain often significantly limits vocational abilities. The pain may limit his or her ability to work even if the patient's back pain did not start as a result of a work injury. The financial implications of disability can be formidable. Even patients who are injured on the job and receive workers' compensation payments can suffer significantly; patients whose pain is of insidious onset or who lack disability income can find themselves in a desperate financial situation. Further, as the pain wears on, financial reserves can become exhausted, leading to worsening debt and an inability to meet obligations. Given the cumulative effects of protracted pain, it is not surprising that Waddell (1987) found that the likelihood of a back pain patient returning to work, regardless of treatment received, is inversely related to the duration of the pain. Only 50% of the patients in Waddell's study returned to work after pain of 6 months duration, 25% returned after 12 months, and virtually no patients returned to work after 2 years of disabling back pain.

Research on spine surgery has confirmed the negative influence of pain duration. Franklin et al. (1994), for example, examined lumbar fusion patients and found that time from injury to fusion, as well as time on work disability during the 6 months prior to fusion, significantly increased the relative risk of poor clinical outcome. Junge, Dvorak, and Ahrens (1995), in examining discectomy patients, found that those with longer duration of low back pain obtained poorer results, and in a follow-up scorecard study, duration of back pain greater than 26 weeks was given a heavy weight in predicting negative results (Junge et al., 1996). Even in patients undergoing cervical discectomy, greater pain duration was found to have a strong negative association with return to work and reported pain level at 2.8 years postoperation (Bhandari, Louw, & Reddy, 1999). It appears, then, that time to surgery is the enemy of recovery, for as pain persists many adverse effects can accumulate, diminishing patients' financial, emotional, and physical resources.

TYPE OF SURGERY

For the chronic pain patient, surgery often seems the answer to a prayer. It promises to remove the source of persistent pain in a quick, final manner, leading to rapid resolution and return to normal function. However, all surgeries are not created equal in terms of their probability of achieving good clinical outcome. Moreover, some spine surgeries carry a higher risk of making matters worse, that is, of postoperative complications or increased chances of reoperation. Spine surgeries (described in chapter 1) vary widely in a number of respects: duration of the procedure itself, number of spine levels involved, whether or not instrumentation is implanted. The term *destructiveness* has been used in categorizing surgery types for the purposes of predicting clinical outcome (Block, 1996). A surgery is considered more destructive to the extent that

- greater amounts of tissue are exposed (e.g., longer incisions, greater tissue retraction),
- greater amounts of tissue are destroyed or removed (e.g., greater number of spine levels are operated on), and
- instrumentation is inserted (e.g., facet screws, cages).

Using this definition some surgeries, such as facet rhizotomy, intradiscal electrothermal therapy (IDET), and arthroscopic and microscopic discectomy could be considered minimally destructive. Procedures such as a circumferential spinal fusion with instrumentation would be considered highly destructive.

It is generally true that more destructive surgeries are associated with poorer outcome and greater chance of reoperation or surgical complication. For example, Franklin et al. (1994) examined lumbar fusion outcome in all workers' compensation patients in Washington state for a 1-year period and found that greater work disability was associated with greater number of levels fused. Similarly, Turner et al. (1992), reviewing all then-extant articles on treatment for herniated lumbar discs, found that there was a trend for more positive outcome in single- versus multiple-level fusions. Further, there was no overall advantage for fusion over surgery without fusion. In addition, this study found that instrumentation, such as rods, plates, and screws, had a fairly substantial failure rate of 7%.

Spine surgeons recognize the importance of destructiveness as a key risk factor and are constantly devising means of reducing it. In the past few years, for example, lumbar laminectomy/discectomy procedures have developed to the point that they are now frequently performed microscopically. Similarly, thoracic spinal fusions, once almost never performed because they required rib removal and extensive removal of the posterior facets, are now beginning to be performed arthroscopically. Perhaps the most instructive example of the decreasing destructiveness of spine surgery is IDET, which has developed as a potential alternative to open spinal fusion in patients with internal disc disease.

The issue of destructiveness, although difficult to circumscribe, is a critical consideration in presurgical psychological screening (PPS). To the extent that the surgery involves more tissue destruction, it necessarily requires more psychological stamina. Even in cases where the spine surgery is effective, the increasing destructiveness of the surgery frequently gives rise to a number of problems:

- Recovery time is more protracted.
- More narcotic medication is required for pain control.
- External appliances, such as back braces, canes, or walkers, may need to be used.
- Pacing of recovery is more difficult (i.e., the patient may have more difficulty determining the speed with which to return to normal functioning).
- The chances of full functional recovery are decreased.

Thus, an evaluation of destructiveness is a key element in PPS. Given the increased opportunities for problems to arise, PPS is more helpful for patients who would undergo relatively destructive procedures. Further, in formulating a recommendation following PPS, the psychologist can consider destructiveness to be a factor reducing the probability of good clinical outcome.

NONORGANIC SIGNS

It has long been recognized that the relationship between tissue damage and subjective pain experience is both enigmatic and complex. One patient may experience intense pain with only minor identifiable tissue damage, whereas another may suffer a severe injury but have no pain. In fact, within the same individual, sensitivity to pain is a fluid concept. In a classic study in pain psychology, Beecher (1956) examined the pain experience of soldiers wounded during the invasion of Italy in World War II. He found that at the time of the injury soldiers experienced less pain, and required less medication, than civilian counterparts who suffered similar types of wounds. However, once the soldiers left the battlefield and went to the infirmary, they experienced pain at a level similar to that of the civilians. Apparently, the exigencies of battle—relief at surviving the wound, fear, and so forth—blocked the experience of pain until the soldiers were in a safe environment, where they then felt the pain.

The issue of sensitivity to pain is one of the overarching themes of chronic pain management. Pain sensitivity concerns the relationship between tissue damage (i.e., nociception) and subjective pain experience. A patient is often considered to be pain sensitive, or to display symptom magnification, when the level of pain experienced, as well as the level of physical disability displayed, is inconsistent with identified physical pathology. The psychologist often makes a determination of pain sensitivity from elevations on the Hypochondriasis (Hs) and Hysteria (Hy) scales of the Minnesota Multiphasic Personality Inventory (MMPI) (see chapter 5). Physicians, however, often attempt to assess symptom magnification through a special adaptation of their classic diagnostic procedure, the physical exam, as developed by Waddell et al. (1980). This procedure relies on five simple standardized tests to specifically identify nonorganic signs separable from and independent of organic pathological conditions:

1. tenderness
   a. superficial—pain caused by a light pinch over the lumbar skin
   b. nonanatomic—deep tenderness to palpation over a wide area of the lumbar skin
2. stimulation
   a. axial loading—low back pain caused when the examiner presses down on the patient's head
   b. rotation—low back pain caused when the examiner rotates the patient's shoulders and pelvis in the same plane
3. distraction: unobtrusive observation of patient behavior to determine findings that occur only on formal examination and are absent at other times; most often observed during prone straight leg raising (patient has greater range of motion when distracted than during formal examination) but also can be observed while the patient is seated
4. regional disturbances: widespread problems not explainable on the basis of accepted neuroanatomy, including
   a. weakness—partial cogwheel "giving way" of many muscle groups inconsistent with localized neurologic basis
   b. sensory—diminished sensation to light touch or pinprick fitting a stocking rather than a dermatomal pattern
5. overreaction: "disproportionate verbalization," facial expression, muscle tension, collapsing, or sweating during examination

If the patient shows three or more of these five types of signs, now often called Waddell signs, the patient's pain is declared to have a nonorganic component.

Waddell's original research and subsequent independent studies have demonstrated that nonorganic signs can be reliably assessed and have significant clinical utility. The signs have shown high interrater reliability (> 80% agreement) and high test-retest reliability (> 85% agreement at 23 days).

They are independent of (i.e., have no correlation with) medical symptoms such as referred leg pain, radiological findings of spinal abnormality, or objective evidence of nerve root compression. The presence of a nonorganic component (at least three of the five signs) was found in about 10% of patients presenting to a general orthopedic clinic but in more than one third of patients referred by surgeons to a spine clinic (Waddell et al., 1980).

There appears to be a strong relationship between nonorganic signs and other independent measures that might be considered to assess pain sensitivity. Waddell et al. (1980) found that nonorganic signs are significantly correlated (r^2 = .35) with MMPI elevations on the Hypochondriasis scale. Reesor and Craig (1998) examined the relationship between nonorganic signs and a number of medical, behavioral, and psychological measures in 80 back pain patients. In this study, *medically incongruent pain* was operationally defined as the presence of two or more Waddell signs, three or more inappropriate symptoms, or a high score on the Ransford Pain Drawing (Ransford, Cairns, & Mooney, 1979). Patients with incongruent pain complaints had greater physical impairment and disability than those with consistent pain complaints (control participants). The incongruent-pain patients were found to have poorer ability to cope with pain as determined by greater scores on the catastrophizing dimension of the Coping Strategies Questionnaire (Rosenstiel & Keefe, 1983) (see chapter 5). Incongruent-pain patients also had greater observed pain behavior when observed during a standardized assessment protocol (Keefe & Block, 1982) and reported a higher level of depression.

Nonorganic signs have been examined in relationship to recovery from back injury. Wernecke, Harris, and Lichter (1993) found that patients displaying nonorganic signs showed diminished response to a work-hardening program—an aggressive physical conditioning program designed to simulate work tasks. Similarly, Lehmann, Russell, and Spratt (1983) found that transcutaneous electrical nerve stimulation was less effective in patients who had nonorganic signs. Further, a number of studies have shown that nonorganic signs predict delayed return to work or recovery from injury (e.g., Lancourt & Kettlehut, 1992). Of particular significance is a study of 55 acute back pain patients that excluded patients having a history of psychological disturbance or comorbid physical conditions (Gaines & Hegman, 1999). Patients having one or more nonorganic signs had a mean return to work time of 58.5 days versus 15.0 days for patients with no organic signs. The two signs most strongly correlated with prolonged return to work were axial loading and rotation. Nonorganic signs have been investigated in several studies on spine surgery. Dzioba and Doxey (1984) found that nonorganic signs constituted a major risk factor for poor surgical results. Sorenson (1992) found atypical pain distribution, one of the signs (sign 4; Waddell et al., 1980) to be a risk factor.

Given the broad range of well-conducted research on nonorganic signs, it is not surprising that many spine surgeons conduct some form of assessment for Waddell's signs during their evaluation of the patient. Examination of these results in the medical chart can provide evidence of pain sensitivity. However, Main and Waddell (1998) suggested that the presence of nonorganic signs should be interpreted cautiously. They urged clinicians to consider the signs a reaction to a physical examination. Their presence does not suggest that the patient is consciously manufacturing or faking pain. Nonorganic signs may be at least partially explained, in some cases, by physical factors not related directly to identifiable organic pathology. For example, patients with soft tissue injuries may develop deconditioning syndrome, which can result in behaviors resembling the nonorganic signs. Finally, clinicians must avoid using the signs as the only basis for concluding that the patient's pain is influenced by factors other than physical pathology, and they should especially avoid overinterpreting the presence of individual signs. Main and Waddell cautioned that interpretation of the signs "should be clarified by identification of other clinical and psychological features that may co-exist at the time of the physical examination" (p. 2369). Fortunately, the psychologist conducting a PPS can provide such independent verification.

PAIN DRAWINGS

Almost every surgeon now includes a pain drawing as part of the patient's intake package. As initially described by Ransford et al. (1976) and modified by Ohnmeiss (2000), the pain drawing consists of front and back outlines of a human figure, along with instructions to the patient for identifying the pain distribution and quality on the outlines (see Figure 3.1). The pain drawing allows the clinician not only to rapidly visualize the areas in which the patient is experiencing pain, but also to assess certain aspects of the patient's perception of the pain. A number of researchers have developed procedures for scoring and classifying the pain drawings; these quantitative procedures hold the keys to the utility of the pain drawing.

The most commonly used scoring method was developed by Ransford et al. (1976), who used a penalty point method to identify pain drawings that are "abnormal," or indicative of pain that is not solely attributable to physical pathology. Penalty points can be scored in three domains. The first domain is poor anatomic localization, indicated in drawings of total leg pain, circumferential foot or thigh pain, or bilateral anterior tibial area pain. The second domain, pain expansion or magnification, is indicated in drawings of back pain radiating to the iliac crest, groin, or anterior perineum; anterior knee pain; or pain drawn outside the outline of the body. The final domain, termed "I particularly hurt here," includes explanatory notes added to the outline, circling of painful areas, use of arrows, or use of multiple pain symbols (see Figure 3.1). A drawing is considered abnormal if it scores three or more points. This system has shown strong interrater reliability ($r^2 = .97$).

PAIN DRAWING

Name _____

Date _____

Where is your pain?
Please mark (using the symbols) the areas on your body where you feel the
following sensations:

	^^^^		oooo		====		xxxx		////
Ache	^^^^	Numbness	oooo	Pins and needles	====	Burning	xxxx	Stabbing	////
	^^^^		oooo		====		xxxx		////

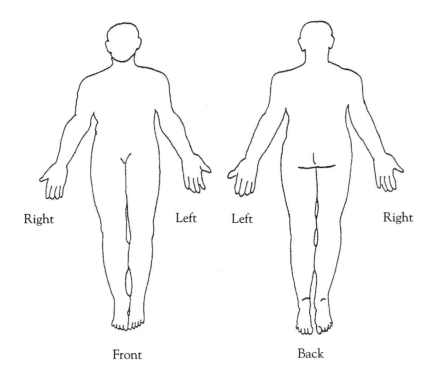

Right		Left	Left		Right

Front   Back

Figure 3.1. Sample form containing a human figure outline used for pain drawings.

Other, less commonly used scoring systems focus on grid scoring techniques
in which the body outlines are divided into regions and the number and
distribution of regions shaded in by the patient are counted (Mann & Brown,
1991; Margolis, Tait, & Krause, 1986).

The Ransford et al. (1976) scoring system, and other techniques for analyzing pain drawings, address a familiar theme—the inconsistent relationship of organic pathology to pain complaint. It should not be surprising, then, that Ransford et al. found that patients having abnormal pain drawings scored higher on the MMPI Hs and Hy scales than did patients with normal drawings, with overall agreement between the MMPI and pain drawings of 87% (for similar results, see Dennis, Rocchio, & Wiltse, 1981; Herron & Pheasant, 1982). Using a scoring system similar to that of Ransford et al. developed by Uden and Landin (1987), Chan, Goodman, Ilstrup, Kunselman, and O'Neill (1993) found that patients who had a high number of Waddell signs also tended to have abnormal pain drawings.

Pain drawings not only seem to be an effective means of measuring pain sensitivity; they have also been found to be predictive of treatment outcome. Uden, Astrom, & Bergenudd (1988) found that patients whose pain drawings were classified as "nonanatomic" had poor outcome following conservative treatment. Takata and Hirotani (1995), investigating patients with lumbar disc herniation, lumbar stenosis, or benign back pain, found that patients who had low scores on the Ransford et al. (1976) penalty point system had better treatment outcome than patients whose scores were high. Most significantly, a number of studies have found that abnormal pain drawings are associated with reduced effectiveness of spine surgery. In the Takata and Hirotani study, surgical patients with atypical pain drawings displayed a less satisfactory responses to surgery, as did the group of patients who underwent conservative treatment. Sorenson (1992) found that discectomy was not as effective in patients whose pain drawings were atypical for herniated discs. Dzioba and Doxey (1984) also found that abnormal pain drawings were associated with reduced surgical outcome. Given that pain drawings are nearly ubiquitous in their use by spine surgeons, this simple source of information is a powerful piece of evidence to consider in PPS.

PREVIOUS SURGERIES

Oaklander and North (2001) defined failed back surgery syndrome as "persistent or recurrent, chronic pain after one or more surgical procedures on the lumbosacral spine" (pp. 1540–1549). Unfortunately, this syndrome is much more common than desirable. Oaklander and North reported that 10% to 40% of all spine surgeries result in this syndrome. For many patients, the next step following failed back surgery is additional surgery. Franklin et al. (1994) found that 23% of patients who underwent lumbar fusion had a subsequent spine surgery within 2 years, and Hoffman et al.'s (1993) review found a 10% reoperation rate with laminectomy/discectomy. These repeat operations are often unsuccessful. North et al. (1993) found a success rate from reoperation of about one third. Pheasant et al. (1979) found that patients with multiple prior operations had a much lower probability of good outcome than did single-surgery patients. Similar results have been obtained by a number of authors (Ciol et al., 1994; Franklin et al., 1994; Turner et al., 1992). Such findings led Waddell (1987) to conclude that the probability of good surgical outcome decreases with each successive surgical intervention.

The not-infrequent failure of reoperation has led to the development of interventional procedures designed not to correct underlying pathology in patients with failed back surgery syndrome, but rather to ameliorate the patient's symptoms by modulating the sensations produced by the pathology. Spinal cord stimulation, the most widely used of these procedures, involves implantation of electrodes along the spinal column to block, reduce, or alter ascending nociceptive input. A trial implant, typically of 1 week's duration, allows the surgeon to predict the effectiveness of the implant. If significant pain relief is achieved during the trial (as it is in approximately 75% of patients), the electrodes are permanently implanted. Results of spinal cord stimulation show that at long-term follow-up, approximately 50% of patients have achieved significant reduction in pain intensity (De La Porte & Van de Kelft, 1993), with a somewhat greater percentage able to reduce medication use and report improvements in lifestyle (see North et al., 1993, for similar results). An implanted continuous infusion morphine pump delivering medication intrathecally or into the epidural space around the spinal cord is another, albeit somewhat less successful and more controversial, technique for reduction of pain sensation for failed back surgery patients.

Fortunately, underlying pathology can be successfully corrected in some patients who have undergone previous spine surgery, and there are some factors that may militate toward successful reoperation. Patients who have responded well to previous spine surgery generally respond better to additional fusion than do those who have not shown such sanguine previous results (Lehmann & Rocca, 1981), suggesting that the coping skills patients apply in their recovery from spine surgery carry over to new injuries. Numerous factors concerning the underlying pathology can also influence surgical results. For example, findings of disc herniation are associated with good surgical results in patients with failed back surgery syndrome (Kim, 1992). Patients with pseudoarthrosis (unstable fusion) seem to have reduced outcome (Lehmann & Rocca, 1981), although when the fusion is successfully corrected the outcome rate of revision surgery can be quite high—81% in one study (Kim & Michelsen, 1992). In line with Waddell's (1987) observation, patients with fewer previous spine surgeries do better in reoperation than do those with a greater number of surgeries. All these influences on reoperation speak to the complexity of considering previous spine surgery as a significant risk factor.

PRIOR MEDICAL UTILIZATION

Just as prior surgery can prejudice outcome, a history of many prior illnesses or nonspine surgeries bodes poorly for recovery from both conservative care and invasive spine procedures. Wiltse and Rocchio (1975) found that high scores on the Cornell Medical Index, a questionnaire that assesses past illness and bodily symptoms, were associated with poor outcome of chemonucleolysis. Hoffmann et al. (1993), in examining multiple surgical outcome studies, found that improved discectomy outcome was generally more likely in patients who had lower numbers of previous hospitalizations. Ciol et al. (1994), examining a Medicare population, found that patients who had relatively greater numbers of previous hospitalizations were at increased risk of lumbar spine reoperations. Similarly, in the conservative treatment of chronic back pain, Deyo and Diehl (1988) found that positive responses to the question, "Do you feel sick all the time?" correlated significantly with poor treatment outcome, including decreased reduction in pain, a higher number of visits to physicians, and compensation seeking.

Such findings suggest that a high level of prior medical utilization may be a risk factor for reduced spine surgery outcome, perhaps because it reflects sensitivity not only to pain but also to physical symptoms in general. That is, some back pain patients may be more likely to attend to and be distressed by unusual physical symptoms, leading to frequent illness complaints and the seeking of medical treatment. Such patients may also be less likely to filter out symptoms or to feel relieved by medical procedures.

Rollman and colleagues (e.g., Lautenbacher & Rollman, 1999) used the term hypervigilance to describe the characteristic of heightened awareness of physical symptoms. Hypervigilance has been demonstrated to occur in a number of medical conditions. Scudds, Rollman, Harth, and McCain (1987), for example, assessed hypervigilance in patients with fibromyalgia, a condition characterized by numerous tender points. Sensitivity to pain at these tender points, as well as at nontender control points, was assessed by the application of pressure to the points. Patients with fibromyalgia had lower pain pressure thresholds at both the tender and the nontender points compared to control participants. Significantly, hypervigilance has been shown to extend beyond the domain of pain. McDermid, Rollman, and McCain (1996) found that fibromyalgia patients presented with brief bursts of white noise tolerated only 66 dB, a level that sounded only moderately loud to control participants. Similarly, summarizing the results of a number of studies, Crowell and Barofsky (1999) reported on findings of hypervigilance in patients with irritable bowel syndromes or nonulcer dyspepsia, a condition characterized by recurrent epigastric pain. Sensitivity in this population was assessed by inflating a gastric balloon with air as a physical stimulus. Both epigastric pain groups perceived gut distension with lower levels of balloon inflation than did control participants. Thus, many studies, across a wide range of pain syndromes, indicate that certain individuals may be highly sensitive to abnormal physical symptoms, increasing the likelihood that they will undergo medical procedures and diminishing their ability to overcome their pain problems.

LIFESTYLE ISSUES

Chronic back pain is the enemy of a healthy lifestyle. Patients in pain sleep poorly. Back pain limits activity and reduces physical strength through the process of deconditioning. In some areas, however, back pain patients exercise choices that can militate for or against improved spine surgery results. Two such areas are smoking and obesity.

Research has indicated a number of connections between smoking and chronic spine problems. Smokers may be predisposed to develop back pain. Hellsing and Bryngelsson (2000) followed soldiers who enlisted for duty in the Swedish army over 20 years. They found, among other factors, that smoking more than 11 cigarettes per day increased the odds of having back pain that interfered with everyday life to about 1.5—about the same increase in odds as having a medium heavy job (in terms of physical effort involved). Scott, Goldberg, Mayo, Stock, and Poîtras (1999), in a retrospective study of more than 2,000 participants, half of whom had a diagnosis of scoliosis, found that there was a significant correlation in smoking and back pain for men with scoliosis and for women who both had and did not have scoliosis. In fact, men with scoliosis who smoked a pack a day for at least 30 years had an odds ratio for significant back pain of 1.85 compared to pain at baseline. Even adolescent smokers are more likely to report back pain than their nonsmoking counterparts (Feldman, Rossignol, Shrier, & Abenhaim, 1999).

It is not surprising, then, that smoking has also been correlated with the development of intervertebral disc problems. An et al. (1994) examined smoking history in spine surgery candidates with disc herniations and in nonsurgical controls. Surgical candidates were much more likely to have a smoking history, whether their disc problems were in the lumbar spine (56% of smokers vs. 37% of nonsmokers) or in the cervical spine (64% of smokers vs. 37% of nonsmokers). The authors concluded that the relative risk for the development of disc disease in smokers is 3.0 for lumbar discs and 3.9 for cervical discs. This result contrasts somewhat with that of Leboeuf-Yde (1999), who reviewed 47 studies examining the relationship of smoking and low back pain (but not disc disease). In the 11 studies with the largest sample sizes ($n > 3,000$), 64% of participants (7 of 11 studies) reported an association between smoking and back pain, the odds ratio ranging from 2.3 to 4.3. Surprisingly, a dose-response relationship between smoking and pain was found in only the largest study ($n > 30,000$). Leboeuf-Yde concluded that smoking should be considered a weak risk factor, and not a cause, in low back pain.

Literature on the relationship of smoking to the outcome of spine surgery is not extensive (Leboeuf-Yde, 2000). Manniche et al. (1994) questioned discectomy patients about smoking history and found that smokers were significantly less likely to achieve good spine surgery results than were nonsmokers; on the other hand, in a study in our laboratory (Block et al., 2001), smoking was not found to significantly influence clinical outcome. C. W.

Brown, Orme, and Richardson (1986) found that smoking may lead not only to failure to achieve good clinical outcome, but may also affect surgical results. For patients undergoing spinal fusion, the authors found that 8% of nonsmokers and 40% of smokers developed pseudoarthrosis (failed fusion). Interestingly, these authors also found that smokers had lower levels of PO_2 and concluded that "Pseudoarthrosis is more likely to develop in smokers because inadequate oxygenation of blood flow to the bone graft appears to result in formation of fibrous tissue rather than bone" (p. 943).

In a similar study, Glassman et al. (1998) found that the pseudoarthrosis rate after posterior lumbar instrumented fusion in smokers who continued to smoke after the surgery was 26.5%, compared to 14.2% in nonsmokers. Interestingly, patients who quit for longer than 6 months following surgery improved their chances of a solid fusion; this group had a pseudoarthrosis rate of 17.1%. Recent studies have found that, at least in the case of fusion patients, the probability of good surgical outcome in smokers may be improved through the use of bone stimulation (Mooney, 1990).

Another aspect of lifestyle, obesity, has long been speculated to be associated with higher risk of failure from spine surgery. The adverse impact of obesity seems logical for a number of reasons. First, surgery is lengthier and more complicated in obese patients. Second, obesity places greater physical stress on the structure of the spine. A large abdomen pulls the lumbar spine forward, increasing strain on discs, facets, and ligaments. In fact, Mayfield (1993) reported that for every pound of excess weight above the waistline, 5 lb of additional pressure is added to the spine.

A number of studies have found that obesity increases the risk for development of back pain. The Hellsing and Bryngelsson (2000) study found that individuals who at military enlistment had a body mass index (body weight divided by the square of height) of greater than 25 had an average odds ratio of 1.45 for significant interference in their lives due to back pain. Similarly Croft, Papageorgiou, Thomas, MacFarlane, and Silman (1999), in a prospective study of 2,715 adults from the general population, found that women with a high body weight (greater than 85.5 kg) had a 1.8 odds ratio for the development of new back pain, although body weight did not increase the men's odds of developing pain. Obesity has not been studied extensively in relation to spine surgery outcome. However, in our study (Block et al., 2001) using a stepwise hierarchical regression model, obesity (defined as greater than 50% above ideal body weight) was the only "medical" risk factor that contributed significantly to the prediction of outcome—a stronger predictor than chronicity, number of previous surgeries, or even type of surgery undergone.

The results of the few studies examining smoking and obesity in relation to spine surgery outcome point to these two issues as moderate risk factors. They also suggest that in evaluation of spine surgery candidates, psychologists should probe for additional lifestyle information. There is evidence that regular physical exercise can greatly improve the outcome of spine surgery (Dolan, Greenfield, Nelson, & Nelson, 2000); the psychologist should therefore assess extent to which the patient engaged in physical exercise before the injury. The patient's perception of his or her healthiness may also be critical to assess. Croft et al. (1999) found that poor self-rated health compared to peers greatly increased the risk for development of back pain in both men and women. Von Korff, Dworkin, & LeResche (1990) found that poorer health status was associated with higher, more persistent, and more disabling pain complaints. Katz et al. (1999), examining patients who underwent decompressive laminectomy/discectomy for degenerative lumbar stenosis, found that better self-rated health status was the strongest predictor of outcome, improving the odds of good outcome by 3.6 to 3.8. In general, then, a healthy lifestyle, including regular exercise, a balanced diet, and abstention from smoking, appears to promote recovery from spine surgery and should be examined as a component of PPS.

CONCLUSION

The psychologist conducting PPS should begin by examining factors in the medical realm. A thorough review of the medical chart provides a great deal of insight into the patient's medical status, and the psychologist can explore in detail during the interview portion of the evaluation any risk factors identified, as well as relevant lifestyle issues. Only a truly biopsychosocial assessment of back pain can allow for effective, individualized treatment plans.

4

BEHAVIORAL AND HISTORICAL INFLUENCES: THE PSYCHOLOGICAL EXAMINATION

For the initial evaluation of back pain patients, spine surgeons rely on two sources of information. The first is the physical examination, a process that involves poking and palpating, measuring and attending, speculating and testing. The physician attempts during the physical exam to "reproduce the patient's symptoms and identify the location of the problem" (Rodriguez, 1993), as well as to determine the consistency of pain complaints. The second source of information is an examination of the patient's medical history, including the course of the pain from onset to present, the patient's perception of the pain and the limitations it causes, and the means the patient uses to keep pain at bay. Using their powers of observation and drawing on years of experience, surgeons can greatly clarify the basis of the pain during the initial medical evaluation, which will also indicate additional, more objective diagnostic tests to obtain further clarity. By showing deep concern for the patient and expertise during this initial information gathering, the surgeon gains patients' confidence and trust, feelings that can be critical to recovery.

The psychological examination of a spine surgery candidate bears many similarities to the medical examination. Interview techniques prod and probe to reveal symptoms of pain and their emotional sequelae. The psychologist brings his or her own powers of observation and years of experience to bear during the interview process in gathering such information as clues to the consistency of pain symptoms, the depth of depression or extent of anxiety experienced, and the effects of pain and medications on cognitive functioning. Effectively timed questions can allow the psychologist to uncover motivations and incentives for recovery. Detailed questioning of the patient's history, not only of pain but also of prior emotional, social, and behavioral problems, can identify significant influences on recovery. Both surgeon and psychologist question the patient about the past and observe the patient's present symptoms in seeking the best route for future recovery.

GOALS OF THE PPS INTERVIEW

The presurgical psychological screening (PPS) interview serves three functions: the gathering of information from the patient, the communication of information to the patient, and assistance in the development of a treatment plan. First, the interview has an information gathering function. The psychologist comes to the interview already having reviewed the research on key risk factors for reduced spine surgery results and after thoroughly familiarizing himself or herself with the patient's medical chart. The interview offers the opportunity to question the patient in detail about identified risk factors and observe his or her answers, allowing for more complete insight and perhaps unearthing plausible explanations that might mitigate a factor's negative influence on treatment outcome. For example, a history of substance abuse is a surgical risk factor. However, questioning the patient about the reasons for abuse may reveal that this problem resulted from a thoughtless physician maintaining the patient on high doses of narcotics for many months or even years without any appreciable treatment gains. In such a case, especially if the patient has overcome the narcotics abuse, the psychologist could rightly consider this risk factor as not especially influential.

The second function of the PPS interview is informational also, but in this case it is to provide the patient with information about the surgery and recovery. The psychologist often gets only one opportunity, the PPS interview, to interact with the patient. It is important to take advantage of this opportunity to convey significant information that may augment recovery. For example, a candidate for spinal fusion who engages in high levels of physical activity may need to be advised to carefully pace his or her recovery, to avoid returning to work too quickly, and especially to avoid taking high levels of narcotics in order to achieve such activity increases. A more indolent patient may need just the opposite advice—to be assiduous, to push as hard as possible to achieve functional gains postoperatively.

Informing the patient about the nature of the surgery, describing the expected recovery course, providing advice for improvements, and so forth require a thorough understanding of the proposed surgery and of the referring physician's approach to rehabilitation. The psychologist must be careful not to overreach in providing this information and must avoid giving the patient advice that will be contradicted by the surgeon. As the psychologist gains expertise and experience with PPS, he or she can become a critical conduit of information to the patient.

The final goal of the PPS interview is to aid in developing a treatment plan that can facilitate the outcome of surgery. By coming to a thorough understanding of the patient's perception of and reaction to pain, the psychologist can make plans for training the patient in coping strategies. Detailed questioning about marital history, including reactive changes in sexuality and marital quality, can help the psychologist determine to what extent the spouse or other support person should be involved in the development of the treatment plan.

Most importantly, when a patient is a questionable surgical risk, the interview may point to ways for further assessing and augmenting the patient's motivation for recovery. For example, when the PPS reveals that a patient who smokes also has fairly high level of identified psychosocial risk, the psychologist may propose a plan to stop smoking, thereby testing the patient's commitment to an active recovery process.

INTERVIEW TECHNIQUES

The first key to a successful interview begins before the patient ever enters the room. The psychologist should review the medical record as thoroughly as possible to understand the pathological basis of the pain and the relative destructiveness of the proposed surgery. By knowing the type of surgery being contemplated, the psychologist is in a better position to weigh the levels of stamina and motivation shown by the patient against those required for rehabilitation and recovery.

The psychologist can also assess motivation in certain aspects of the medical record. The log of medication use may indicate when the patient has stronger desires for maintaining rather than controlling narcotic consumption, if patterns of giving excuses for lost medication or rapidly escalating doses of narcotics are seen. Noncompliance with recommended conservative treatments is often well documented in the medical record and can be a source for significant discussion during the interview. Review of the medical record sets the stage for the interview, allowing the psychologist to understand the nature of the patient's pain and the proposed treatment, as well as providing clues to the patient's motivations and frustrations in overcoming the pain.

Once the PPS interview begins, it is important that the psychologist begin by explaining to the patient the rationale for the evaluation. Most patients who seek surgery for spine pain have little recognition of the importance of a psychological assessment within the evaluation process. They understandably see the pain as a direct result of a physical injury or underlying pathological process. Therefore, they are often confused, or even hostile, when referred for a mental health evaluation.

The explanation of the rationale for the evaluation should be straightforward. The psychologist should inform the patient that PPS is a routine procedure, very frequently ordered by surgeons, that can help maximize the effectiveness of the surgery. The psychologist should explain to the patient that the experience of chronic pain can create many emotional and interpersonal difficulties and that some of these can make recovery from spine surgery more difficult. He or she can observe that by uncovering and discussing the ways in which pain has affected their lives, many patients have felt a sense of relief, lessening their sense of desperation. Not infrequently, patients have received conflicting information from physicians or have developed poor relationships with health care providers. The interview can be presented as an opportunity for patients to discuss such problems, increasing their confidence and trust in their care providers. In short, the psychologist can establish the interview as a means of addressing not simply the pain, but also the person in pain.

To enhance the success of PPS, it is critical that the psychologist use a previously prepared semistructured interview format and a form for recording patient responses during the interview. These tools help ensure that none of the specific information required to arrive at a surgical prognosis will be missed. Each psychologist needs to develop an interview format that elicits these key pieces of data, while blending with his or her own interviewing style.

The real advantage of the semistructured interview format is that it allows the psychologist to pursue topics with the patient in a nonlinear fashion. For example, most spine surgery candidates are initially reluctant to discuss emotional or interpersonal problems. For such patients the early phases of the interview can focus on the history of the injury, including the pain sensations experienced and previous medical treatments. Other patients, with perhaps higher levels of distress, are more eager to talk about the impact of the pain on their lives and to discuss their worries and fears. The semistructured interview allows patient needs and personality to guide the timing and depth of questions. As the interview proceeds, a quick glance at the prepared interview response form will prompt the psychologist to ask questions that fill in any missing data (see Block, 1996, for a sample interview form).

The final key component of the PPS interview is observation of the patient. Patients in pain are likely to show it in many ways. Patients sit and move uncomfortably, shifting their weight and grimacing. They may wince, gasp in pain, or cry out. They may display signs of depression—a sloppy appearance, exhaustion, tearfulness, softened speech. Angry behavior—resistance, yelling, tension—is also often seen. Of particular importance is the relationship between observed behavior and patient reports of pain and of emotional state. Patients who state that they are severely depressed but appear relaxed, display a full range of affect, and laugh and smile throughout the interview may be disingenuous in their reports of emotional distress. On the other hand, some more stoic patients who refuse to acknowledge their emotional distress may exhibit obvious behavioral indications of depression or anxiety.

One of the most important areas for observation during the interview involves the consistency between the patient's report of pain sensation and the level of pain behavior he or she displays. The psychologist should take note when a patient who reports extreme pain appears to sit and move comfortably. Keefe and Block (1982) found that it is possible to systematically observe and quantify the pain behaviors low back pain patients display and that such behaviors correlate strongly with pain report. In this study, patients were videotaped while engaging in a series of movements, including sitting, standing, walking, and reclining. Videotapes were scored by trained observers using a time-sampling procedure for the presence of five operationally defined pain behaviors:

1. bracing—using a limb to abnormally support weight;
2. guarding—stiff, interrupted movement;
3. grimacing—a facial expression of pain;
4. rubbing—touching the affected area; and
5. sighing—an exaggerated exhalation of pain.

Overall interobserver reliability was quite high, in the .85 to .95 range. Most importantly, these behaviors correlated strongly ($r = .67–.81$) with patient pain reports on a 0 to 10 scale (for replications and extensions of this study, see Baumstark et al., 1993, Buckelew et al., 1994; McDaniel et al., 1986). Although it is not possible for most psychologists conducting PPS to observe pain behavior in such a systematic fashion, it is important to be alert for the consistency of pain behaviors not only with reported pain levels, but also in different settings and conditions of observation. Unobtrusive observation of the patient in the waiting room, while walking down the hall, and after completing the interview may raise questions about the level of pain the patient is experiencing or confirm the pain's severity.

CONTENT OF THE INTERVIEW

Behavioral Factors

Pain is more than just a noxious sensation. Pain also has strong effects on behavior. Functional activities, such as walking, sitting, lifting, and working, may be severely limited. Individuals observing a person in pain can tell that pain is being experienced by the moans, grimaces, and limping the person displays. Spine pain patients also verbalize their experience in letting others know that they need medical attention.

It was in the pioneering work of Fordyce (1976) that behavioral aspects of chronic pain were first appreciated. According to Fordyce, chronic pain behaviors are like any others in that they are amenable to reinforcement (i.e., rewards and punishments) provided by others and the social environment. Although pain behaviors arise from damaged tissues, when family members, employers, or the legal system provides incentives for such behaviors, the behaviors may be maintained "long after the original nociceptive stimulus has been resolved" (Fordyce, 1976, p. 59). In other words, if the patient's pain behaviors lead to desirable consequences, then according to this perspective the pain behaviors will strengthen, consuming more of the patient's life and becoming more resistant to intervention.

Early research on the behavioral aspects of pain supported such a perspective. Cairns and Pasino (1977), for example, systematically applied social rewards to pain-related behavior within the context of a multidisciplinary, noninvasive treatment program. Staff members were trained to reward the patient with praise for increases in certain therapeutic activities (e.g., riding on a stationary bicycle) but not to reward other behaviors (e.g., walking on a track). Results showed that only rewarded behaviors increased, whereas nonrewarded behaviors did not change. When reinforcement was shifted, so that a previously nonreinforced behavior was then praised, that behavior increased, while previously rewarded behaviors decreased when staff ignored them.

The notion that pain behaviors are responsive to reward and punishment has provided a strong direction for research in chronic pain. There is also clear evidence that behavioral factors can exert significant influence on recovery from spine surgery.

Vocational Factors

Spine injuries culminating in surgery often occur on the job. Individuals in certain job classifications are particularly vulnerable. People whose jobs involve long-distance driving requirements (Kelsey & Golden, 1988), such as traveling salespeople, are at particularly high risk for back injuries, as are those whose jobs involve frequent heavy lifting, bending, and twisting (see Battie & Bigos, 1991, for other vocational predictors of back pain complaints).

However, psychosocial aspects of employment also predict the development of spine problems. The most dramatic research in this area was the seminal study by Bigos et al. (1991) of 3,000 aircraft employees followed for a period of 4 years. The experimenters found that job dissatisfaction was strongly associated with back injuries. Those workers who expressed strong agreement with the statement "I hardly ever enjoy the tasks involved in my job" were 2.5 times more likely to report back pain than were those who expressed high levels of job satisfaction. In numerous subsequent studies, occupational dissatisfaction, as well as job stress, have been found to predict the development of back problems.

Marras, Davis, Heaney, Maronitis, & Allread (2000), in an ingenious study, identified one pathway through which vocational factors such stress or dissatisfaction may lead to back problems. In this study, volunteer participants (not complaining of spine pain) were required to perform a standardized lifting task. Spine compression and surface electromyography (EMG) readings of the low back musculature were taken during the lifting task. All participants were required to perform several repetitions of the task under two different conditions. During the "unstressed condition," participants received extensive praise and encouragement from the experimenter, whereas during the "stressed condition," the experimenter constantly criticized and belittled the participants. Results showed that under the stressed condition, participants had greater lumbar disc compression and showed greater lateral sheer than under the unstressed condition. These results were particularly true for women and for individuals who scored high on introversion and intuition on the Myers-Briggs Type Indicator. Surface EMG activity in the erector spinae muscles was also higher under the stressed condition. The authors suggested that "the cumulative effect of stress on muscle activity and spinal loads may prove to be a significant mechanism by which stress leads to low back pain" (p. 3051).

The results of the Marras et al. (1999) study were corroborated by an evaluation of 17,000 workers in Sweden (Vingard et al., 2000). In this study, a relative risk of 2.8 for reporting back pain was found for participants whose jobs contained a combination of heavy physical loads and high reported job strain, compared to those without such vocational conditions. It appears, then, that physical and psychosocial aspects of work can combine to increase the likelihood of developing spine problems.

Vocational factors also exert a strong influence on the outcome of conservative treatment. Fishbain, Cutler, Rosomoff, Khalil, and Steele-Rosomoff (1997) examined variables predicting work status among 128 back pain patients 30 months after they were treated at a multidisciplinary center. They derived a regression equation consisting of six significant predictors that correctly classified 75% of the patients. Three of these significant predictor variables related to work: perceived job stress, belief that work was dangerous, and the patient's intent to work. DeGood and Kiernan (1996) also found that attitude toward the employer, specifically in regard to a spine injury, affected the outcome of conservative spine treatment. Patients who blamed their employers for the injury had much poorer treatment results than did patients who assigned blame to other individuals, to themselves, or to no one in particular.

There has been a paucity of research examining the influence of occupational stress and strain on the outcome of spine surgery. The notable exception is the recent study by Schade, Semmer, Main, Hora, and Boos (1999) examining a host of variables predicting 2-year outcome of lumbar discectomy for 46 patients. In this study, several psychological aspects of work had strong associations with outcome. High levels of job satisfaction, a low level of occupational mental stress, and "job-related resignation" (acceptance that one must work even though the job is not desirable) were significant positive predictors of return to work. These same factors, to varying degrees, also predicted pain relief and overall outcome using Stauffer and Coventry (1972) criteria.

The results of the studies by Marras et al. (1999) and Vingard et al. (2000) suggest that individuals who perceive their work environments as being aversive, especially if their jobs involve heavy physical demands, may be particularly at risk for poor outcome from spine surgery. Although this notion has not been fully explored, several studies (e.g., R. A. Davis, 1994; Junge et al., 1995) have found that patients with physically intense jobs showed reduced surgical results. It remains to be seen how physical and psychosocial aspects of work might interact to influence recovery.

Although research is scarce specifically relating spine surgery outcome to psychosocial aspects of work (such as occupational stress, job satisfaction, and job-related resignation), the implications of the larger body of research in this area are clear. To the extent that patients enjoy their jobs, feel respect from their supervisors, do not hold their employers responsible for their injuries, and do not perceive their jobs as highly stressful, they are more likely to be responsive to both surgical and noninvasive spine treatment. Perhaps for patients who are not so favorably disposed toward their work, the incentives for experiencing or reporting improvements as a results of treatment are lacking, leading them to be less motivated for rehabilitation, more discouraged about the future, and more aware of their pain and limitations.

Workers' Compensation

Individuals who experience the onset of back pain while working, by definition, fall within the purview of workers' compensation. Such patients find themselves in a unique legal and medical situation. They are frequently sent initially to a company doctor, and their subsequent choices and control over their medical care are typically significantly limited. The workers' compensation insurance carrier often directs patients to designated specialists or otherwise restricts physician choice. Employers retain ultimate discretion in determining whether the patient should return to work after a spine injury. Frequently patients are required by employers to receive an unrestricted work release, something most physicians are initially reluctant to provide. Further, in most states, complicated workers' compensation laws place burdensome regulations on medical treatment, including preauthorization of treatments, specification of the types of treatments allowed, and a requirement of second and third opinions. Finally, for patients with severe injuries or those whose surgical recovery requires them to miss work, earned wages are replaced by temporary total disability payments.

In study after study patients whose injuries placed them within the workers' compensation system have tended to have poorer results from spine surgery. Klekamp et al. (1998), for example, examined 82 patients who underwent lumbar discectomy and found that 81% of non-workers' compensation patients achieved a good result, compared with only 29% of workers' compensation patients. Glassman et al. (1998) similarly found that workers' compensation patients fared poorer than non-workers' compensation patients in response to lumbar fusion procedures. Knox and Chapman (1993) found that workers' compensation patients with discogram-concordant pain reproduction had worse outcomes of anterior lumbar interbody fusion surgery than did non-workers' compensation patients. Diminished surgical outcome was found in a number of other studies, including R. A. Davis (1994), Greenough and Fraser (1989), Haddad (1987), Hudgins (1976), and V. M. Taylor et al. (2000). Such results led Frymoyer and Cats-Baril (1987) to state that "compensability" is one of the strongest predictors of excessive disability among back pain patients.

One might conclude, from the studies on workers' compensation, that surgical outcome for job-injured patients often is influenced more by the economic incentives to remain disabled than by the effectiveness of the surgery in correcting pathophysiology. After all, job-injured patients receive total disability payments from their employers while receiving treatment. Sometimes these payments provide even greater income than when the patient was working, especially if the patient has additional private disability policies that pay mortgage, automobile, or credit card debts. Certainly, such financial incentives can be powerful, but it is more often the case that employees receive substantially less income while on workers' compensation than while they are working. The average worker receives workers' compensation benefits equal to two-thirds of wages, and even with tax breaks the income level is rarely greater than 85% of wages (Block, 1992).

In fact, patients receiving workers' compensation experience a plethora of difficulties that may diminish surgical response. Workplace-related factors such as blaming the employer for the injury, job dissatisfaction, and occupational stress predispose individuals to seek medical care for job-related injuries and also can influence surgical outcome. Delays in treatment caused by cumbersome workers's compensation regulations or uncaring insurance adjusters can increase the extent of injury or the time required for recovery. Financial stress caused by the injury can divert the patient's focus away from rehabilitation efforts and place it instead on economic survival. These and numerous other factors may combine to make the behavioral disincentives for recovery almost insurmountable.

Dworkin, Handlin, Richlin, Brand, and Vannucci (1985) attempted to untangle the effects of workers' compensation, employment status, time off work, and litigation on short- and long-term noninvasive treatment response among 454 chronic pain patients. In univariate analyses, both compensation benefits and time off work predicted short-term outcome, but in a multiple regression analysis, only time off work predicted short-term results. Similarly, long-term results were predicted only by time off work. Such results imply that although workers' compensation status is a significant risk factor for reduced spine surgery results, this effect may be mediated by the many physical and emotional problems faced by patients with job-related injuries.

Litigation

Patients who are in pain have many reasons to seek legal recourse. Often injuries make them unable to work or significantly decrease their ability to function in their jobs. Litigation may be the only way to recoup some of this lost income. In some states, it is necessary to retain an attorney to receive workers' compensation benefits. Patients applying for social security disability benefits frequently find their applications repeatedly denied until they obtain legal representation and appear before an administrative law judge. Perhaps most significantly, the patient in pain frequently desires retribution against the individuals or institutions perceived as causing the injury. Litigation, then, can be an expression of anger.

It has long been speculated that for some patients, pain and disability are cynically related to litigation and other purely economic benefits derived from injuries. Kennedy (1946), for example, coined the term "compensation neurosis" to describe "a state of mind born out of fear, kept alive by avarice, and cured by verdict." For patients with such a "neurosis," treatment effectiveness would seem to be inversely related to financial compensation.

There is some evidence that litigants do have poorer surgical response. Finneson and Cooper (1979) found that both a history of lawsuits and secondary gain predicted reduced discectomy results. V. M. Taylor et al. (2000) found that whereas about two-thirds of fusion patients reported improvements in functional ability and quality of life at 1 year following surgery, several variables, including consultation with an attorney, contributed significantly to a multiple regression equation predicting reduced results. Klekamp et al. (1998) found that at 40 weeks following laminectomy/discectomy, 73% of patients who lacked legal representation achieved good results, compared to 17% of those with attorneys. Junge et al. (1995), in a Swiss study, found reduced discectomy results for patients applying for or receiving disability pensions, compared to results for nonapplicants. Similar reductions in surgical outcome have been found in a number of other studies (R. A. Davis, 1994; Glassman et al., 1998; Manniche et al., 1994).

Although these results make clear that litigation is associated with diminished surgical outcome, such results do not necessarily imply that litigating patients are malingering. The *DSM-IV* (American Psychiatric Association, 1994) defines malingering as "the intentional production of false or grossly exaggerated physical or psychological symptoms, motivated by external incentives" (p. 683). Malingering

> should be suspected if *any combination* [italics added] of the following is noted:
> 1. Medico-legal context of representation
> 2. Marked discrepancy between the person's claimed stress or disability and the objective findings
> 3. Lack of cooperation during the diagnostic evaluation and in complying with prescribed treatment regimen
> 4. The presence of Antisocial Personality Disorder. (p. 683)

This definition acknowledges that simply being represented by council does not make one a malingerer. The spine surgery candidate who has an objectively identified pathophysiologic basis for the pain, has been previously compliant, and is not antisocial should not be suspected of malingering. In fact, most surgeons report that malingering occurs only rarely. F. Leavitt and Sweet (1986), in a large survey of neurosurgeons and orthopedic surgeons, found that most believed malingering occurred in fewer than 5% of patients.

Malingering and deception among pain patients are extremely difficult to determine. The patient's pain experience is essentially subjective and cannot be directly measured. Craig, Hill, and McMurtry (1999) provided some guidelines for identifying malingering, pointing out that such a determination should be made only after examining in detail multiple information sources, including the patient's history, verbal behavior and nonverbal expression (preferably via unobtrusive observation or surveillance), and psychometric testing. Most difficult of all is to reach the conclusion that there is conscious intent behind the production of symptoms. Perhaps it is safest to conclude as Chapman (1978) did that financial incentives may make many litigating patients "somatically hypervigilant," or acutely aware of their pain.

Interpersonal Factors

Chronic pain can turn a family upside down. Because most spine surgery candidates are either unable to work or must significantly restrict work activities, family income is often drastically decreased, leading to overwhelming changes in lifestyle and, perhaps, the stress of phone calls from collections agencies. Almost inevitably there are significant role changes. A nonworking spouse may suddenly be forced to seek employment. Child care responsibilities may shift. Sexual activity may cease to exist.

In the face of the misery created by chronic pain, it is difficult for a spouse to determine how to cope and to help the patient. The patient's moans, groans, grimaces, and complaints may call forth conflicting visceral responses in the partner (Block, 1981). The desire to encourage the patient to take pain-relieving narcotics is counterbalanced by the knowledge that such medications can be addicting. The uninjured partner, exhausted after a long day of work making up for lost income, knows that rest is not possible, for if he or she does not take over most of the household chores, the patient will have to engage in activities that will increase pain. Perhaps most significantly, the partner must be attentive to the patient's physical and emotional needs, but may feel as though the patient cannot be burdened by listening and providing support in turn.

Spousal reactions are not merely multiply determined and emotionally charged; the spouse's response may also exert a significant influence on the patient's pain and recovery. Fordyce's (1976) behavioral conceptualization states that chronic pain behavior can increase if it is rewarded and will decrease or extinguish if rewards are withheld. A substantial body of research examining spousal response provides support for this viewpoint.

Block, Kremer, and Gaylor (1980) drew on operant learning theory (Skinner, 1974) in the design of a study assessing the influence of spousal response on pain behavior. Numerous operant studies have shown that when behavior is rewarded in the presence of particular environmental conditions, then the behavior tends to be exhibited if those conditions are present and is not exhibited in other conditions. A child, for example, is rewarded for using the toilet, so that hopefully urination and defecation occur only there and not in other situations. The conditions under which behavior is rewarded are termed "discriminative stimuli."

Block, Kremer, and Gaylor (1980) argued that it is the spouse who has the most frequent and potentially most powerful means to reward pain behavior. If the patient's grimacing, limping, or groaning frequently cause the spouse to attend to the patient, and especially if the spouse is generally less responsive to the patient at other times, then the spouse may become a "discriminative stimulus" for the patient to display pain behaviors. To test this implication of learning theory, the researchers asked chronic pain patients to rate how frequently their spouses showed various responses to pain behaviors. For example, did the spouse bring medications, tell the patient to avoid exertion, or take over household responsibilities? Based on these ratings, patients were divided into two groups—those with solicitous (pain-rewarding) spouses and those with nonsolicitous spouses. All patients in this study were also given a structured interview about their pain and treatment history. The interview was conducted under two different conditions of observation. During half of the interview, the patient was aware that the spouse was observing the process through a two-way mirror. During the other half of the interview, the patient was aware that an unfamiliar individual, the ward clerk, was observing. In each half of the interview the patient was asked to numerically rate current and average pain level. Results showed that spousal presence influenced pain report. Patients with solicitous spouses reported greater pain when the spouse was observing than when the ward clerk was observing. Those with nonsolicitous spouses showed the opposite pattern. Thus, in line with the predictions of learning theory, pain behavior is affected by rewards, and the spouse who provides pain-contingent reinforcement can become a discriminative stimulus triggering increases in the patient's pain behavior.

Many subsequent studies have confirmed and extended the results of the Block et al. (1980) study. Lousberg, Schmidt, & Groenman (1992) found that patients with solicitous spouses showed diminished physical exercise in the presence of the spouse. Kerns et al. (1991) used the Multidimensional Pain Inventory (MPI; Kerns, Turk, & Rudy, 1985) to measure spousal solicitousness and then videotaped chronic pain patients and their spouses, as well as control couples, as they performed a series of tasks such as sweeping the floor or changing bed linens. Patient and spouse behaviors were coded using a systematic behavioral observation system. Results showed that patients displayed higher rates of pain behavior during the tasks than did controls, and patients' spouses showed more solicitous behavior than did control spouses. Spousal solicitous behavior also correlated significantly with solicitousness as measured by the MPI.

Romano et al. (1995) also videotaped and coded patient–spouse interaction during household tasks. They found that solicitous spouse responses were significant predictors of the rate of overt pain behaviors among patients reporting high pain levels, and solicitousness also predicted disability among depressed pain patients.

Given the strong effects of spousal solicitousness on pain behavior, it would seem likely that spine surgery outcome would be influenced by patient–spouse interaction. Block et al. (2001) included spousal solicitousness in the measures they examined in predicting the outcome of spine surgery. Solicitousness contributed significantly to the regression equation.

Solicitousness takes on a different meaning, however, in the postoperative period. Certainly anyone who has just undergone surgery needs assistance and concern, especially from the spouse. Many of the spousal behaviors (e.g., bringing the patient medication, taking over household responsibilities) that might be seen as reinforcing disability in chronic pain patients might be necessary and psychologically beneficial for a patient who has just undergone spine surgery. Indeed, the spouse who does not engage in such behaviors might be perceived as nonsupportive by the postoperative spine surgery patient. A feeling of being supported (loved and cared for and willingly assisted) by the spouse is critical to recovery in many illnesses (for reviews, see Cohen, 1988; Uchino, Cacioppo, & Kiecolt-Glaser, 1996). Schiaffino and Revenson (1995), for example, found that individuals with arthritis who had high levels of support from their spouses had low levels of depression over an 18-month period. Similarly, Mutran, Reitzes, Mossey, and Fernandez (1995), examining recovery from hip fracture surgery, found that patients with low levels of support achieved less improvement in walking ability at 2 months following surgery than patients with high levels of support. Finally, and most significantly, Schade et al. (1999) found that social support from the spouse was significantly associated with greater pain relief in patients undergoing lumbar discectomy.

There are many reasons that the spouse of a chronic pain patient may be nonsupportive. The stresses and uncertainty surrounding a person in pain can be almost overwhelming. A patient who is normally a strong, active person may be transformed into a depressed, withdrawn, drug-dependent shadow of his or her former self. When there is marital distress before the injury, the pain will likely worsen it. Whatever the cause, research has demonstrated that marital dissatisfaction is common and deleterious in chronic pain syndromes. A number of studies have shown that spouses, especially wives, of back pain patients tend to be dissatisfied with their marriages and to be depressed (Romano, Turner, & Clancy, 1989; Schwartz, Slater, Birchler, & Atkinson, 1991). Dissatisfied spouses tend to attribute the sufferer's pain to psychological rather than physical problems (Block & Boyer, 1984) and to have more negative outcome expectations for patients (Block, Boyer, & Silbert, 1985). Sexual disturbances also frequently occur (Maruta & Osborne, 1976).

Many aspects of the marital relationship, then, can influence the course of recovery. Spousal solicitousness is associated with increased disability and pain and with reduced outcome, whereas spousal support is associated with improved health and surgical recovery. Yet for a patient to feel supported, it may be necessary for the spouse to act in solicitous fashion during the postoperative period, doing all that can be done to keep the patient out of pain, away from excess activity, and relieved of household responsibility. Wacholz and Block (2000), in a preliminary study, attempted to tease out the effects of these two factors on surgical recovery. Forty-two spine surgery patients were followed for 6 months after surgery. Spousal solicitousness was assessed using the MPI, and spousal support was assessed using a modified version of the Social Provisions Questionnaire (Cutrona & Russell, 1987; Paulsen & Altmaier, 1995). Results showed that neither solicitousness nor support had main effects on recovery. However, a significant interaction of these two factors was obtained, whereby patients whose spouses were low on support and high on solicitousness showed the least recovery of function. However, patients whose spouses were both solicitous and supportive showed rapid recovery, comparable to those whose spouses were not solicitous. Thus, it appears that for the spouse to avoid the negative effects of solicitousness on recovery from surgery, such behavior must occur within the context of a high level of overall support. If spouses attend only to the pain behavior and ignore the patient at other times (leading to a lowered sense of overall support), recovery from surgery is likely to be adversely affected.

Historical Factors

Whereas interpersonal, vocational, and financial elements of the patient's current environment can have a significant impact on pain and recovery, other influences have their roots in the past. Problems that occurred perhaps many years previously can return to haunt a patient in pain, affecting his or her ability to cope with problems and limiting options for managing the pain. Such historical factors as abuse and abandonment, substance abuse, and previous psychological problems can be adequately explored only within the context of a psychological interview and require the psychologist to ask questions in a gentle, sensitive, nonjudgmental, and direct manner.

Abuse and Abandonment

If marital dissatisfaction and lack of support commonly accompany chronic pain, far more harmful relationships are also frequently seen. Haber and Roos (1985) found, for example, that over half of the patients they evaluated for entrance into a multidisciplinary pain program had been victims of physical or sexual abuse, and for over 90% of these patients the abuse had occurred during their adult years. A history of sexual abuse is common in many chronic pain syndromes besides back pain. Walker et al. (1988) found that 64% of patients with chronic pelvic pain had been sexual abuse victims before age 14, results essentially corroborated by Reiter and Gambone (1990) and R. J. Gross, Doerr, Caldirola, Guzinski, & Ripley (1980). Curran et al. (1995), reviewing the history of 206 patients with chronic orofacial pain, found that approximately 69% reported a history of physical or sexual abuse and that patients with such a history had higher depression scores on psychometric testing.

A recent study by Linton (1997) suggests that the experiences of sexual and physical abuse may predispose individuals, especially women, to develop chronic pain. In a general population survey of approximately 1,000 participants in Sweden, respondents were queried about abuse experiences and also about any pain symptoms they may have had. Respondents were divided into three categories for analysis: no pain, mild pain, and pronounced pain. A fourth group, composed of chronic pain patients, was given the same questionnaire for comparison purposes. For women, the prevalence of sexual abuse was 46% among respondents with pronounced pain but only 23% among the no-pain group. Physical abuse was less frequent but still significantly more commonly reported in the pronounced-pain group. The pronounced-pain group had approximately the same overall abuse rate (35%) as did the chronic pain patient group. Further analyses demonstrated that for women, physical abuse increased the risk for developing pronounced pain by a factor of 5, and sexual abuse increased the risk by a factor of 4. There was no clear link between abuse and chronic pain in men. Linton suggested that abuse may affect pain by altering perception and one's ability to cope with the pain. . . . Since abused patients have been found to have higher levels of depression, daily hassles, and affective distress, and lower levels of perceived control as compared to their non-abused counterparts, they are not able to cope with pain in an effective way, and thus the chance of developing chronic problems is increased. (p. 52)

The unfortunate legacy of abuse apparently also can affect the outcome of spine surgery. Schofferman et al. (1992) conducted interviews of 100 consecutive patients who subsequently underwent lumbar spine surgery. Patients were questioned about their history of five types of childhood abuse and abandonment, including physical abuse, sexual abuse, substance abuse by a caregiver, abandonment, and emotional abuse or neglect. Surgical outcome was evaluated at a mean of 13 months and was considered unsuccessful if the patient had repeat surgery, failed to return to work or functional ability, required continued analgesics, or had further medical testing. Results demonstrated that patients who reported no instances of childhood abuse or abandonment had a 95% surgical success rate. The success rate was 73% for those reporting one or two categories of abuse or abandonment and 15% among those reporting three or more abuse categories. Thus, it appears that individuals who undergo early emotionally traumatic experiences are both at increased risk for developing chronic pain and less likely to respond to medical and surgical treatment.

Substance Abuse

One of the most significant changes in the management of chronic pain over the past 20 years has been the increasing willingness of physicians to prescribe opioid medications for relief. Following the lead of Fordyce (1976), in the 1970s and 1980s most pain management treatment centers viewed pain medications, particularly narcotics, from a behavioral perspective. It was felt that pain medications, particularly those prescribed on an as-needed (prn) basis, acted to reinforce in the long term the very pain perception and pain behavior they relieved in the short term. In other words, pain medication, by providing rapid escape from noxious sensations, was seen as rewarding the experience of pain and the action of pill taking. Therefore, pain medications were often switched from a prn to a time-contingent basis, and pain medication was delivered in a pain cocktail preparation in which decreasing doses of narcotics were suspended, without the patient's knowledge of dosage amount, until completely eliminated. White and Sanders (1985) found that such an approach was quite effective. Addicted chronic pain patients who were placed on a time-contingent cocktail were able to eliminate narcotic use over 5 days and reported less pain and better mood at the conclusion of the study than a control group who continued to receive the narcotic at baseline rates on a prn basis.

The beliefs that narcotics reinforce pain and are strongly addictive are reflected in the attitudes of the general population. Morris (1999) cited the results of a survey from the Mayday fund finding that "people would rather bear pain than take action to relieve it. A full 82% agreed with the erroneous statement that 'It is easy to get addicted to pain medication'" (p. 128). Research, however, demonstrates that addiction to pain medication is more the exception than the rule. Portenoy (1994), examining the results of studies involving over 25,000 participants without a history of drug dependence, found only seven cases of addiction caused by the treatment. Moulin, Iezzi, Amireah, and Merskey (1996) found that morphine can be effectively used to reduce chronic pain without diminishing cognitive function. Merskey and Moulin (1999), in providing a more detailed review of opioid use, stated, "These data strongly suggest that the overall risk of addiction among patients with no prior history of drug abuse is actually quite low" (p. 160). Given such results, chronic opioid therapy has become more acceptable as an alternative in the treatment of chronic pain. It is most often safe and effective and may have positive psychological effects.

On the other hand, it is clear that opioid medications do have some potential for creating addiction, especially if misused. Further, some chronic pain patients abuse other substances, such as alcohol or street drugs. Some studies have found that substance abuse has deleterious effects on the outcome of spine surgery. In a rather gut-wrenching self-examination of the causes for failure of multiple spine surgeries in 30 of their patients, Spengler, Freeman, Westbrook, and Miller (1980) found that 25 of the patients had been "continually abusing medication or alcohol" (p. 358). The authors concluded that "detoxification alone can result in marked improvement in pain behavior. . . . Therefore, treatment decisions should be deferred until after detoxification has occurred" (p. 359). Uomoto, Turner, and Herron (1988) performed a discriminant analysis of factors predicting the outcome of laminectomy/discectomy, finding that a history of alcohol abuse significantly correlated with reduced results.

Unfortunately, it is often quite difficult to accurately determine substance abuse among spine surgery candidates, for a number of reasons. First, patients are often reluctant to report their excessive use of legal and, especially, illegal substances. Such information often may need to be obtained from family members or by questioning the patient about arrest records or lapses in employment. Further, in the case of prescription medication, the changing acceptability of chronic opioid therapy somewhat clouds the picture for determining whether the spine surgery candidate is abusing medication. After all, some physicians still believe that any use of opioids is unacceptable, whereas others routinely maintain chronic pain patients on doses similar to those given to terminal cancer patients.

In determining abuse, one must keep in mind its definition. According to Merskey and Moulin (1999), psychological dependence or addiction can be defined as compulsive drug use despite harm, an overwhelming preoccupation with securing a good supply, and the tendency to relapse after withdrawal. Addiction is a behavioral pattern of drug use, in which medication is taken for its psychic effects rather than for its pain-relieving effects. (p. 160)

The *DSM-IV* (American Psychiatric Association, 1994) adds several criteria to be considered in determining whether substance abuse exists, including increasing tolerance of medication, the presence of withdrawal symptoms, and persistent unsuccessful efforts to reduce medication.

Merskey and Moulin (1999) examined the *DSM-IV* definitions and concluded that most spine surgery candidates do not fit the definition of substance abusers. Even when the PPS reveals that a patient is using high dosages of narcotics, if the medication use pattern is compliant with the physician's prescription and if the medication is effective in providing pain relief and improving the patient's functional ability, it cannot be said that the patient is abusing the pain medication. However, if on detailed questioning a patient reveals a history of abuse of prescription medication, street drugs, or alcohol, the psychologist must examine the patient's current medication use carefully. In fact, a certain limited number of patients with a patent pathophysiological basis for the pain take opioids as much for the euphoria as for the pain relief. When the PPS interview reveals such patterns, and particularly when a patient violates a medication contract, calls early for prescriptions, or provides implausible explanations for the loss of prescribed medication, the psychologist should consider the possibility that substance abuse will compromise surgical outcome.

Prior Psychological Problems

Diagnosable psychological problems are common among patients experiencing chronic pain. For example, Kinney, Gatchel, Polatin, Fogarty, and Mayer (1993), using standardized interview techniques, found that virtually every chronic pain patient they assessed had a diagnosable mental health disorder, whereas only 61% of acute pain patients had such problems. The most common mental health disorders in chronic pain patients are depression (30% to 54%; Robinson & Riley, 1999), anxiety disorders (30.9%, vs. 14.3% of controls; Fishbain, Goldberg, Meagher, Steele, & Rosomoff, 1986), and personality disorders (40% to 50%; Fishbain et al., 1986; Polatin, Kinney, Gatchel, Lillo, & Mayer, 1993; Reich, Tupen, & Abramowitz, 1987).

Although the existence of diagnosable psychological problems among chronic back pain patients is indisputable, the etiology of such difficulties is controversial. Some have argued that psychological disturbance is primarily a reaction to pain (Gamsa, 1994). Such speculation receives support from two lines of studies: (a) those that show an increase in psychological distress with increasing pain chronicity (Magni et al., 1986) and (b) those showing that treatment-related pain relief is accompanied by a reduction in emotional difficulty. In the second category are studies such as those of Schade et al. (1999), who found that lumbar discectomy led to relief of pain in 83% of patients and return to full-time work in 81%, with patients also showing a significant decline in anxiety and a trend toward a decline in depression.

Psychological problems have also been theorized to predispose patients to the development of chronic pain. This line of speculation is supported by longitudinal studies showing that individuals with documented psychological difficulties are prone to develop pain problems. Bigos et al. (1991), for example, found that employees with high scores on the Hypochondriasis and Hysteria scales of the Minnesota Multiphasic Personality Inventory were at significant risk of developing occupational back pain complaints over a 4-year period compared to those without such elevations. Further, several studies have shown that patients with psychological problems preceding back injury have diminished response to spine surgery. In a study of patients undergoing lumbar discectomy and spinal fusion, Block et al. (2001) found that a history of psychological treatment prior to the spine injury contributed significantly to a regression equation of reduced surgical outcome. Similar results were obtained by Keel (1984). Manniche et al. (1994) also found that "poor psychological background" was included among the factors having a deleterious influence on spine surgery results.

Although many patients presenting for PPS have diagnosable mental health problems, it may be quite difficult to disentangle the temporal relationship of the pain and the emotional distress. Most patients evaluated for PPS have not received any mental health intervention in the past; however, many will admit to a history of significant depression or anxiety. Further, for patients who have taken antidepressant medication prescribed by a primary care physician, it is not clear whether pre-existing psychological problems reached a diagnosable level. To complicate matters further, patients with personality disorders are often unaware or loath to admit that they have a diagnosable condition. Yet personality disorders, by definition, have an onset no later than early adulthood, so for most patients such disorders predate the onset of pain. Only a detailed, sensitive probing of the patient's history during the PPS interview will enable the psychologist to determine the nature and course of emotional and personality-related issues and to assess their probable influence on the course of recovery. In general, to the extent that problems are more chronic, intense, and pervasive, they can be expected to have a substantial negative effect on surgical outcome.

CONCLUSION

The diagnostic interview, always considered the cornerstone of psychological evaluation, is no less critical to PPS. The interview is the place where the nomothetic and the idiographic intersect—where the psychologist uncovers surgical risk factors and comes to understand the meaning of these factors in each patient's case. Further, observation of the patient's behavior, facial expression, and affect allow the psychologist to assess the consistency of the patient's presentation, a key element in considering surgical prognosis.

Behavioral factors—those influences that provide incentives to remain disabled and disincentives to recovery—can be uncovered during the interview by examining the patient's social, vocational, and legal situations. The influence and continuity of historically significant events in the patient's life, such as childhood abuse and abandonment and substance abuse, can be assessed with the necessary sensitivity only through the interview process. The insight gained during the interview can then be combined with the more objective data gleaned from psychometric testing to determine the likelihood that a patient will have diminished response to spine surgery.

5

PERSONALITY AND EMOTIONAL ISSUES: USE OF PSYCHOMETRIC TESTING

Injury to the spine can be the starting point of a descent into despair, dysfunction, financial ruin, and dissolution of relationships. Or, injury can be no more than a minor obstacle on one's life journey. Which path a given patient takes depends on many factors. The physical nature of the injury and the physician's ability to recognize and appropriately treat the injury are fundamental to recovery. However, injury to the spine is much more than physical. The sequelae of injury resonate in almost every area of life, and all of a patient's fortitude and resources are called on in recovery. Unfortunately, some patients are poorly equipped to meet the demands of injury and recovery. Some become so depressed by an injury, so drained of motivation, sleep, and cognitive abilities, that they lack the strength to fight the injury. Others, reared in conditions of abuse, isolation, or abandonment, may have such a poor self-image that the injury only reinforces their preconceived notions of ineffectuality. Still others may worry and obsess about their condition to such an extent that the pain becomes amplified and appears to be inescapable.

The experience of back pain is a stress unique in many ways. Most patients enjoy high levels of activity, lack of concern about health, and a relatively stable psychosocial environment before the onset of pain. Suddenly, pain thrusts such patients into an unknown world, where contact with doctors and insurance companies is frequent, money and work are hard to maintain, and uncertainty about the cause and cure of the pain abounds. Yet patients' responses to pain are determined not merely by its distinctiveness, but also by its similarity to other problems the patient has faced. In fact, response to back pain is strongly influenced by the patients' individual *personality*, defined as "deeply ingrained patterns of behaviors, which include the way one relates to, perceives and thinks about the environment and oneself" (American Psychiatric Association, 1987, p. 1). In other words, the perception of pain and of oneself as experiencing pain and the strategies one uses to overcome pain grow out of the patterns one uses to deal with life in general.

Any stress as all-encompassing and overwhelming as pain is bound to call forth a strong emotional response. Depression, anxiety, and anger are fairly normal responses to such major changes. Personality lays the foundation for such emotions, but emotions, in and of themselves, also play a large role in determining the impact of pain. That is, even though emotional distress in the wake of chronic pain is common, untreated distress can undo even the most effective surgery.

The impact of pain and the patient's ability to respond to surgery are affected not only by the patient's personality and emotional reactions, but also by the ways that the patient thinks about and copes with the pain. *Coping strategies*—that is, specific thoughts and behaviors used to manage pain and reactions to pain (Brown & Nicassio, 1987)—have been found in research to influence pain perception and response in widely disparate arenas. For example, studies showing that amount of time a participant can tolerate experimentally induced pain (e.g., the application of heat or cold to the skin) can be increased by instructions to imagine being in a pleasant place and can be reduced by instructions to attend closely to the length of time that the pain stimulus has been applied (Hilgard & Hilgard, 1975). Other studies have shown that cancer pain and chemotherapy-related nausea can be reduced through the use of relaxation skills (Redd & Jacobsen, 2001).

Pain coping strategies, together with personality and emotion, form the triad that is the focus of this chapter. Although these three areas may seem difficult to examine because of their subjective nature, psychology offers a well-defined and standardized approach to the identification of such subjective phenomena through the use of psychometric testing. Psychometric tests are extremely useful devices both within the context of presurgical psychological screening (PPS) and in psychological evaluation in general. Many aspects of a patient's presentation are necessarily subjective; feelings, sensations, and thoughts cannot be viewed by another and are difficult to describe. Yet psychometric testing can enable a psychologist to make objective, standardized assessment of subjective phenomena. According to a recent discussion by Meyer et al. (2001), psychometric testing "is a relatively straightforward process wherein a particular scale is administered to obtain a specific score. Subsequently, a descriptive meaning can be applied to the score on the basis of normative . . . findings" (p. 143).

Before gaining widespread use, psychometric tests go through rigid, carefully constructed test development standards, including assessment of large numbers of individuals in a variety of situations and across time. Psychometric testing, then, can produce reliable and reproducible results that provide for objective measurement of the subjective phenomena of personality, emotion, and coping style.

Psychometric testing within the context of PPS has three major uses. First, it is a very efficient means of gathering a great deal of information about the patient. Even tests that are lengthy, such as the Minnesota Multiphasic Personality Inventory (MMPI) and its revision the MMPI-2, obtain much more information in a standardized fashion than can be obtained in a comparable period of time through a clinical interview. Thus, a second goal of testing can be seen—it provides a check on the clinical impressions the psychologist obtains during the interview. With some frequency patients' test results may contradict the psychologist's impressions. A patient who displays no emotional distress during the interview, for example, may report extreme anger or anxiety. Alternatively, a patient may be tearful throughout the clinical interview, but in testing may not report excessive levels of depression. An examination of interview results together with those from testing will provide the psychologist with a much more comprehensive knowledge of the patient and of situations that exert significant sway over the patient's behavior patterns.

The third function of psychometric testing is that it can contribute to the individualization and selection of treatments. The objective, quantitative measures these tests obtain of personality, emotion, and coping style can be linked to research examining the outcome of spine surgery. Such research has determined the psychological characteristics of patients most likely to respond well and poorly to spine surgery. The objective measurement provided by psychometric testing, in combination with data from a clinical interview and examination of the medical chart, allow the psychologist to determine surgical prognosis. Such a comprehensive evaluation, relying both on objective data and professional insight, can indicate whether ancillary treatments might facilitate surgical results or whether alternatives to surgery should be investigated.

MMPI-2 AND OTHER TESTS OF PERSONALITY AND EMOTION

The MMPI and its revision, the MMPI-2, are by far the most widely used psychometric test and have had over 50 years of research and application. In the area of chronic pain, and especially in the prediction of spine surgery outcome, the MMPI has proven invaluable. On the MMPI-2 each patient's results are given as a series of elevations on three validity scales and

10 clinical scales (see Graham, 1990). These scales are the most extensively researched. In addition, the MMPI-2 generates scores on numerous supplementary scales, and researchers frequently develop their own scales by selecting and combining specific items chosen from the full administration of the MMPI. Research using the MMPI-2 has consistently demonstrated the existence of three or four modal personality profiles displayed by chronic pain patients (Bradley, Prokop, Gentry, Van der Heide, & Prieto, 1981; Keller & Butcher, 1991).

There is a growing body of research examining the relationship of MMPI scale elevations to spine surgery results. These studies are the main focus of the current chapter (see Table 5.1). In all of these studies, the MMPI or MMPI-2 was given to patients with identified physical pathology to account for their back pain complaints. Patients then underwent spine surgery of varying types. Outcome was examined after a minimum of 6 months to determine whether the surgery was either successful in correcting underlying physical pathology (surgical outcome) or successful in reducing symptoms (clinical outcome). Clinical outcome typically was assessed using some variant of the Stauffer and Coventry (1972) criteria. Often patients were categorized into good, fair, or poor outcome categories depending on the changes they showed in these four criteria.

The MMPI and MMPI-2 studies reviewed in this chapter vary greatly in terms of experimental procedure. Much of the research is retrospective rather than prospective. Although in some cases the patients completed standardized outcome measures such as the Dallas Pain Questionnaire (see Gatchel, Polatin, & Kinney, 1995) or the Oswestry Disability Index (Fairbank, Couper, Davies, & O'Brien, 1980), in most cases the researchers developed their own follow-up questionnaires for the specific study. Further, in some cases, surgeons' global estimates of clinical success or failure, rather patient reports, were used. Thus, some studies are far weaker than others. However, the overall results from Table 5.1 are clear: Several MMPI clinical scales are consistently associated with reduced spine surgery results.

In this chapter we will discuss the research on each of these scales and examine the concepts embodied in the scales. We will also review research using instruments other than the MMPI and relate PPS research to studies on general chronic pain syndromes. One note on scoring: Elevations considered to be clinically significant vary between the MMPI and MMPI-2. On the former elevations of T score greater than 70 are considered significant, whereas on the MMPI-2 the significance cutoff is 65. We follow those conventions in the studies described in this chapter unless otherwise noted.

PAIN SENSITIVITY

Examination of Table 5.1 reveals that the most common MMPI scale elevations associated with reduced spine surgery results are found on Hs (Hy-

TABLE 5.1
Studies Examining the Relationship of MMPI to Spine Surgery Outcome

Authors	Participants and Treatment	Evaluation Interval	MMPI Results
Block et al. (2001)[a]	118 laminectomy/ discectomy patients, 86 fusion patients	Mean 8.6 months	L, D, Hy, Pd, Pt, and Sc showed significant r^2 with outcome
Cashion & Lynch (1979)	78 laminectomy/ discectomy patients (no previous surgery)	1 year	Significant differences between good and bad outcome on Hs, D, K, F, and Es
Doxey et al. (1988); Dzioba & Doxey (1984)	116 workers' compensation patients (no previous surgery): 74 received surgery, 43 did not	1 year	Correlation with poor outcome: Hs = .48, Ma = .36, Pt = .35
Kuperman et al. (1979)	37 discectomy patients (no previous surgery)	1 year	Hs, Hy, and D showed significant r^2 with outcome; r^2 of Hs + Hy + D with outcome = .58
Long (1981)	44 surgery patients referred because of suspected nonorganic factors	6–18 months	Hy, Hs, and Pd higher in poor outcome group; success rate higher in patients with no elevations
Pheasant et al. (1979)	90 patients, unspecified various procedures	6 months, 1 year	Hs and Hy higher in poor outcome group but correlated .29 with outcome
Riley et al. (1995)[a]	71 fusion patients (39% had previous surgery, 37% received workers' compensation)	Mean 20 months	Cluster analysis: poorest outcome in patients with high Hs + Hy and depressed-pathological
Smith & Duerksen (1979)	31 patients, various procedures (3 had previous surgery)	Unclear	Correlation with poor outcome: Hs = .73, Hy = .57, D = .59; combined Hs + Hy + D = .83
Sorenson & Mors (1988); Sorenson (1992)	57 discectomy (no previous surgery)	6 and 24 months, 5 years	R^2 with poor outcome: Hs = .37, D = .37, Hy = .47; also, Sc and Ma combined into SM scale = .69
Spengler et al. (1990)	84 discectomy patients (no previous surgery)	1 year or more	Hs + Hy significantly associated with poor outcome; also Pd and Sc
Turner et al. (1986); Uomoto et al. (1988); Herron et al. (1992)	106 discectomy patients (25 had previous surgery)	1 year	Discriminant function using MMPI predicted 69.7% of outcome; function included Hs, K, and L
Wiltse & Rocchio (1975)	130 chemonucleolysis patients (no previous surgery)	1 year	Success predicted by Hs + Hy, by physical findings; R^2 with poor outcome on combined MMPI + psychosocial factors = .73

[a]Study conducted using the MMPI-2.

Note. Abbreviations refer to scales of the Minnesota Multiphasic Personality Inventory (MMPI). D = Depression; Es = Ego Strength; Hs = Hypochondriasis; Hy = Hysteria; Ma = Hypomania; Pd = Psychopathic Deviate; Pt = Psychesthenia; Sc = Schizophrenia.

pochondriasis) and Hy (Hysteria). In fact, every study listed in the table found at least one of these scales to be a significant predictor. In several cases, elevations on one or both scales are the strongest identified predictor of outcome, even compared to physical variables. For example, Spengler et al. (1990) found that elevations on scales Hs and Hy contributed 26% to a multiple regression equation against clinical outcome, whereas imaging studies contributed only 10% and neurological signs only 3%. Similarly, in regression analysis performed in our laboratory (Block et al., 2001), Hy was the strongest predictor of clinical outcome, exceeding such medical factors as length of injury, type of surgery performed, and number of previous spine surgeries.

Profiles displaying elevations on Hs and Hy are common among chronic pain patients in general. Keller and Butcher (1991) found that 38% of men and 45% of women with chronic pain displayed profiles with elevations on these two scales only, far outdistancing the next most frequent MMPI profile. Bradley et al. (1981) obtained similar results. Elevations of Hs or Hy or both not only are very common in chronic pain syndromes, but also are associated both with the development of chronic pain and with reduced conservative treatment outcome. Bigos et al. (1991), in a prospective study of 3,000 Boeing employees, found that patients who scored in the upper quintile on Hy were twice as likely to develop back problems as patients who scored low on this scale (see Hansen, Biering-Sorensen, & Schroll, 1995, for similar results). Gatchel, Polatin, Mayer, and Garcy (1994), prospectively examining 421 acute back pain patients, found that patients with elevated Hy scores were less likely to be working at 1-year follow-up than were low Hy scorers. High scores on Hy are also associated with reduced likelihood of improvement in some conservative treatment programs (McCreary, Turner, & Dawson, 1979).

It is not surprising that Hs and Hy elevations are both common among chronic pain patients and can have adverse effects on recovery. After all, both scales were originally designed to assess patients whose psychopathology is manifested in physical symptoms. Hs elevations were designed to assess hypochondriasis—that is, "pre-occupation with the body and concomitant fears of illness and disease . . . [which are] . . . not of delusional quality, but are quite consistent" (Graham, 1990, p. 38). The Hy scale was developed to assess "hysterical" reactions to stress situations—that is, "involuntary psychogenic loss or disorder of function" (Graham, 1990, p. 43). Both of these concepts imply an inconsistent relationship between organic pathology and physical symptoms. The hypochondriac, according to the classic definition, has physical symptoms and remains convinced of the presence of illness, even in the face of overwhelming medical evidence to the contrary. The hysteric develops physical symptoms under stress that have no organic basis.

The concepts of hypochondriasis and especially of hysteria have their roots in classic psychoanalysis. Freud (Breuer & Freud, 1895) considered that at least some instances of pain could be purely psychogenic,—or having a mental but not an organic basis. Psychogenic pain can occur when a patient experiences psychological conflicts that are highly emotionally charged. Rather than experience distressing anxiety, the conflict is "converted" into physical symptoms. Conversion allows the psychological conflict to be repressed into the unconscious, where it can cause the patient no further distress. Treatment of such pain, then, involves allowing the patient to become aware of repressed conflicts through the process of psychoanalysis. Breuer and Freud stated, "individual hysterical symptoms immediately disappear . . . without returning, if we succeed . . . in thoroughly awakening the memories of the causal process with its accompanying affects, and if the patient . . . gives verbal expression to that affect" (pp. 59–60).

Early research on the use of the MMPI with chronic pain patients was based on such psychoanalytic concepts. Engel (1959), describing the "pain-prone patient," suggested that conversion plays a large role in the etiology and maintenance of nonorganic pain complaints. Hanvik (1950) compared MMPI profiles of patients with "organic" pain to those of patients with "functional" pain (i.e., no clear-cut organic findings). The functional group was found to have higher scores on Hy and Hs than the organic group. Similar results were reported in several other studies (Freeman, Calsyn, & Loucks, 1976; see Keel, 1984, for a review).

At their extremes, the concepts of hysteria and hypochondriasis have little relevance to PPS. After all, patients who undergo screening for spine surgery have some pathological condition underlying their pain complaints and disability, or the surgeon would never consider operating. The presence of an underlying organic condition would, thus, seem to exclude hysteria or hypochondriasis from consideration. For the purposes of PPS it may be more useful to consider these two concepts as reflecting excessive sensitivity to pain rather than the cause of pain. In other words, in the face of organic pathology and concomitant nociception, individuals who have characteristics reflected in high Hs and Hy scores may be more likely to experience high pain levels, and to be more functionally disabled, than those with low scores.

Such an interpretation of elevated Hs and Hy scores in spine surgery candidates receives support from a number of experimental studies showing that some chronic pain patients tend to perceive or report pain with a lower level of nociceptive input than do others. Schmidt (1987; Schmidt & Brands, 1986), for example, subjected chronic pain patients and control participants to the cold pressor test (immersion of the forearm into a bath of ice water). The pain patients reported pain after a shorter period of time and tolerated less total immersion time than did the control group.

A study in our laboratory provides even stronger support for the concept of excessive pain sensitivity (Block et al., 1996). In this study, as a normal part of their diagnostic regimen for spine surgery, patients underwent discography. As noted in chapter 1, this is a procedure that involves injection of radiographic contrast material into the nucleus of intervertebral discs suspected of being degenerated or disrupted. Most often, injection of a damaged disc provokes the patient's normally occurring pain, whereas injection of a normal disc is not pain provocative (Vanharanta et al., 1987). In the Block et al. study, all patients had three lumbar disc levels injected, including the discs that were suspected of being damaged as well as at least one level suspected of being normal. Patients were also given the MMPI-2 prior to discography. Results showed that although pain reproduction almost always occurred on injection of the damaged discs, a number of patients reported pain reproduction on injection of normal discs. Patients who displayed such "discordant" pain reproduction when normal discs were injected were much more likely to have elevated Hs and Hy (T > 75) scores than were patients who evinced only "concordant" pain reproduction. Thus, it appears that pain sensitivity, as assessed by the MMPI Hs and Hy scales, may predispose patients toward negative spine surgery results; even when surgery corrects the underlying pathology, patients with such characteristics may be unable to perceive any physical improvement.

DEPRESSION

Patients experiencing chronic spine pain often have a host of related symptoms. The pain makes it difficult to sleep; inability to find a comfortable position in bed, worries about financial difficulties caused by the injury and about upcoming surgery, and even gastrointestinal distress caused by anti-inflammatory medication can make it nearly impossible to get more than a few hours sleep. Pain is distracting, often leading to memory and concentration difficulties. The general feeling of mental dullness is further enhanced by the narcotic medications surgical candidates frequently use. Because patients with spine pain have difficulty with most movement, they frequently move slowly and carefully, spending most of their time at home and away from others and from activities they enjoy. Sexual activity is often the last thing on their minds, as it is sure to provoke an increase in pain. Understandably, these symptoms accompanying chronic spine pain may lead to feelings of despair, hopelessness, and even suicidal ideation.

These symptoms are very similar to those of clinical depression (Cavanaugh, Clark, & Gibbons, 1983). In fact, depression has been found in up to 85% of chronic pain patients (Lindsay & Wyckoff, 1981). Unfortunately, depression (assessed by MMPI scale D) may not bode well for the outcome of spine surgery. At least five studies using the MMPI have found a significant correlation between scale D elevations and reduced spine surgery results (see Table 5.1). Several other studies using different measures of depression have obtained similar results. Junge et al. (1996) found that elevated scores on the Beck Depression Inventory (BDI; Beck, Ward, Mendelsohn,

Mock, & Erbaugh, 1961) were predictive of diminished spine surgery success, particularly in patients who had only disc herniation. Similarly, Kjelby-Wendt, Styf, and Carlsson (1999), examining discectomy results, found that patient satisfaction with surgery results was strongly related to BDI scores—elevated BDI scores were found preoperatively in 55% of unsatisfied patients but only in 18% of satisfied patients. Schade et al. (1999) found that depression scores assessed by a simple Likert scale were strongly negatively correlated with return to work, as well as overall recovery, using the Stauffer and Coventry (1972) criteria. Katz et al. (1999) found that a three-item measure of depression drawn from the Rand Health Insurance study had a significant negative correlation with symptom severity and satisfaction with outcome 2 years after decompressive laminectomy/discectomy. Finally, Trief et al. (2000) found that high scores on the Zung Depression Inventory (Zung, 1965) were associated with little reduction of back pain and greater work disability as a result of spine surgery.

The relationship between depression and spine surgery outcome, however, is complex. A number of MMPI studies found no predictive value of elevated scale D scores (see Table 5.1). Further, several studies using the Distress and Risk Assessment Method (DRAM; Main et al., 1992) also yielded negative results. The DRAM measures both depression and pain sensitivity. If depression is an especially strong predictor of spine surgery results, then the DRAM measure should also show a strong relationship to outcome. Indeed, the original Main et al. study found that high scores on the DRAM were predictive of reduced surgery results, a result more recently corroborated by Trief et al. (2000). On the other hand, Hobby et al. (2001), examining patients who underwent lumbar discectomy, failed to find that outcome was predicted by DRAM scores. Similarly, Tandon et al. (1999) found that the DRAM scores did not have an association with improvement as a result of posterior lumbar interbody fusion. Thus, the relationship of depression to surgical outcome warrants closer consideration.

There are certainly many reasons why a patient experiencing pain would become depressed. Decreased functional ability, deconditioning, and loss of strength lead to diminished ability to engage in enjoyable activities, such as athletics, recreation, and interaction with family members. As Haythornthwaite, Seiber, and Kerns (1991) suggested, reduced activity, reduced reinforcement, somatic symptoms, and depression may all interact to create a downward physical and emotional spiral. Further, the patient often experiences a loss of control over many aspects of life, including health, money, work, and medical treatment. Finally, the protracted nature and noxious qualities of the pain itself may strip patients of their general emotional control.

Just as depression is a frequent and somewhat natural reaction to pain, the effects of depression may make it more difficult to recover from pain. Depressed individuals tend to have a low threshold for experimentally induced pain (Merskey, 1965) and to be more likely to focus on negative rather than positive events (Seligman, 1975). Depressed patients also tend to interpret events more negatively and to interpret a given sensation as painful (Geisser & Colwell, 1999).

Finally, a study in our laboratory found that depressed patients were not likely to recognize improvement when it occurred (Kremer, Block, & Atkinson, 1983). In this study, staff members systematically observed chronic pain patients on an inpatient pain unit on a time-sampling basis throughout their treatment. Staff members recorded once an hour whether they observed the patient to be sitting, standing, walking, or reclining. Patients also recorded on an hourly basis how much time they spent in these four positions. The results revealed that although all patients showed an improvement in "up time" (standing and walking), some patients systematically underreported their improvement. A path analysis of the data indicated two factors that correlated strongly with underreporting of improvement: chronicity of pain complaints and scores on the Beck Depression Inventory. Apparently, then, depression in chronic pain patients may alter their ability not only to improve, but also to recognize such improvements.

Given the widespread nature of depression in chronic pain patients and the concomitant effects of depression on motivation and cognition, why should some studies fail to find depression as a factor associated with reduced spine surgery results? One strongly plausible answer to this question may arise from the source of the depression. Whereas depression in many cases may be situational and reactive in nature, a number of studies have shown that individuals who are depressed are also at risk for developing chronic pain. For example, Atkinson, Slater, Patterson, Grant, and Garfin (1991), in a systematic study of depressed male Veterans Administration chronic pain patients, found that 42% of patients experienced the onset of depression prior to the onset of pain, whereas 58% experienced depression after the pain began. Polatin et al. (1993) reported that 39% of the chronic low back pain patients they evaluated displayed symptoms of pre-existing depression. A review by Linton (2000) of research on psychosocial risk factors found that in 14 of the 16 reviewed studies, depression increased the risk for developing back pain problems.

Unfortunately, in the area of recovery from spine surgery, no examination has been made of the relative risk to recovery for patients with a preinjury history of depression versus those whose depression is reactive. However, it seems likely that patients with protracted pre-existing depressive symptoms would be more likely to retain such symptoms in the postoperative period. They may, for example, continue to display low motivation, sleep disturbance, and inability to perceive improvements, delaying and diminishing surgical results. Such a conclusion is bolstered by two studies on the DRAM. Hobby et al. (2001), studying discectomy, and Tandon et al. (1999), studying lumbar fusion, both failed to find that high preoperative scores on the

DRAM were associated with reduction in spine surgery effectiveness. However, in both of these studies there was a strong correlation between surgical outcome and a decline in DRAM scores from before surgery to after surgery. Although neither of these studies distinguished between reactive and chronic depression, for most patients examined a decline in pain and improvement in functional ability as a result of surgery were accompanied by a decline in emotional distress. However, emotional distress did not decline for all patients in either of the two studies. In the Hobby et al. study, 48% of patients were classified as distressed preoperatively, and 18% remained distressed following surgery. In the Tandon et al. study, although there was a significant decline in DRAM scores following surgery, 17 of the 55 patients remained distressed at follow-up. Further, disability, as measured by the Oswestry, was more severe in patients whose DRAM scores worsened postoperatively.

Thus, patients who have chronic depression are at risk for the development of pain problems and are much less likely to perceive improvements in their condition. Chronically depressed patients, then, likely account for the bulk of individuals who remained distressed and disabled at follow-up in both of these studies. Taken together, these results indicate that the subset of patients whose chronic depression predated the onset of back pain are less likely to experience sanguine emotional changes as a result of surgery and are more likely to have depression interfere with surgical recovery.

Anger

It has long been known that pain can induce anger. Niehoff (1999) reported on early studies by Ulrich and Azrin (1962) demonstrating that rats who had electric shock applied to their tails or feet became very aggressive, fighting fiercely with other rats or, in the absence of live victims, attacking inanimate objects such as tennis balls or rubber hoses. Humans are no less immune to hostile feelings, and patients with chronic back pain frequently experience intense anger (Turk & Fernandez, 1995). Fernandez, Clark, and Ruddick-Davis (1999) reported on a study in which chronic pain patients rated the frequency with which they had experienced six emotions during the previous 30 days. Although fear, sadness, shame, guilt, and envy were all experienced commonly, anger was reported to be experienced the most frequently, an average of about 70% of the time (fear was the second most frequent, about 61% of the time).

Unfortunately, the common feeling of anger may have negative consequences for recovery from spine surgery. The MMPI scale that comes closest to assessing anger is Pd (Psychopathic Deviate). As described by Graham (1990), the significant characteristics of patients with elevations on this scale are hostility, aggressiveness, and rebelliousness toward authority. Elevations on scale Pd were found in three studies to be associated with reduced surgical results (Table 5.1; see also Herron et al., 1992). In a perhaps more direct test,

Trief et al. (2000) examined the relationship of spine surgery results to scores on the Cook-Medley Hostility subscale of the MMPI-2. The authors found that at one year following surgery, patients who had high presurgical hostility scores were significantly less likely to be working and had reported less improvement in daily activities than did patients who had scored low on this scale.

There are, of course, many foci for the anger experienced by a chronic back pain patient. Patients who are injured in a motor vehicle accident are frequently angry with the other driver. Patients often express hostility toward previous health care providers for failing to cure the pain. DeGood and Kiernan (1996) found that many chronic back pain patients blame their employers for the pain and that such a blame pattern was associated with poor response to past surgical and conservative treatment, as well as high levels of overall mood disturbance. The long list of those whom the patient may blame also includes attorneys, insurance companies, mental health workers, significant others, God, oneself, and "the whole world" (Fernandez & Turk, 1995). When one is suffering, it appears, anger is both common and virulent.

There are many reasons that anger may have a negative impact on the reduction of pain. As Fernandez and Turk (1995) suggested, anger may lead to maladaptive lifestyle changes, such as lack of physical exercise, excessive use of alcohol or drugs, and generally poor health habits. Further, anger may lead to general health problems; this emotion has been found to be associated with many health conditions, including cardiovascular disease, asthma, and headaches. Indeed, a study of over 17,000 spine pain patients by Fanuele, Birkmeyer, Abdu, Tosteson, and Weinstein (2000) found that many had a high incidence of comorbid medical conditions. Drawing on data from the National Spine Network's Health Survey Questionnaire, these authors found that 46% of patients had comorbid nonspinal illnesses, a level similar to that of patients with coronary heart disease and worse than patients with cancer, lupus, or chronic obstructive pulmonary disease. Although the causes for such comorbid conditions are certainly complex and difficult to disentangle, given the strong empirical support for a link between anger and adverse health changes in the general population, it seems likely that anger may play some role in negatively influencing the health status of spine pain patients.

The effects of anger go far beyond indirect effects on health, for anger often motivates individuals to act in ways that seek short-term gratification over long-term gain. Individuals with road rage, for example, in a fit of anger over some perceived error or offense by another driver, may attempt to stop and attack that driver, risking a jail term for assault or a retaliatory attack. Similarly, anger leads some parents to explode at their children with little provocation or to abuse them verbally or physically. So the experience of intense anger may expose spine pain patients to interpersonal conflict and isolation, potentially compromising their recovery. If some patients' needs for vindication are strong enough, it seems plausible that they might continue to experience or complain of pain even after they have made a complete physical recovery. Further, angry patients may have difficulties complying with medical treatment; as Fernandez and Turk (1995) noted,

> any treatment . . . requires mutual trust, acceptance and co-operation between patient and therapist. . . . If the pain patient is cynical, mistrustful and hostile, then the therapeutic alliance will be undermined and the treatment goals will be less readily attainable. . . . Anger may lead to a vicious circle in which treatment fails, thus aggravating the levels of frustration and anger. The patient is thus trapped in a self-perpetuating rut of failure and frustration. (p. 172)

Although it seems clear that anger can be a direct reaction to pain, the pattern Fernandez and Turk (1995) described implies that for many patients, anger is a much more chronic problem and may be component of a personality disorder. As with depression, it seems likely that chronic anger bodes especially poorly for surgical outcome.

Anxiety

The prospect of spine surgery can give rise to much trepidation. Patients often know of or hear about individuals who have had surgery, only to have a worsening of symptoms. Discussion among patients in the waiting room of a busy spine surgeon will almost certainly reveal stories of patients for whom multiple invasive procedures have failed, leading to progressively greater disability. The surgery candidate's anxiety may be heightened by the fear of undergoing anesthesia, with the frequently expressed concern about "not waking up afterward." The patient is almost certainly aware that once the surgery is completed, the pace and extent of recovery are quite variable. In turn, many fear (in some cases, realistically) either that they will be unable to recover enough to perform their job duties or, worse, that their employers will terminate their jobs. Anxiety, then, may become quite intense as the date of surgery approaches.

Anxiety is most closely associated with the MMPI scale Pt (Psychesthenia). According to Keller and Butcher (1991), elevations on this scale indicate "anxiety, phobic pre-occupations, tendency to intellectualize, obsessiveness, compulsiveness" (p. 28). Elevations on scale Pt have been associated with diminished spine surgery results in a number of studies (see Table 5.1). In our own study, Pt was a significant predictor of outcome and contributed heavily to a regression equation differentiating patients who achieved poor outcome from those who achieved good or fair results (Block et al., 2001).

A number of studies using other, perhaps more direct measures of anxiety have corroborated its negative influence on recovery. Kjelby-Wendt et al. (1999), examining discectomy patients, divided participants into "discontented" and "contented" groups, based in large part on presurgical scores on the State-Trait Anxiety Inventory (STAI; Spielberger, Gorusch, & Lushene, 1983). At follow-up 6 to 12 months following surgery, they found that discontented patients achieved poorer discectomy outcome than did contented patients, including poorer lumbar range of motion and greater than twice the duration of postoperative sick leave. Trief et al. (2000) found that elevated STAI state anxiety scores were significantly associated with lower return to work and less change in reported pain. Schade et al. (1999), in their study of discectomy results, found that "occupational mental stress" had a significant negative correlation with return to work and near significant negative correlations with improvement in activities of daily living and reduction in pain. Anxiety in its many guises, then, seems to militate against surgical effectiveness.

A growing body of research provides evidence that anxiety may affect recovery from surgery because it directly influences the experience of pain. In studies of experimentally induced pain, anxiety has been found to reduce the threshold for pain perception and pain tolerance (Chapman, 1978). Several studies have shown that anxiety can also increase awareness of chronic pain. For example, McCracken, Gross, Aiken, and Carnrike (1996) found that anxiety accounted for 16% to 54% of the variance in pain report, disability, and pain-related behavior among chronic pain patients. Moreover, Marras et al.'s results suggest that stress and anxiety on the job can have physical effects, such as increased muscle tension in the lumbar spine, that can increase pain and predispose an individual to back injury. Anxiety and stress, then, appear to heighten both physiological conditions that may contribute to pain and awareness of pain sensations.

Beyond pain perception, anxiety may negatively influence spine surgery outcome by negatively influencing healing. An exciting review by Kiecolt-Glaser, Page, Marucha, MacCallum, and Glaser (1998) suggested a number of pathways through which such adverse effects may occur. First, anxiety and stress can slow wound healing by reducing production of proinflammatory cytokines such as interleukin 1. Further, anxious individuals may require greater amounts of anesthetic. Just as with anger, people who are anxious may engage in negative health behaviors such as high levels of alcohol consumption or overeating—behaviors that can influence the course of the surgery itself. Patients who are heavy drinkers may require stronger anesthetics, and spine surgery often requires greater time and involves more extensive tissue damage for patients who are obese. Finally, anxiety is associated with greater amounts of postsurgical pain, and such increased noxious sensations can down-regulate immune function, again compromising the healing process. Thus, anxiety has the potential to interfere with recovery from spine surgery by influencing the surgical process itself, postoperative healing, and sensitivity to pain in both the immediate postoperative period

TABLE 5.2
Personality Disorder Descriptions

Disorder	Description
Paranoid	Unwarranted tendency to interpret the actions of people as deliberately demeaning or threatening
Schizoid	Indifference to social relatedness and a restricted range of emotional experience and expression
Schizotypal	Deficits in interpersonal relatedness and peculiarities of ideation, appearance, and behavior
Antisocial	Irresponsible and antisocial behavior (often beginning as a conduct disorder before age 15)
Borderline	Instability of mood, interpersonal relationships, and self-image
Histrionic	Excessive emotionality and attention-seeking
Narcissistic	Grandiosity (in fantasy or behavior), lack of empathy, and hypersensitivity to the evaluation of others
Avoidant	Social discomfort, fear of negative evaluation, and timidity
Dependent	Submissive and dependent behavior
Compulsive	Perfectionism and inflexibility
Passive-aggressive	Resistance to demands for adequate social and occupational performance

Note. Summarized from American Psychiatric Association, 1994, *Diagnostic and Statistical Manual of Mental Disorders,* 4th ed., Washington, DC: Author.

and for many months thereafter (see chapter 7 for a more complete discussion of the effects of stress on healing).

Personality Disorders

It is clear that pain is an undesirable condition, sufficient in itself to produce intense emotions in even the most well adjusted of individuals. Patients who have intense, chronic emotional and personality problems may have an especially problematic course of recovery. Such individuals often have characteristics that fit the definition of a personality disorder. According to the *Diagnostic and Statistical Manual of Mental Disorders*, fourth edition (*DSM-IV*), personality disorders exist when "normal" personality traits are "inflexible and maladaptive and cause significant functional impairment or subjective distress" (p. 630; American Psychiatric Association, 1994). The *DSM-IV* lists a number of personality disorders, the major characteristics of which are summarized in Table 5.2.

Recently developed interview techniques such as the Structured Clinical Interview for *DSM-III-R* (Spitzer, Williams, Gibbon, & First, 1988), the Personality Disorder Evaluation (Loranger, Lehmann-Susman, Oldham, & Russakof, 1985), and the Semistructured Interview for *DSM-IV* Personality Disorders (Pfohl, Blum, & Simmerman, 1995) allow for accurate and fairly reliable diagnosis of personality disorders in a research setting. Unfortunately, research using such instruments demonstrates that personality disorders are very common among individuals with chronic pain. Fishbain et al. (1986)

studied 182 patients with chronic pain, 90% of whom had back or neck pain, and found that 58% fit a personality disorder diagnosis. Other studies have found personality disorders in 31% (Weisberg, Gallagher, & Gorin, 1996) to 51% (Polatin et al., 1993) of pain patients.

There is no extant research examining the relationship of diagnosed personality disorders to spine surgery outcome. However, patients with personality disorders could present special challenges to health care providers (see also Gatchel & Weisberg, 2000). For example, many of the personality disorders presented in Table 5.2 involve problems with anger. Paranoid personality disorder, found in up to 33% of individuals with chronic pain (Polatin et al., 1993), involves unwarranted tendencies to interpret the actions of people as deliberately demeaning or threatening (see also Gatchel, Garofalo, Ellis, & Holt, 1996, who found paranoid personality disorder in 18% of temporamandibular pain patients). Patients with paranoid personality disorder have been described as "unable to accept responsibility . . . suspicious, mistrustful, hypersensitive" (Weisberg & Keefe, 1997, p. 3).

In the Fishbain et al. (1988) study, the most frequently observed personality disorder was the passive-aggressive type, occurring in 14.9% of the chronic pain population studied. Significantly, 24.7% of the male workers' compensation patients fit the criteria for this personality disorder, compared with 0% of the male non-workers' compensation patients.

Passive-aggressive personality disorder (PAPD) involves resistance to demands for adequate social and occupational performance. Individuals with PAPD often resist authority by dawdling, acting in ways that are inconsistent with statements, and enlisting others to both resist and criticize authority figures. Spine pain patients with either paranoid or passive-aggressive personality disorders, then, may fail to establish trust in their health care team and may have diminished motivation for improvement as a result of spine surgery. If postoperative intervention occurs within a group setting, patients with PAPD may actually cause other patients to fail.

Several other personality disorders that occur among chronic pain patients may be linked to poor response to invasive treatment. Histrionic personality disorder, occurring in up to 12% of pain patients (Fishbain et al., 1986), involves dramatic, attention-seeking behavior and impaired functioning coupled with a tendency to experience vague physical symptoms when under stress. The difficulties involved in recovering from surgery and the multiple opportunities for drawing attention to their disabled state may cause some patients with histrionic personality disorder to have difficulty acknowledging a decrease in pain as a result of surgery.

Borderline personality disorder, occurring in up to 15% of individuals with chronic pain (Polatin et al., 1993), also has the potential to adversely influence recovery. Patients with this diagnosis have tumultuous and unstable relationships and shift dramatically and rapidly from overvaluing to devaluing others. They tend to have poor self-images and are quite impulsive. Patients with borderline personality disorder, then, may have difficulty maintaining a consistent relationship with their surgeons and health care team. At some minor perceived slight or offense, they may respond to clinicians very negatively and refuse suggestions or help in a dramatic fashion. Such a pattern may make surgical recovery much more difficult.

Personality disorders, which clearly have the potential to create significant interference with recovery, remain uncharted territory in spine surgery research. However, given the highly problematic emotional and behavioral patterns displayed by patients with personality disorders, recognition of these conditions is a critical component of PPS. The paucity of research on this topic suggests that personality disorders should not be considered a primary risk factor for reduced surgical outcome, but rather should influence suggestions for pre- and postoperative patient management through their inclusion as "adverse clinical features" (see Exhibit 6.2).

Gatchel, Polatin, Mayer, and Garcy (1994) examined the effect of personality disorders on the conservative treatment of chronic pain. They found that patients with diagnosed personality disorders showed a return-to-work rate equivalent to that of patients without such conditions and that there were no significant differences in the return-to-work rates of patients with differing types of personality disorders. This study suggests that appropriate management may enable the health care team to assist these patients in overcoming emotional and behavioral obstacles to recovery.

Multiple MMPI Scale Elevations

Emotional and personality problems are complex and rarely restricted to a single intense emotional experience such as anxiety or anger. Examining multiple-scale MMPI profile patterns can help psychologists consider such issues in all their complexity. Much recent research has used cluster analysis techniques to identify modal patterns of MMPI elevations among chronic pain patients. Keller and Butcher (1991), for example, identified three consistent profiles among both male and female chronic pain patients: a cluster of elevations on scales Hs, D, and Hy; a pattern with elevations on many scales; and a pattern in which all scales were within normal limits. Research by Bradley and colleagues (Bradley et al., 1981) obtained somewhat similar results, finding a four-cluster solution for women and a three-cluster solution for men. In both sexes a pattern of Hs, Hy, and D elevations was common. A second common profile in both sexes was all scale results within normal limits, although borderline elevations or less than 2 standard deviations above the mean were obtained on scales K (validity), Hs, and Hy. A third but less frequently seen pattern in both sexes was multiple scale elevations. Finally, in women only a group having elevations on scales Hs and Hy but not scale D was found.

Two studies have applied cluster analysis techniques in examining MMPI-2 profiles of spine surgery candidates. Riley et al. (1995) examined the profiles of 201 candidates, 71 of whom underwent spine fusion. A four-cluster solution was obtained and the outcome of surgery at 6 months follow-up was analyzed by MMPI cluster type. The largest group, having all MMPI scales within normal limits, obtained significant improvement. Similar results were obtained by the second group, which had elevations on scales Hs, D, and Hy (termed the "triad" group). A third cluster, with elevations on scales Hs and Hy only (termed the "V" group), achieved poorer results than did the normal and triad groups. Finally, a group of four patients having multiple elevations (the "depressed-pathological" group) also had diminished surgical results.

Research in our laboratory (Block & Ohnmeiss, 2000) also applied cluster analytic techniques to the MMPI-2 profiles of spine surgery candidates to determine profiles associated with diminished outcome. A three-cluster solution was found in examining the profiles of 222 participants, 60% of whom underwent discectomy and 40% of whom underwent spinal fusion. The modal MMPI-2 profiles obtained in this study are displayed in Figure 5.1. The three clusters obtained are a within normal limits group, a triad-type profile, and a depressed-pathological profile. As in the Riley et al. (1995) study, outcome varied by MMPI profile type. A group of 22 patients formed the depressed-pathological group, which obtained the least improvements in functional ability and pain reduction. The within normal limits group of 114 patients achieved the best surgery results. The remaining patients ($n = 86$) with the triad profile achieved less pain improvement but similar improvement in functional ability when compared to the within normal limits group.

The results of MMPI cluster analysis for chronic pain patients, whether candidates for spine surgery or for noninvasive treatment, show similarity across many studies. Patients with minimal psychopathology, approximately 50% of those tested, have had the best results. Patients with a high degree of psychopathology (approximately 15% of patients) have had significantly diminished surgery results. Patients with tendencies toward excessive pain sensitivity (Hs and Hy elevations), whether or not accompanied by depression (D elevations), obtain mixed results. This final group of patients presents the greatest challenge to PPS. In determining surgical prognosis for pain-sensitive patients, it becomes critical to determine whether aspects of the patient's background and environment may combine with such characteristics to make improvement difficult to achieve.

COPING STRATEGIES

The studies reviewed thus far in this chapter emphasize the negative sequelae of chronic pain. Intense emotional responses to chronic pain can

MMPI 3 Cluster Solution

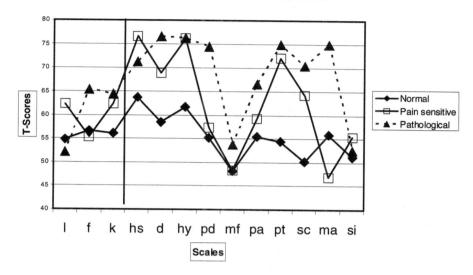

Figure 5.1. Three-cluster solution of MMPI results. MMPI = Minnesota Multiphasic Personality Inventory; Hs = Hypochondriasis; D = Depression; Hy = Hysteria; Pd = Psychopathic Deviate; Mf = Masculine/feminine; Pa = Paranoia; Pt = Psychesthenia; Sc = Schizophrenia; Ma = Hypomania; Si = Social introversion.

worsen its impact, militating against sanguine outcome for spine surgery. Individuals with certain long-standing personality characteristics seem particularly affected by and unable to recover from the pain. However, the majority of patients who undergo spine surgery recover well, giving testimony to the fact that for many, chronic spine pain is a condition that can be dealt with relatively objectively and with limited emotional impact.

The question of why some individuals can handle the experience of chronic pain with relative ease while others experience extreme distress has stimulated the largest body of research in psychosocial aspects of chronic pain. This question has been addressed through an examination of "pain coping" strategies. The concept of coping is derived from the conceptual model Lazarus and Folkman (1984) developed to describe the ways in which individuals deal with stress. According to this model, stress has its origins in the relationship between life events and the individual's responses to those events. Stress occurs when a person appraises an event as taxing or exceeding his or her resources or as endangering his or her well-being. According to this model, pain is stressful only when an individual appraises it as such. *Pain coping,* then, refers to the specific thoughts and behaviors people use to manage their pain or their reaction to pain (G. K. Brown & Nicassio, 1987) so that they do not perceive the pain as exceeding their available resources.

A number of questionnaires have been developed to assess coping strategies, especially as they relate to pain. These include the Ways of Coping

Checklist (Folkman & Lazarus, 1985), the Vanderbilt Pain Management Inventory (G. K. Brown & Nicassio, 1987), the Cognitive Coping Strategies Inventory (Butler, Damarin, Beaulieu, Schwebel, & Thorn, 1989), and the Coping Strategies Questionnaire (CSQ; Rosenstiel & Keefe, 1983). These questionnaires assess coping thoughts and activities that fall into the following general areas (there is some variation in terminology; see Boothby, Thorn, Stroud, & Jensen, 1999; Rosenstiel & Keefe, 1983):

- positive self-statements—telling oneself that one can handle the pain (e.g., "I see the pain as a challenge and don't let it bother me");
- praying/hoping—telling oneself to hope and pray that the pain will get better someday (e.g., "I have faith in my doctors that someday there will be a cure for my pain");
- reinterpreting the pain sensation—imagining something that, if real, would be inconsistent with the experience of pain (e.g., "I don't think of it as pain, but as a dull or warm feeling");
- ignoring—denying that the pain hurts or affects one in any way (e.g., "I tell myself it doesn't hurt");
- diverting attention—thinking of things that distract one from the pain (e.g., "I try to read a book or magazine to take my mind off the pain");
- catastrophizing—exaggerated negative self-statements (e.g., "the pain is awful, and it overwhelms me"); and
- increasing activities—engaging in active behaviors that divert one's attention from the pain (e.g., exercising or reading when in pain).

Several major articles have reviewed the large body of research on coping with chronic pain (most notably, Boothby et al., 1999; M. P. Jensen, Turner, Romano, & Karoly, 1991). Although the results of these studies are, as might be expected, not completely uniform, Boothby et al. suggested that several general conclusions can be reached: In general, positive self-statements are associated with lower pain levels, less depressed mood, and higher levels of general activity among pain patients. Catastrophizing, on the other hand, is associated with higher levels of psychological distress, poorer physical functioning and increased disability, higher ratings of pain intensity, and more interference with daily activities. Less consistent is the association of praying/hoping with greater pain-related dysfunction. For the other pain coping strategies, the results are less clear or consistent.

The use of coping strategies in spine surgery candidates has been examined in two studies, both using the CSQ. A. R. Gross (1986) examined pain intensity, sleep disturbance, and patient-rated surgical outcome in 50 laminectomy/discectomy patients who were given the CSQ prior to surgery. Patients who scored high on a factor termed "loss of control" (combining high scores on the catastrophizing scale and low scores on the pain control scale) had greater postoperative pain and reported poorer surgical outcome than did those who scored low on this scale. High scores on the "self-reliance factor" (combining high scores on the pain control scale and low scores on the praying/hoping scale) were positively associated with reported surgical outcome and negatively associated with postoperative pain and sleep disturbance.

Block et al. (2001), as part of a PPS study, gave the CSQ preoperatively to 204 patients who underwent spine surgery. A hierarchical regression analysis found that the CSQ self-reliance factor was a significant contributor to the regression equation predicting overall surgical outcome. Taken together with the study by A. R. Gross (1986), these results indicate that the ways in which a patient copes with pain can have a strong influence on the outcome of spine surgery.

The coping strategies of surgical candidates may differ from those of patients in conservative chronic pain treatment programs, whose pain does not have a pathological basis amenable to invasive treatment. It is the goal of many conservative treatment programs to help patients realize that increases in pain are to be expected and that they can minimize the impact of such pain increases through coping strategies such as hypnosis, relaxation, or alteration of their conception of the pain. The patient undergoing spine surgery, however, is in a somewhat different position. Although the use of distraction, relaxation, or cognitive techniques may help the patient limit medication use and maintain emotional stability, such techniques must be used judiciously. The pathology leading to spine surgery is, in fact, a threat to well-being and must be respected as such. Patients need to be alert to the limits of coping and to the importance of attending both to changes in the quality of pain and to significant increases in pain intensity.

Without such a balanced approach to coping, surgical candidates run the risk of worsening the pathophysiological basis of the pain. For example, during the preoperative period, the development of pain or numbness radiating down the leg in a new distribution may signify symptoms related to disc herniation. Even more significantly, spine fusion patients need to be wary of excessive pain during the postoperative period. Not infrequently, in their eagerness to return to normal function, some patients ignore or use distraction techniques to cope with pain to such an extent that they can become quite active, endangering the fusion consolidation process and leading to the development of pseudoarthrosis.

Coping, then, is a double-edged sword for the spine surgery patient. Judicious use of positive self-statements and pain control techniques can improve emotional stability, minimize medication use, and improve functional abilities. Catastrophizing, on the other hand, can worsen the emotional and sensory impact of the spine injury. However, patients whose pain coping strategies are especially effective need to beware, lest they become either oblivious to alterations in pain sensation or cavalier about activity restrictions.

The research reviewed in this chapter suggests that psychometric testing is a critical component of PPS. Psychometric testing, normally, should be given to the patient after completion of the interview. Accurate, non-defensive test responses are much more likely if the patient has established a relationship with the psychologist prior to test completion. Otherwise certain test items may be perceived as invasive or unnecessary. Instructions to the patient should make it clear that psychometric tests are a standard and critical component of the evaluation, and that the results will help the psychologist to better understand the patient's concerns and feelings.

Although, obviously, the MMPI (and the MMPI-2) have the strongest research support, they are not necessarily the choice for all patients, nor for all clinicians. For example, time constraints will sometimes not be sufficient for MMPI completion. A good alternative, then, is the SCL-90. This test, of course, does not provide the depth nor breadth of information provided by the MMPI, so if SCL-90 results are highly aberrant, or in conflict with the evaluator's impression, it is wise to have the patient return and complete an MMPI.

Regardless of the specific tests used, we suggest that, in conducting PPS, tests should be included that:

1. Assess personality issues and emotional states (both reactive and acute), including:
   a. Pain sensitivity
   b. Depression
   c. Anger
   d. Anxiety
2. Assess pain coping techniques and strategies including:
   a. Catastrophizing
   b. Sense of control over pain

CONCLUSION

Psychometric testing constitutes the most systematically researched, objective, and consistent component of PPS. Research using psychometric testing demonstrates that personality and emotional issues play a strong role in influencing surgical outcome. Pain coping, another key to recovery from spine injury, can be identified by psychometric testing. Thus, the time and energy required for completion of psychometric tests are justified by the significant insight they provide into surgical responsiveness and provide direction for adjunctive psychological treatment.

Unfortunately, insurers are becoming increasingly draconian in denying authorization of the use of psychometric testing in general. The studies reviewed in this chapter indicate that such an approach is shortsighted, because the inclusion of psychometric testing within PPS provides key objective criteria for identifying patients unlikely to benefit from spine surgery. Providing noninvasive alternative treatments for high-risk patients both helps the patients avoid a worsening of their pain and saves the insurer the expense of futile interventions.

6

THE MIND–BODY INTERFACE: ESTABLISHING SURGICAL PROGNOSIS

The factors influencing back pain, from its genesis to its subjective experience and overt expression and ultimately to its reduction, are shrouded in mystery. Pain is a private epiphenomenon, a culmination of both physical and psychosocial events. It can never be directly assessed. The studies reviewed in Part 2 (chapters 2–6) underscore the complexities involved in deciphering the enigmatic nature of pain. Even though sophisticated medical diagnostic testing can identify a putative pathophysiological basis for the pain, the surgeon can never be certain that such testing identifies all "pain generators."

Further, surgical approaches that successfully eliminate the identified physical cause of the pain often fail to improve the patient's lot. Pain sensations, decreased function, and use of narcotics may persist, even when apparently perfect surgical correction is obtained, because psychosocial factors often exert a stronger influence on the reduction of pain than do physical factors. In some ways this is not surprising; like emotions and perceptions, pain is a subjective experience and although such a conclusion is possibly obvious, the implications are far-reaching. To most effectively eliminate or reduce the pain, the patient's health care providers must assess these subjectively experienced psychological phenomena with much care, knowledge, and attention to detail. The mysteries of back pain are best investigated by approaches that jointly identify both the physical and mental factors involved in its etiology and maintenance.

Previous chapters have reviewed studies that contribute to a detailed understanding of the interaction of mind and body on back pain. The manner in which one draws on these studies to render a decision about surgical prognosis is the topic of this chapter. As noted in chapter 2, several researchers have developed so-called scorecard methods for addressing medical and psychosocial influences on spine surgery. Such approaches define a list of risk factors, assigning weights to each, so that the clinician can tally the results. Some researchers have assigned weights to risk factors based on their assumptions about the relative importance of each factor (e.g., Spengler et al., 1990; Wiltse & Rocchio, 1975). Other researchers' risk factor weights were empirically derived (e.g., Junge et al., 1996). In all scorecard methods, patients whose scores place them on the wrong side of a numerically defined threshold are determined to be poor surgical candidates.

In developing our scorecard approach to presurgical psychological screening (PPS), we had five goals in mind:

1. We sought to develop a scorecard based on the risk factors identified in multiple studies.
2. We wished to include a very broad range of psychosocial risk factors (most previous scorecards use only one or two psychosocial risk factors).
3. We decided to provide a three-tiered decision on prognosis (good, fair, and poor) and not simply a pass-or-fail decision.
4. We felt the need for a means of decision making that is not completely driven by numerical risk factor totals, but that rather includes consideration of "adverse clinical features"— aspects of a patient's case that, although not quantitatively circumscribable, the psychologist can identify as having significant potential to affect surgical outcome.
5. We structured our approach to allow PPS to guide interventions. Our discussion of the approach particularly emphasizes the fair prognosis patients, for whom psychological interventions may make a critical difference in recovery.

Our initial approach to PPS used a 2 x 2 decision matrix (see Figure 6.1). In this decision matrix, each risk factor was assigned an a priori weight. Psychosocial risk factor scores were tallied separately from medical risk factor scores. Separate high-risk thresholds were defined for the medical and psychosocial dimensions. Surgical prognosis was then based on the quadrant into which the patient's total scores fell. Patients whose scores were below the risk threshold on both medical and psychosocial dimensions were pro-

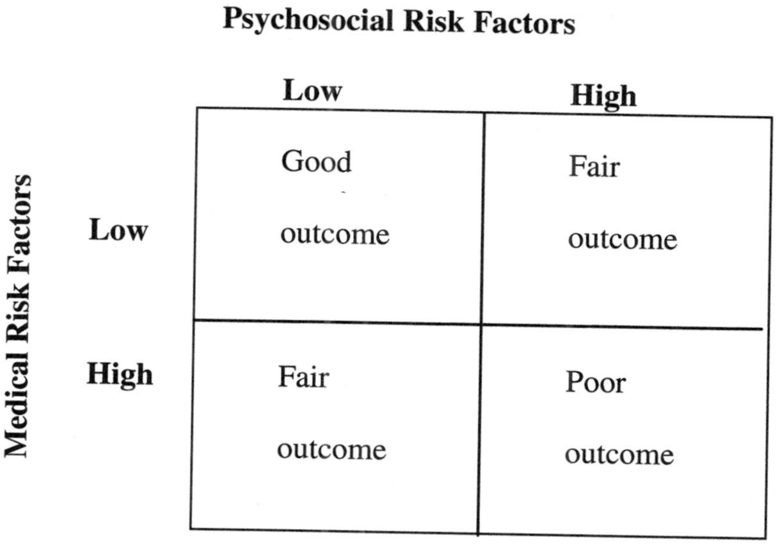

Psychosocial Risk Factors

Figure 6.1. Original model for determining surgical prognosis on the basis of psychosocial and medical risk factors.

jected to have a good prognosis, and those whose scores fell above the risk threshold on both dimensions were projected to have a poor prognosis. Those whose scores fell above the risk threshold on one dimension and below on the other were projected to have a fair prognosis.

Block et al. (2001) examined the effectiveness of this model in predicting surgical outcome for 204 patients (118 laminectomy/discectomy, 86 spinal fusion). The numbers and percentages of patients falling into each quadrant are listed in Table 6.1, which shows that the majority of patients fell into the fair prognosis group. Results at a mean of 8 months following surgery were then examined comparing different aspects of outcome for the three prognosis groups using a series of repeated measures ANOVAs. Three major outcome measures were used: functional impairment (assessed by the Oswestry Disability Index; Fairbank et al., 1980); pain report (using the visual pain analog scale), and continued medication use. Overall outcome was assessed by combining the three measures. Results demonstrated that the poor prognosis group had a significantly worse overall outcome than did the fair or good prognosis groups and fared the worst on specific outcome measures of decrease in pain report and reduction of medication. There was also a trend ($p = .06$) for the poor prognosis group to evince less improvement in functional ability. By comparing patients' PPS prognoses to the overall outcome obtained, we assessed the predictive power of this PPS scorecard, which achieved an 82% accuracy rate. Particularly noteworthy was that 82.3% of patients in the poor prognosis group achieved poor outcome, compared to 17% of patients in the good prognosis group.

TABLE 6.1
Relationship Between Prognosis and Outcome for Original Presurgical
Psychological Screening Scorecard

Prognosis	Outcome			
	Good	Fair	Poor	Total
Good	24	4	3	31
Fair	19	78	23	120
Poor	6	3	44	53
Total	49	85	70	204

We continued analysis of the PPS scorecard using hierarchical regression analyses to determine the variables that contributed significantly to overall outcome. Table 6.2 displays the results of this unforced hierarchical regression equation that achieved statistic significance. The psychometric test data contributed most significantly to the equation, followed by four variables from the interview set. Only one medical risk factor, obesity (greater than 50% above ideal body weight), contributed significantly. Overall, the hierarchical regression equation was only slightly more effective at predicting outcome (84.3% correctly classified) than was the PPS scorecard (82.8% correctly classified). This result supports the effectiveness of the scorecard approach and demonstrates that patients who have a poor prognosis will very likely fail to improve as a result of spine surgery.

PPS Algorithm

Our results (Block et al., 2001) support a conclusion of several previous groups of researchers: Psychosocial factors are most often found to be stronger predictors of surgical outcome than are medical diagnostic factors. In our study, diagnosis, type of surgery, and duration of pain did not contribute uniquely to the hierarchical regression equation, whereas psychometric and interview data did. Wiltse and Rocchio (1979) found that elevated Hypochondriasis (Hs) and Hysteria (Hy) scores on the Minnesota Multiphasic Personality Inventory (MMPI) were the best predictors of operative success in chemonucleolysis patients, correlating .60 with outcome. Dzioba and Doxey (1984) found that MMPI Hs scores, nonorganic signs, and abnormal pain drawing scores significantly predicted lumbar surgery outcome, whereas factors such as type of operative procedure, postoperative complications, chronicity, and preoperative diagnosis were not predictive. Similarly, Spengler et al. (1990) performed a regression analysis predicting outcome in lumbar discectomy patients and found that MMPI scores contributed far more to the overall outcome prediction than did the medical factors or neurological signs, "sciatic-tension" signs, or imaging studies.

TABLE 6.2
Hierarchical Regression Analyses

Step	Variable	Significance
1. Psychological test data (78.4% correctly classified)	MMPI-L	.062
	MMPI-Depression	.001
	MMPI-Hysteria	.049
	MMPI-Psychopathic Deviate	.024
	MMPI-Psychesthenia	.001
	MMPI-Scizophrenia	.025
	CSQ-Self-Reliance	.001
2. Psychological interview data (83.3% correctly classified)	Workers' compensation	.009
	Heavy job	.031
	Spousal solicitousness	.003
	Preinjury psychological dysfunction	.008
3. Medical risk factors (84.3% correctly classified)	Obesity	.047

Note. All predictors with significance level < .10 are displayed. MMPI = Minnesota Multiphasic Personality Inventory; CSQ = Coping Skills Questionnaire.

The results of these studies led us to refine our original PPS scorecard. The psychosocial risk factors in the revised scorecard and their weights and assessment scores, along with selected references, are listed in Table 6.3. Each risk factor is assigned a weight based on the extent of research literature supporting it: 2 if the factor is considered a strong risk factor and 1 if it is considered a moderate risk factor. A similar weighting scheme is used for the medical risk factors (see Table 6.4). These weights are very similar to those used in our original PPS model.

Reflecting the studies that demonstrate psychosocial factors to be the strongest predictors of spine surgery outcome, we have replaced the 2 x 2 matrix (Figure 6.1) with a PPS prognosis algorithm, as displayed in Figure 6.2. This algorithm adds several major new features. First, the algorithm places psychosocial risk factors in the primary position—they are to be considered before medical risk factors. Second, an information set termed *adverse clinical features* is explicitly included within the algorithm. Finally, each path in the algorithm leads directly to a set of general treatment recommendations, in addition to the projection of surgery outcome.

The first step in determining prognosis is to total the weights of identified psychosocial risk factors. To accomplish this, the psychologist should figure the interview and testing risk factors separately using the weights shown in Figure 6.2. Note that for testing, the maximum total number of risk points is 6: 4 maximum from the personality and emotional factors assessed by the MMPI or substitute test, plus 2 if the patient has a high score on the

TABLE 6.3
Revised PPS Scorecard: Psychosocial Risk Factors

Factor Name	Weight[a]	Data Source	Selected References
Job dissatisfaction	2	Interview	Bigos et al., 1991; Schade et al., 1999
Workers' compensation	2	Interview	Klekamp et al., 1998; Glassman et al., 1998
Litigation	2	Interview	V. M. Taylor et al., 2000; Junge et al., 1995
Spousal solicitousness	1	Interview	Block et al., 2001
No spousal support	1	Interview	Schade et al., 1999
Abuse and abandonment	1	Interview	Schofferman et al., 1992
Substance abuse	2	Interview	Spengler et al., 1980; Uomoto et al., 1988
History of psychological disturbance	2	Interview	Block et al., 2001; Manniche et al., 1994
Pain sensitivity	2	MMPI-Hs MMPI-Hy	Turner et al., 1992; Wiltse & Rocchio, 1975
Depression Chronic Reactive	 2 1	MMPI-Pd, BDI	Junge et al., 1996; Trief et al., 2000; Block et al., 2001; Sorenson, 1992
Anger	2	MMPI	Dvorak et al., 1988; Herron et al., 1992
Anxiety	2	MMPI, STAI	Doxey et al., 1988; Kjelby-Wendt et al., 1999
Depressed-pathological profile	4	MMPI	Riley et al., 1995; Block & Ohnmeiss, 2000

[a]Determined by extent of literature support.
Note. 1 = moderate risk; 2 = strong risk. PPS = presurgical psychological screening; MMPI = Minnesota Multiphasic Personality Inventory; Hs = Hypochondriasis; Hy = Hysteria; Pd = Psychopathic Deviate; BDI = Beck Depression Inventory; STAI = State-Trait Anxiety Inventory.

catastrophizing scale of the Coping Strategies Questionnaire (CSQ). (To provide for a conservative measure of psychological distress, the cutoff scores for significant elevations are $T > 75$ if using the MMPI and $T > 70$ if using the MMPI-2.) The interview and testing risk points are summed to derive a total level of psychosocial risk.

Three different prognoses may be arrived at depending on the level of psychosocial risk obtained. Patients with minimal psychosocial difficulties (0–3 points) are projected to have a good prognosis, regardless of the level of medical risk factors identified. For patients whose level of psychosocial risk is either moderate (4–7 points) or high (8+ points), medical risk factors are next examined, and fair surgical prognosis is the best obtainable. For patients

TABLE 6.4
Revised PPS Scorecard: Medical Risk Factors

Risk Factor	Weight[a]	Selected References
Duration of pain		Junge et al., 1996; Bhandari et al., 1999;
6–12 months	1	Franklin et al., 1994
< 12 months	2	
Type of surgery: Highly destructive[b]	2	Turner et al., 1992; Franklin et al., 1994
Nonorganic signs	2	Dzioba & Doxey, 1984; Sorenson, 1992
Pain drawing abnormal	2	Takata & Hirotani, 1995; Dzioba & Doxey, 1984
Previous surgeries		North et al., 1993; Pheasant et al., 1979; Ciol et al., 1994; Turner et al., 1992
2 or more	2	
1	1	
Prior medical problems	2	Hoffman et al., 1993; Ciol et al., 1994
Smoking (fusion patients)	2	C. W. Brown et al., 1986; Glassman et al., 2000
Obesity	1	Block et al., 2001

[a]Determined by extent of literature support. 1= moderate risk; 2 = strong risk. [b]Highly destructive surgery.
Note. PPS = presurgical psychological screening.

with a moderate psychosocial risk level and a low medical risk level (0–5 points), surgical prognosis is deemed good, with no need to examine any other aspects of the case, although there may be a call for additional psycho-therapy, especially in the postoperative period. For all remaining patients, psychologists should assess a third source of information, adverse clinical features.

Adverse clinical features are those aspects of the patient's case not explicitly included on the PPS risk factor scorecard that, in the psychologist's judgment, can be expected to negatively influence surgical results. These factors, listed in Exhibit 6.1, are somewhat impressionistic and quantifiable only in the loosest sense of the word. Their identification relies on the expertise and insight of the examiner, especially during the interview phase of the evaluation. The presence of any of these features should give the examiner pause, as is seen in Figure 6.2. To the extent that such features are found in patients with a high level of both psychosocial and medical risk, they are cause for recommending that the patient receive no treatment and simply be discharged. When adverse clinical features are found in a patient who has moderate psychosocial risk and high medical risk, surgery should be delayed until the patient's compliance and motivation can be tested through presurgical intervention. Such intervention is also suggested for patients who have a high level of psychosocial risk but a low level of medical risk.

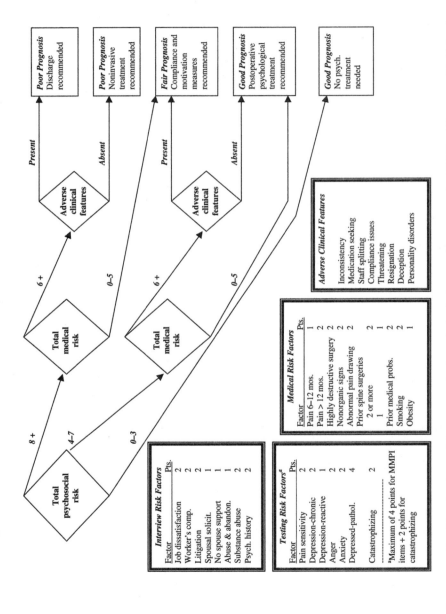

Figure 6.2. Algorithm for determining presurgical psychological screening prognosis. MMPI = Minnesota Multiphasic Personality Inventory.

EXHIBIT 6.1
Adverse Clinical Features

Inconsistency: Observed pain behavior is much lower than would be expected based on patient pain report or is dramatically exaggerated. High levels of pain behavior are observed in one setting but not in another.

Medication seeking: Medical chart indicates pattern of early prescriptions and excuses for narcotic medication loss, or patient's focus during the interview is on getting the psychologist to help obtain narcotics.

Staff splitting: Patient complains unjustifiably about other staff members, noteworthy especially if combined with an obsequious attitude toward the examiner.

Noncompliance or minimal compliance: History of active or passive resistance to treatment plans, often seen in numerous missed appointments, late arrivals, or refusal to undertake treatment suggestions.

Threatening behavior: Patient demands surgery with the implication or statement that if surgery does not occur, drastic actions will follow, such as suicide, divorce, or even homicide.

Defeatist resignation: Patient wants to have the surgery yet states a belief that surgery will be ineffective, that the surgeon is incompetent, that he or she is likely to die during surgery, or that the diagnosis is incorrect.

Deception: Patient describes or implies activities intended to deceive health care providers, employers, or insurers.

Personality disorders: Major disorders that can be expected to compromise surgical outcome include borderline, histrionic, narcissistic, passive-aggressive, and antisocial disorders. Caution is advised if other personality disorders are identified.

Compliance and Motivation Measures

The PPS prognosis clearly identifies the psychologist's recommendations to the referring surgeon regarding the advisability of proceeding with surgery. For the patient with a good prognosis, the outlook is positive, and the chances that psychosocial factors may interfere with surgical recovery are slim. As noted earlier, in most studies, patients with low levels of psychosocial risk achieve good results in at least 80% to 90% of cases. For the poor prognosis patient, the opposite results are likely—in our study fewer than 20% of poor prognosis patients achieved good surgical results (Block et al., 2001). The recommendations concerning surgery are not as immediately apparent for the remaining group of patients, those with a fair prognosis (about 30% of patients). We recommend that psychologists take additional steps to assess and improve the motivation of patients with a fair prognosis before giving a final recommendation concerning surgery.

Compliance and motivation measures are clinical recommendations the psychologist makes that are tailored to address problems noted in the PPS that might interfere with surgery (see Exhibit 6.2). These recommendations should center on relatively rapidly changeable behaviors and patterns rather than long-term personality issues. For example, in patients with a noncom-

EXHIBIT 6.2
Compliance and Motivation Target Behaviors and Rationale

Reduction of narcotic medications: Improves the effectiveness of medications given postoperatively to control pain.

Weight reduction: Reduces physical load on spine, thereby improving surgical effectiveness.

Smoking cessation: Increases speed and improves probability of solid bone growth in fusion patients; speeds healing.

Active participation in aerobic exercise program: Reverses deconditioning, leading to more rapid postoperative recovery.

Active participation in relaxation training program: Improves ability to control stress, thereby improving healing.

Family behavioral medicine psychotherapy sessions: Reduces reactive marital distress; reduces spousal solicitousness; improves feeling of support.

Required timely attendance at all scheduled appointments: Demonstrates patient motivation.

Proper use of antidepressant medication: Treats biochemical depression, thereby improving outcome.

---

pliance history, the psychologist might suggest requiring absolute adherence to treatment recommendations and punctual attendance at all scheduled appointments. Likewise, the psychologist might recommend requiring patients who present with reactive clinical depression to begin both a course of antidepressant medication and cognitive-behavioral intervention (discussed in chapter 9). Smokers may be required to terminate or reduce cigarette use. For patients overusing narcotic medications, a reduction to low-level use may be demanded. Longer-term personality issues, such as pain sensitivity or personality disorders, are not appropriate as direct targets for presurgical motivation and compliance measures.

The psychologist should introduce the recommended motivation and compliance measures to the patient after the PPS is completed, during a separately scheduled feedback session if possible. During this session the patient and psychologist discuss the patient's risk factors for reduced surgical outcome and the recommendations for improving the probability of a good response. Together, they decide on the sorts of behavioral changes that are feasible and acceptable to the patient and that can make an actual difference in surgical outcome. The patient's spine surgery preparation program (described in part 3) often has as its core these behavior change suggestions. Once the patient and psychologist have agreed on the measures the patient will undertake, the psychologist must make clear to the patient that his or her recommendations to the surgeon will depend on the patient's successful execution of these recommendations. The psychologist and patient agree on a firm time frame for completion of the measures, most often 6 weeks or less.

The psychologist should communicate to the patient that successful completion of the measures demonstrates the patient's willingness to take an active and positive role in his or her recovery from the spine surgery. In this way, the motivation and compliance measures contain both carrot and stick—they improve the patient's chances of success and, if not completed, may be the cause of refusal for surgery, with a recommendation for noninvasive treatment or, in extreme cases, for discharge without treatment.

PPS RECOMMENDATIONS

Recommendations to the Surgeon

PPS is not unlike a number of other medical diagnostic tests in that the relationship between pain and pathology is often far from clear. Tests such as computed tomography with discography, myelography, magnetic resonance imaging, and radiographs produce shadows, images, and patterns. The physician then examines the test results, intuiting, on the basis of years of training and experience, the relationship between identified pathology and pain. Successful completion of PPS requires a similar ability to bring informed interpretation to specific test results. In other words, the psychologist must rapidly deduce, from esoteric and complex psychosocial factors, conclusions that are simple and straightforward. For PPS results to be useful to the surgeon, the psychologist must present them in a manner that is similar to other diagnostic tests. The results and recommendations should be clear and specific, and they must be given to the surgeon quickly so that medical decision-making is not delayed.

Psychologists are trained to produce evaluation reports with great depth and understanding. Five- to ten-page reports, detailing much of the patient's life, are not uncommon. Yet to the surgeon such reports are mostly superfluous. For the surgeon's purposes, a brief summary of results, in a format similar to the one contained in Exhibit 6.3, provides the needed information. The advantage of such a summary is that it can be completed very rapidly in just a few minutes after the evaluation so that the physician can get the PPS results the same day. A more complete report can follow later. In cases where a delay in recommendations is necessary—for patients requiring motivation and compliance measures, or when one session has not been sufficient to obtain all necessary information—the PPS summary sheet rapidly informs the surgeon of the reasons for this delay. The report can be amended later, when full information is obtained or at the completion of the motivation and compliance period.

Recommendations to the Patient

At some point, either after the initial PPS session or at the completion of motivation and compliance measures, the psychologist must face the some-

EXHIBIT 6.3
Presurgical Psychological Screening Summary Form

Patient: _____

Referring MD: _____ Surgery Type: _____

Our evaluation of this patient reveals the following level of psychosocial risk for reduced outcome of spine surgery:

Low Risk   **Medium Risk**   **High Risk**

Major identified risk factors are (4 maximum):

1. _____

2. _____

3. _____

4. _____

Recommendation for surgery (if being performed primarily for pain relief):

- Proceed with surgery, no need for psychological treatment
- Proceed with surgery, psychotherapy: pre-op ____, post-op ____
- Hold on surgery pending outcome of psychotherapy
- Hold on surgery, with following recommendations:
  _____
- Avoid surgery if possible.

Additional Recommendations: _____

_____

_____   _____
          Psychologist   Date

---

times daunting task of informing the patient of PPS results. Whether the recommendation is to proceed with surgery, to pursue noninvasive treatments, or to avoid treatment altogether, the psychologist can offer the patient a great deal of information, feedback, and guidance after conducting the PPS. When the psychologist recommends proceeding with surgery, he or she can offer advice about identified risk factors. For example, to the patient who is under pressure because of financial strains or employer demands to return to work rapidly after surgery, the psychologist should emphasize the importance of activity pacing. Most patients will benefit from a discussion of the importance of stress management and proper sleep to the healing process. Even though psychotherapy is outside the purview of PPS, the psychologist can provide the patient with a presurgery preparation program that will undoubtedly lead to more realistic expectations and a more successful recovery.

We strongly recommend that, despite any trepidation concerning the patient's response, the evaluating psychologist schedule a follow-up meeting with high-risk patients to explain the rationale for the recommendation not to proceed with surgery. In this session, the psychologist should state the major risk factors identified and explain how research has shown these factors to decrease the probability of spine surgery being effective. The high incidence rate of failed back surgery syndrome in patients with similar psychosocial profiles should also be a focus of conversation. Discussion of noninvasive alternative treatments, such as functional restoration programs or chronic pain programs, can demonstrate to the patient that his or her situation is not hopeless. It is surprising how many patients presented with such information are relieved to know that more effective treatment alternatives may be available. Many patients feel that noninvasive treatments offer them much greater control over their bodies and their destinies. The psychologist can emphasize that in the long run, effort given to such treatments may not only reduce the patient's pain and dysfunction, but also forestall a recurrence or worsening of the underlying spinal problems.

The patient for whom discharge without treatment is recommended may be displeased. Some patients are firm in the belief that surgery is the only solution; the psychologist should explain to such patients that the results of extensive research demonstrate that patients with a high level of psychosocial risk, regardless of the identified pathophysiologic basis of the pain, have greatly reduced chances of obtaining good surgical results. Patients in this group, thus, may be helped to realize the problems that their psychosocial difficulties create for recovery. The psychologist can recommend self-help books and community resources to lessen the patient's distress and improve the patient's condition. It may help the patient to discuss the situation with others who have experienced failed back surgery syndrome, so referral to a chronic pain support group (the American Chronic Pain Association, for example, conducts such groups) may be quite valuable. Of course, the psychologist should reiterate that the decision to operate rests solely with the surgeon and that PPS results are only one of many diagnostic tests that the surgeon will consider in making this decision. The psychologist should encourage the patient to return to the surgeon to discuss the PPS results in the context of all medical diagnostic testing.

CONCLUSION

As devastating as are the sequelae of chronic pain, failed spine surgery can be even more disastrous. When surgery is ineffective, the patient's hopes for recovery are often dashed, leading to progressive declines in emotional stability and interpersonal relationships. As the patient seeks ever more invasive solutions to the pain, the costs of care can dramatically escalate. Spine surgery itself can cost from $15,000 to $50,000 and up, so that the total cost of care in a failed spine surgery case can easily exceed $100,000. For employers, failed spine surgeries lead to the protracted absence of valuable employees and may produce large costs in disability payments. Truly, failed spine surgery is a nightmare that all involved wish to avoid.

Results of research on PPS demonstrate that psychosocial factors are frequently the strongest predictors of reduced surgical outcome. The studies reviewed in part 2 indicate that about 20% to 30% of patients have a high level of psychosocial risk. For these patients, the probability of obtaining good outcome is quite low, with only about 20% of high-risk patients achieving acceptable surgical results. Thus, the careful and judicious use of PPS can help avoid failed back surgery syndrome.

In this chapter we presented a systematic PPS approach that identifies and quantifies surgical risk factors. The approach involves rules for combining these risk factors, while taking into account adverse clinical features, to arrive at a surgical prognosis. Use of the algorithm provided in this chapter allows for a systematic, replicable, and scientifically valid means of identifying patients likely to be nonresponsive to spine surgery. The approach presented in this chapter can help clinicians and patients avoid futile, costly, and even disastrous surgeries and can help guide the travels of patients for whom the path to recovery passes through the operating room.

III

PREPARING THE PATIENT FOR SPINE SURGERY

7

THE PSYCHONEUROIMMUNOLOGY
OF SPINE SURGERY

With the decision to proceed with spine surgery, the patient has completed another stage of the odyssey to back pain relief. First, the surgeon identified the physical causes of the pain, explained them to the patient, and discussed surgical solutions. A thorough presurgical psychological screening (PPS) evaluation identified any psychosocial factors that might influence surgery outcome, relief of pain, and recovery of function. The psychologist has declared the patient an acceptable surgical candidate, and the surgeon has decided to proceed with the intended treatment. There remains one final step in the presurgical stage of the odyssey: preparation of the patient for surgery. A large body of research demonstrates that patient preparation may have a larger effect on surgical outcome than all the previously conducted medical and psychological diagnostics.

Surgery is a physically traumatic event. Tissues are cut and removed, and sometimes bone or hardware is inserted to replace the removed tissues. Anesthesia exerts effects on the patient that may linger long after the patient has left the hospital. Strong narcotic medications are given to relieve pain, but these sometimes cause side effects, such as constipation or cognitive confusion, or even create dependence. Thus, the healing process after spine surgery is complicated and problematic, but patients can be prepared beforehand to manage the psychosocial factors that can influence this process.

Surgical preparation of the patient rests on an understanding of the many ways psychosocial factors can influence the process of recovery after surgery. There are two major, overlapping phases of this recovery, both of which need to be considered in developing surgical preparation techniques. The first phase involves postsurgical healing. During this phase, physiological processes must occur that overcome not only the physical basis of the pain, but also the trauma of the surgery. Next, aggressive rehabilitation is required to overcome the cumulative effects of months of injury and inactivity. This phase involves physical and mental exercises that help the patient improve stamina, recognize and build on small gains, and develop incentives for recovery.

In this chapter we focus primarily on the ways in which psychosocial factors can influence the first of these phases—the postsurgical healing process. Until recently, researchers faced a "black box" problem when trying to investigate such psychological influences on post-surgical healing. They had no way to adequately measure the intricate inner workings of a surgical patient's various body systems. Thus, most of the research was correlational in nature, and the psychophysiological links between presurgical variables (and interventions) and postoperative outcomes could only be speculated on. With the emergence of the field of psychoneuroimmunology (PNI), investigators are now able to directly measure physiological processes within the human "black box," suggesting ways in which psychosocial factors can affect wound healing and postoperative outcome. The science of PNI basically focuses on connections between the central nervous system ("mind") and the immune system ("body"; Hafen, Karren, Frandsen, & Smith, 1996).

Kiecolt-Glaser et al. (1998) developed a biobehavioral conceptual model linking psychological variables with immune system function, wound healing, and subsequent short-term postoperative recovery. This conceptual model, illustrated in Figure 7.1, involves the following components:

- The patient's attitude toward the spine surgery and premorbid personality significantly influence emotions during the spine surgery decision-making process. In turn, emotions have a direct effect on stress hormones and, thus, modulate immune function.
- A patient's psychological status (including both cognitive and emotional factors) influences the type and amount of anesthetic necessary. These medications in turn have influences on the patient's immune and endocrine system.
- Health behaviors and health status have a significant influence over the surgery process, including immune and endocrine func-

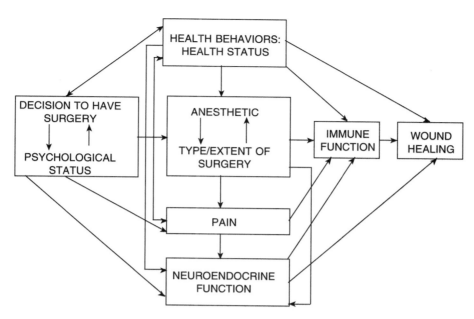

Figure 7.1. A biobehavioral model of the psychological, behavioral, and biological pathways that influence wound healing. From "Psychological Influences on Surgical Recovery: Perspectives from Psychoneuroimmunology," by J. K. Kiecolt-Glaser, G. G. Page, P. T. Marucha, R. C. McCallum, and R. Glaser, 1998, *American Psychologist, 53,* p. 1210. Copyright © 1998 by the American Psychological Association. Reprinted with permission of the authors.

tion, wound healing, and overall postoperative rehabilitation. Patients under stress may be likely to increase destructive coping behaviors such as smoking, alcohol use, and overeating. These potentially self-destructive behaviors can have a deleterious effect not only on immune and neuroendocrine function, but also on postoperative physical recovery.

- Inadequately controlled pain has been found to have adverse effects on immune and endocrine function (Liebeskind, 1991), which can impair wound healing and overall recovery from the spine surgery.

Later in this chapter we discuss the PNI model of Kiecolt-Glaser et al. (1998) in detail and review some background research in this area. This model is helpful not only to the psychologist, but also to the patient and physician; it demonstrates to the psychologist the biobehavioral pathways influencing the healing process, which the psychologist can use in increasing the patient's motivation and active preparation for surgery, and it provides surgeons with a firm rationale relative to wound healing in support of psychological preparation for spine surgery. A program of preparation for surgery interventions is indeed valuable from a physical, psychological, and behavioral standpoint.

THE IMMUNE AND NEUROENDOCRINE SYSTEMS

The biobehavioral healing model rests on a thorough understanding of the functioning of the immune and neuroendocrine systems and the mechanisms of wound healing. To appreciate the research findings in the areas of PNI and surgery, psychologists need some understanding of these important body systems. Following is a brief overview of the immune and neuroendocrine systems; more detailed information can be found elsewhere (Benjamini, Sunshine, & Leskowitz, 1996; S. Cohen & Herbert, 1996; Kiecolt-Glaser & Glaser, 1995; O'Leary, 1990; Page, 1996; Rabin, 1999; Spence, 1982).

Immune System

The immune system is the body's primary defense against attackers from both within the body and without. According to Kiecolt-Glaser and Glaser (1992), the immune system has two primary functions: to distinguish between "self" and "non-self" and then to inactivate, destroy, or eliminate foreign substances that are identified as not naturally part of the body ("non-self").

The immune system comprises organs that are found throughout the body. These are generally termed the "lymphoid" organs because they are involved with the development and deployment of lymphocytes (small white blood cells that modulate the immune system response). Lymphoid organs include the bone marrow, the thymus, the lymph nodes, the spleen, the tonsils, the appendix, and lymphoid tissue in the small intestine known as Peyer's patches.

The bone marrow produces cells that will eventually become lymphocytes. There are two major types of lymphocytes: T-lymphocytes and B-lymphocytes. B-lymphocytes (so named because they were first discovered in a chicken gland called the bursa) develop outside the thymus. The B-lymphocytes, or B-cells, produce circulating antibodies. Antibodies are proteins (belonging to a family of proteins called immunoglobulins) that attack bacteria, viruses, and other foreign invaders (called antigens). Each specific antibody matches a specific invading antigen. The antibodies are capable of inactivating the antigens, making them incapable of causing disease. Antibodies "fit" specific antigens, commonly described "as a key fits a lock." Each antibody will attack only a single kind of antigen, and each B-lymphocyte produces only one kind of antibody.

The other major class of lymphocytes are the T-lymphocytes, or T-cells. Some of the cells produced in the bone marrow, termed *stem* cells, migrate to the thymus, an organ that lies high up just beneath the breastbone. These stem cells multiply in the thymus and develop into T-cells (their named is derived from the fact that they develop in the thymus gland). T-cells do not secrete antibodies but are essential for antibody production.

There are several different groups of T-cells, and these have different functions. *Helper T-cells* stimulate B-lymphocytes to produce antibodies, and they also "turn on" other T-cells. *Suppressor T-cells* "turn off" the helper T-cells when an adequate amount of antibodies have been produced. Helper and suppressor T-cells communicate with each other by producing chemical messengers such as interferons, interleukins, and others. In a healthy person, the helper:suppressor cell ratio should be in balance. Patients with immunodeficiency diseases have low ratios (too few helper cells relative to suppressor cells), and people with autoimmune diseases have high ratios.

Other groups of T-cells have different functions. Cytotoxic (literally, cell-killing) T-cells, along with blood cells termed *natural killer* (NK) cells, patrol the body constantly searching for hazardous abnormal cells. Once these cells are discovered, the cytotoxic T-cells attach themselves and release toxic chemicals to destroy them. Like antibodies, each cytotoxic T-cell is designed to attack a specific target. Thus, there are cytotoxic T-cells that are specific to cancer cells, to cells that have been infected by viruses, and to transplanted tissue and organs. The activity of cytotoxic T-cells is one reason why immunosuppressant medication must be given as part of organ transplantation procedures. The NK cells are called *natural* because they will go into action without prior stimulation by a specific antigen. Normal cells are generally resistant to NK cell activity; however, tumor cells and cells infected with a virus are susceptible. Therefore, NK cells are thought to play a critical role in the immune system's response to cancer. In contrast to cytotoxic T-cells, NK cells attack a broad range of targets, including tumor cells and a variety of infectious microbes.

Other important components of the immune system include the macrophages and monocytes, which are cells that act as scavengers (or phagocytes). These cells envelop and destroy microorganisms and other antigenic particles within the body. Monocytes circulate in the blood, and macrophages are found within the body tissues. Granulocytes are phagocytes that are also capable of destroying invaders. These chemicals contribute to the inflammatory response and are also responsible for allergy symptoms.

Neuroendocrine System

Surgical stress can affect the neuroendocrine system and thereby influence wound healing. The endocrine system is composed of various glands located throughout the body. The major endocrine glands include the pineal, pituitary, thyroid, parathyroids, thymus, adrenals, pancreas, ovaries, and testes. The pituitary gland is considered the "master gland" because its hormones regulate several other endocrine glands and affect a number of body activities. The nervous and endocrine systems are intimately related (hence the term *neuroendocrine*).

One function of the endocrine system is to secrete hormones when the body is under stress. Hormones can be thought of as chemical messengers that influence organs in the body (target organs). The body releases two main hormone groups in response to stress: the catecholamines and the corticosteroids. There are two different types of catecholamines: adrenaline (or epinephrine) and norepinephrine. The catecholamines cause significant physical changes such as rapid heartbeat, constriction of blood vessels, hyperventilation, and blood thickening with more rapid coagulation. These changes have been termed the *fight or flight response* and basically prepare the body for a physically threatening situation. This response is adaptive when one is being chased by a tiger or running from a fire; unfortunately, this physical stress reaction is unhealthy when it is in response to a nonphysically threatening situation (emotional stress) or is sustained over a longer period of time (as when facing surgery or chronic anxiety). Catecholamine levels that are too high, such as in chronic stress, can cause a variety of medical problems such as muscle tremors, diabetes, heart attack, and stroke. In addition, unhealthily elevated catecholamine levels significantly suppress the immune response, resulting in an increased susceptibility to infection and delayed wound healing.

Corticosteroids, the other major hormone group secreted in response to stress, include cortisone and cortisol. Similar to the catecholamines, increased levels of corticosteroids are adaptive in response to a physical threat but may be unhealthy under other circumstances. For example, cortisone has a number of negative effects (Hafen et al., 1996):

- Cortisone stimulates the kidneys to produce renin, a hormone that increases blood pressure.
- The cells lining blood vessels can be damaged, causing the body to respond by secreting more cholesterol in an attempt to repair arterial tears. Subsequently, the accumulation of plaque and cholesterol can lead to atherosclerosis and heart problems.
- Cortisone inhibits vitamin D activity, resulting in a loss of calcium.
- Cortisone causes the liver to overproduce glucose, which over the long term can increase the risk of diabetes.

The effects of elevated cortisol over a longer term may also create myriad physical problems, such as the following (Hafen et al., 1996; McEwen, 1990):

- progressive nerve loss in certain parts of the brain;
- shrinkage of the spleen and thymus, which are essential for the production of white blood cells;
- a breakdown of lymphoid tissues in the thymus and lymph nodes, which in turn reduces the level of helper T-cells and increases the level of suppressor T-cells,
- inhibition of the production of NK cells; and
- a reduction in interferon, important for fighting off viruses.

THE PROCESS OF WOUND HEALING

Beyond the acute stress of the surgery process, a surgical patient who has been under chronic stress is likely to be at even greater risk for slower wound healing, postoperative complications, and a longer than normal recovery period. As discussed by Hubner et al. (1996), wound repair progresses through several stages: inflammation, vasoconstriction, blood coagulation, platelet activation, and activation of platelet-derived growth factors. Of course, any type of surgery produces a wound, and the body will respond by initiating this healing process.

The initial stage of wound healing is an inflammatory response (see chapter 11). The inflammatory response is important for its contribution to pain, immunity, and the beginning of wound healing. Tissue damage caused by the surgical procedure results in a local release of substances (e.g., substance P, bradykinin, serotonin, calcitonin, prostaglandins, and histamine, among others) that result in the inflammatory response, characterized by vasoconstriction, blood coagulation, increased capillary permeability, and sensitization of peripheral afferent nerve fibers resulting in allodynia and hyperalgesia (Page, 1996; Van De Kerkhof, Van Bergen, Spruijt, & Kuiper, 1994; Woolf, 1994). Through a variety of mechanisms (see Kiecolt-Glaser et al., 1998, for a review), other physical responses also occur, including local (Schweizer, Feige, Fontana, Muller, & Dinarello, 1988) and systemic hyperalgesia, as well as flu-like symptoms (Watkins et al., 1994, 1995). The flu-like symptoms, such as fever and malaise, are due to activation of the hepatic vagus or the central nervous system (Page, 1996; Watkins et al., 1994, 1995). The hyperalgesia is due to the sensitization of nociceptive fibers that decrease the threshold necessary to initiate impulse transmission (Woolf, 1994). In other words, the surgical patient is physically more susceptible to painful stimuli (i.e., everything hurts more).

The wound repair process, as described by Hubner et al. (1996), results in the migration of phagocytes to the damaged site to begin the process of cell recruitment and replication necessary for tissue regeneration and capillary regrowth. A patient's immune function plays a critical role early in the wound healing process. Certain cytokines are essential to protect the person from infection and prepare the injured tissue for repair and remodeling (Lowry, 1993). As Hubner et al. pointed out, success in the later stages of wound repair is highly dependent on initial events.

Immune and Neuroendocrine Influences on Wound Healing

Stress has been found to influence immune (Glaser & Kiecolt-Glaser, 1994; Herbert & Cohen, 1993) and neuroendocrine function, which in turn has an impact on wound healing (Kiecolt-Glaser et al., 1998). Immune function plays a critical role in the early stages of tissue damage repair. In addition to other variables, the tissue damaging component of surgery has been shown to induce immune and neuroendocrine changes (see Page, 1996, for review). For instance, immune suppression during surgery is evidenced by suppression of natural killer cell activity (Pollock, Lotzova, & Stanford, 1991), lymphocyte proliferation responses, and changes in lymphocyte populations (Tonnessen, Brinklov, Christensen, Olesen, & Madsen, 1987). In general, stress suppresses the immune system's ability to maintain natural killer cells and lymphocytes. Stress has been shown to increase the number of circulating white blood cells but decrease the number of circulating B-cells, T-cells, helper T-cells, suppressor T-cells, cytotoxic T-cells, and large granular lymphocytes (Goliszek, 1987; Hafen et al., 1996). All of these factors make a person more susceptible to infection and disease and slow the wound healing process.

The stress of surgery also affects the neuroendocrine system. Stress-related changes in the hypothalamic-pituitary-adrenal (HPA) axis can have important consequences for the wound healing process. For instance, elevations in glucocorticoids can temporarily suppress proinflammatory cytokines, which are essential to the early stages of wound healing because they protect a person from infection and prepare the injured tissue for repair (Kiecolt-Glaser et al., 1998).

Another neuroendocrine factor in wound healing is the action of growth hormone (GH). Much of a person's daily GH release has been found to occur during deep sleep (Veldhuis & Iranmanesh, 1996). Although acute stressors have been found to result in temporary increases in GH (Kiecolt-Glaser, Malarkey, Cacioppo, & Glaser, 1994), more chronic stress that disrupts the sleep cycle can lessen GH secretion. This is important because GH has been found to be a factor in enhancing wound healing (Veldhuis & Iranmanesh, 1996). GH is a macrophage activator (Zwilling, 1994) important for improved protection from infection after tissue damage.

Stress and Wound Healing

A great many studies, on both animals and humans, have documented the negative effects of stress on wound healing. In a series of nicely designed studies, family members who provided care for a relative with Alzheimer's disease were studied and compared with a well-matched control group (Kiecolt-Glaser et al., 1998; Kiecolt-Glaser et al., 1994; Kiecolt-Glaser, Dura, Speicher, Trask, & Glaser, 1991; Kiecolt-Glaser, Glaser, Gravenstein, Malarkey, & Sheridan, 1996). The caregiver group was assumed to be under more chronically stressful conditions. The results demonstrated that the caregivers had poorer immune function. In one of the studies directly related to wound healing, a small standardized wound (removal of a small piece of skin from the inner arm below the elbow) was made. The healing process was carefully monitored for the caregiver and the control groups. Consistent with differences in immune function, it was found that the caregiver group took an average of 9 days longer than controls to completely heal. Photographic data of wound size demonstrated that the largest differences occurred early in the healing process. Thus, it appears that the early stages of wound repair were most significantly slowed by immune system deficiencies (for a complete discussion of this issue, see Kiecolt-Glaser et al., 1998; Kiecolt-Glaser, Marucha, Malarkey, Mercado, & Glaser, 1995).

A subsequent study using mice compared a stress group (placed in restraints) and a nonstressed group. A standardized punch biopsy wound was created and the healing process monitored. The stressed mice healed an average of 27% more slowly than the control group (Padgett, Marucha, & Sheridan, 1998). Again, it appeared that major differences occurred early in the wound healing process. Assessment of serum corticosterone in the two groups indicated that the stress group may have had a disruption of the neuroendocrine homeostasis (or balance) that modulates wound healing.

In another study, biopsy scalpel wounds were created in the hard palate of 11 volunteer dental students during their summer vacation and then again during their first major examination (Marucha, Kiecolt-Glaser, & Favagehi, 1998). The investigators were able to establish a rate of healing for each individual by measuring the size of the wound initially and at the point of final healing. The healing rate during the high stress examination period was 10.91 days; the rate during vacation was 7.82 days. Thus, wounds placed 3 days before a major test healed an average of 40% more slowly than those placed during summer vacation. The researchers noted that this slower pattern of healing during stress was uniform across all participants. Certain measures of immune function were also investigated during the course of the study. It was found that there was a 71% decline in certain immune cell indices from the low stress period to the high stress period (see Marucha et al., 1998, for details). This study extended previous research in demonstrating that similar delays in wound healing can occur in response to acute stressors (an examination) and to chronic stressors (Alzheimer's caregiving).

As Kiecolt-Glaser et al. (1998) pointed out, the results of these studies have broad implications for surgical recovery. The combined results from this series of studies demonstrate that surgical patients who have been under chronic stress are at risk for slowed wound healing and for infection due to immunosuppression; further, the short-term stress of the surgery process, in and of itself, has the potential to hamper wound healing. These findings have special implications for the chronic back pain patient who undergoes spine surgery. That individual's immune system is confronted not only with the stress of chronic pain, but also with the situational stress of the surgery.

INFLUENCE OF PAIN ON NEUROENDOCRINE AND IMMUNE FUNCTION

Virtually all surgical procedures are associated with mild to severe postoperative pain. In the case of spine surgery, the neuroendocrine and immune systems of the vast majority of patients are assaulted by both chronic and acute pain. An important area of PNI research is whether pain contributes to neuroendocrine and immune function changes. In animal studies, painful stressors that do not cause tissue damage (e.g., foot shock and tail shock) have been shown to suppress immune function including NK cell activity, lymphocyte proliferation responses, and specific antibody production (Liebeskind, 1991; Pezzone, Dohanics, & Rabin, 1994). Neuroendocrine changes have also been demonstrated, including elevated corticosteroid (Pezzone et al., 1994) and plasma beta-endorphin levels (Sacerdote, Manfredi, Bianchi, & Panerai, 1994).

Research suggests a connection between the sympathetic nervous system (SNS), the HPA axis, and the immune system (Kiecolt-Glaser et al., 1998; Koltun et al., 1996) in response to painful stress such as surgery. SNS and HPA axis activation postoperatively is indicated by elevations in plasma levels of epinephrine, cortisol, and beta-endorphin (Salomaki, Leppaluoto, Laitinen, Vuolteenaho, & Nuutinen, 1993). In addition, immunosuppression during surgery is evidenced by a decrease in NK cell activity (Pollock et al., 1991), lymphocyte proliferation, and changes in the lymphocyte population (Tonnessen et al., 1987).

Although these results cannot firmly verify the role of pain as a factor in neuroendocrine and immune changes in response to surgical stress, there are further findings that support such a conclusion (for reviews, see Kiecolt-Glaser et al., 1998; Page, 1996). Multiple studies have demonstrated that anesthetic techniques used to block transmission of nociceptive impulses locally (Pasqualucci et al., 1994), at the spinal cord level (Koltun et al., 1996; Salomaki et al., 1993; Tonnessen & Wahlgreen, 1988), or through systemic anesthetic (Anand, Sippel, Aynsley-Green, 1987; Kehlet, 1984) significantly reduce the neuroendocrine or immune response to surgery. Further, at least two prospective studies have found that epidural anesthesia is associated with a significant reduction in the incidence of postoperative infections, suggesting that immune function suppression may have been blocked (Cuschieri, Morran, Howie, & McArdle, 1985; Yeager, Glass, Neff, & Brinck-Johnsen, 1987); this finding would seem to indicate that adequate pain control via the epidural anesthesia resulted in attenuation of the immunosuppressive effect of surgery.

In other research approaches to this issue, successfully controlling postoperative pain with systemic opioids has been associated with a reduction in plasma cortisol levels (Moller, Dinesen, Sondergard, Knigge, & Kehlet, 1988), and pain control with narcotic anesthesia has been shown to suppress the hormonal response to surgery (Lacoumenta et al., 1987). Taken together, this line of research suggests that adequate pain control helps attenuate deleterious neuroendocrine and immunological reactions to surgery. Unfortunately, postoperative pain control is commonly inadequate, and a preparation for spine surgery program can help successfully address this problem.

HEALTH HABITS, HEALTH STATUS, AND SURGERY

The studies thus far reviewed demonstrate that many factors can affect the surgical healing process, including stress (both acute and chronic), the physical trauma of surgery and resulting tissue damage, and pain. Health behaviors and health status also influence wound healing.

Generally, when individuals experience heightened distress, as when facing surgery, they are more likely to engage in harmful behaviors across all dimensions, such as alcohol abuse and smoking (Steptoe, Wardle, Pollard, Canaan, & Davies, 1996). Such behaviors can be viewed as self-destructive coping techniques, because they can interact with aspects of health status (e.g., age and physical deconditioning) to negatively influence surgical healing and recovery.

Increased Alcohol Use

Any impending surgery can be stressful for the patient depending on the extent of the operation and the meaning the procedure carries with it. For instance, a hernia repair has a meaning quite different than a spinal fusion. For instance, a person who is having a hernia repair will likely not have been disabled prior to the surgery and can expect a fairly predictable and complete course of recovery. On the other hand, the spinal fusion patient will likely have been disabled to some degree preoperatively and the outcome is less certain relative to the extent of return to function. Patients who are preparing to undergo a spine operation are often under acute situational stress associated with the surgery process as well as more chronic stress related to the impact of their back pain on their lives. Patients may increase their alcohol intake as a mechanism for coping with the ongoing stress or as a method of self-medicating for pain, sleep loss, and anxiety (see Block, Kremer, & Fernandez, 1999; Spengler, Freeman, Westbrook, & Miller, 1980).

Preoperative alcohol abuse has been found to slow wound healing directly due to a slowing of cell migration and deposition of collagen at the wound site (Benveniste & Thut, 1981). Several other effects of alcohol can lower the body's ability to heal from a surgery, including sleep disruption, increased depression and anxiety, increased smoking due to diminished impulse control, poor nutrition, subclinical cardiac dysfunction, and amplified endocrine changes in response to surgery (Kehlet, 1997).

Smoking

As demonstrated in a myriad of studies (see S. E. Porter & Hanley, 2001, for a review), smoking (especially chronic) causes a host of problems related to wound healing and spine surgery outcome (Slosar, Perkins, & Snook, 2002). Some researchers have speculated that smoking impairs wound healing after surgery primarily due to a decrease in blood flow to the injured tissues (vasoconstriction) and moderate blood levels of carbon monoxide (Leow & Maibach, 1998; Mosely & Finseth, 1977). In other studies, nicotine has been shown to affect a variety of other bodily functions that relate to wound healing; decreases have been found in the proliferation of cells within the extracellular matrix and epithelial regeneration (Sherwin & Gastwirth, 1990). In addition, Jorgensen, Kallehave, Christensen, Siana, and Gottrup (1998) demonstrated that collagen synthesis was hindered in the wounds of smokers relative to a nonsmoking control group. Collagen is the primary determinant of the flexible strength in a wound that is healing. Silverstein (1992) stated that smoking diminishes proliferation of fibroblasts and macrophages, causes vasoconstriction that reduces blood flow to the injured tissue, and can inhibit enzyme systems for oxidative metabolism and transport. This decreased availability of nutrients important for wound repair, along with the immune system suppression, results in slowed healing time among smokers and an increased rate of postoperative infections (Silverstein, 1992).

Several studies specifically relate to smokers and spine surgery. Some investigators believe that in long-term smokers, the intervertebral discs are malnourished due to vascular and hematologic changes (Ernst, 1993). Researchers postulate that the vertebra and vertebral disc normally have a limited blood supply and are not able to compensate for the decrease in blood flow that occurs in chronic smokers. Over time, the diminished delivery of oxygen and nutrients to these spine structures leaves them more vulnerable to injury and less able to heal after a surgery. Hanley and Shapiro (1989) found a negative impact on the postoperative success of lumbar discectomies to treat severe radiculopathies in patients who were chronic smokers of 15 years or more. Smoking may also lead to a higher rate of postoperative wound infections (Calderone, Garland, Capen, & Oster, 1996; Capen, Calderone, & Green, 1996). Thalgott, Cotler, Sasso, LaRocca, and Gardner (1991) retrospectively reviewed 32 cases of patients who had undergone spinal surgery and found that of those who sustained an infection after spinal fusion and instrumentation, 90% were cigarette smokers. Of special importance to the field of spine surgery is the effect of smoking on the healing of bone, which specifically relates to a patient's recovery from a spinal fusion. As discussed in chapter 3, smoking is associated with an increased risk of pseudoarthrosis (nonunion) for spinal fusion patients (C. W. Brown, Orme, & Richardson, 1986; Carpenter, Dietz, Leung, Hanscom, & Wagner, 1996).

There are a variety of explanations for these results. As discussed previously, one idea is that smoking causes vasoconstriction, which diminishes the blood supply to the area of bone growth. Another theory is that smoking impairs osteoblast function, resulting in defective bone healing (de Vernejoul, Bielakoff, & Herve, 1983). Campanile, Hautmann, and Lotti (1998) suggested that there are a variety of negative effects due to smoking that hamper bone growth including the vasoconstrictive and platelet-activating properties of nicotine, the hypoxia-promoting effects of carbon monoxide, and the inhibition of oxidative metabolism at the cellular level by hydrogen cyanide.

If a spinal fusion is being considered for a patient who smokes, there are no clear guidelines about preoperative cessation of cigarette consumption (Fardon & Whitesides, 2002; Porter & Hanley, 2001). Suggestions range from at least 12 hours to 60 days before surgery. The recommendation of cessation for at least 60 days is based on studies showing that a nonsmoker can make 1 cm of bone in 2 months but that a smoker needs an average of 3 months to make the same amount of bone (Whitesides, Hanley, & Fellrath, 1994). Of course, it is also important that the patient abstain from smoking postoperatively while the fusion is healing.

Physical Deconditioning Syndrome

Deconditioning or deactivation syndrome (discussed in detail in chapter 11) occurs when a patient manages back pain by limiting normal activities, restricting exercise, or engaging in extensive bed rest. Deconditioning syndrome can result in a number of unhealthy occurrences affecting virtually every body system (see Bortz, 1984) and specifically the spinal musculature. In a group of patients who were three months postoperative for spine surgery, muscle strength was at 50% of gender-specific "normal" values (see Gatchel, 1991a, for a review). In addition, healing tissue that is completely immobilized postoperatively tends to become an amorphous, nonfunctional scar with low strength and a vulnerability to reinjury (see Gatchel, 1991a). For this reason spine surgeons recommend some type of movement on a regular basis beginning very shortly even after a major spine surgery. Of course, the movement guidelines are designed to facilitate the healing process without putting the surgery results at risk. When done properly, this movement allows the tissues to heal in a stronger and more flexible manner.

Age

As a person gets older, the risk is associated with surgery increases. In the area of psychoneuroimmunology, several factors appear to be involved (Kiecolt-Glaser et al., 1998). First, immune function and, in particular, the action of the cellular immune response diminish with age (Verhoef, 1990). With this diminished immune response, the older patient is more susceptible to infectious complications. In fact, infection is one of the primary factors in surgical mortality in the elderly population (Thomas & Ritchie, 1995).

To further complicate matters, it appears that depression and distress interact more strongly in the older person to promote immune system downregulation. Several studies have demonstrated that older adults show greater immunological impairments in response to stress or depression relative to a younger population (Herbert & Cohen, 1993; Kiecolt-Glaser et al., 1996).

Linn and Jensen (1983) compared older and younger adults on a number of immunological variables before and after elective surgery. They found that the two groups did not differ immunologically prior to the surgery, but the older group showed more depression of the immune response after surgery. In addition, older persons are more likely to have other medical problems, and these can affect recovery from a spine surgery.

CONCLUSION

The field of psychoneuroimmunology contributes to our understanding of how a variety of factors can negatively affect wound healing and spine surgery outcome. PNI research also points to psychological preparation techniques that can enhance spine surgery outcomes. PNI research is likely to continue to provide exciting findings in the area of surgery preparation. An understanding of PNI can help the clinician convince both patients and physicians involved in spine surgery of the usefulness of psychological preparation in maximizing surgery results.

8

CONCEPTUAL MODELS OF SURGERY PREPARATION

Over the past 30 years, more than 200 research studies with thousands of patients have found that psychological preparation for surgery can have the following beneficial effects:

- decreased patient distress before and after surgery;
- reduced report of pain;
- decreased need for pain medications perioperatively and post-operatively;
- fewer postoperative complications and a quicker return to health;
- shorter stay in the hospital;
- enhanced overall patient satisfaction;
- empowerment of the patient to take more responsibility for recovery, thus reducing health care demands; and
- potential savings of thousands of dollars per surgery.

Psychological preparation for spine surgery (and many other operations) addresses two major needs. First, the physical and emotional stress of surgery can negatively influence outcome, and a number of psychological interventions can alleviate these effects. As Horne, Vatmanidis, and Careri (1994) observed, "Invasive medical and surgical procedures can be extremely distressing and can adversely affect the patient's ability to cope, even when the actual procedures are not a real threat in a medical or biological sense" (p. 5). Thus, even if the surgery has a high probability of a positive outcome, it often has negative individual and social effects. Deleterious physical, emotional, and economic consequences of surgery affect not only the patient, but also his or her family, friends, and work associates (Contrada, Leventhal, & Anderson, 1994). A psychological preparation for surgery program provides spine surgery candidates with treatments that can help address the negative effects of the surgical experience and promote both physical and emotional healing.

Four excellent reviews of research on surgery preparation across a wide range of medical conditions are the meta-analytic studies of Johnston and Vogele (1993), Devine and Cook (1983, 1986), and Devine (1992; see also reviews by Contrada et al., 1994; Deardorff & Reeves, 1997; Johnston & Wallace, 1990; Mumford, Schlesinger, & Glass, 1982; Prokop, Bradley, Burish, Anderson, & Fox, 1991; Suls & Wan, 1989). Johnston and Vogele identified 38 outcome studies on preparation for surgery that met specific design criteria, including random assignment. The studies were grouped by the preparation techniques used: procedural intervention, sensory intervention, behavioral instruction, cognitive intervention, relaxation, hypnosis, and emotion-focused intervention. Outcomes were assessed across a number of variables, including negative affect, pain, pain medication use, length of stay, recovery, physiological indices, satisfaction, and costs. The authors concluded that "significant benefits can be obtained on all of the major outcome variables that have been explored" (p. 252). Further, they stated, "There is now substantial agreement that psychological preparation for surgery is beneficial to patients" (p. 245).

In two sequential investigations, Devine and Cook (1986) and Devine (1992) completed meta-analyses on 102 and 191 studies, respectively. Inclusion criteria were an experimental design in which a psychological or educational intervention for surgery preparation was completed by adult patients who were to be hospitalized for elective surgery. Outcome measures included length of stay, medical complications, respiratory function tests, and resumption of activities. Patients receiving surgery preparation techniques generally did better than controls on all outcome dimensions.

TREND TOWARD OUTPATIENT SURGERY

Because of changes in the health care system, surgery preparation interventions now address an urgent need: The significant trend toward outpatient surgery places much more responsibility on patients and their families to perform pre- and postoperative activities that would previously have been done by hospital staff. This trend affects all types of surgery, including spine surgery.

Both the United States and Great Britain (see Contrada et al., 1994; Mitchell, 1997) have seen an increase in the number of outpatient surgeries. Well over half of all surgical procedures in the United States are now performed on an outpatient basis, and this trend is predicted to continue (Contrada et al., 1994; Mitchell, 1997). In fact, in our own outpatient surgery center, many of the minimally invasive spine surgeries preiously done in the hospital are now done safely on an outpatient basis. This trend is driven by several factors. In the United States, one of the primary factors has been skyrocketing health care costs. By moving away from the traditional fee-for-service delivery of health care, managed care systems can control inpatient admissions and shift as many procedures as possible to same-day surgery programs. Because approximately three quarters of all Americans with health insurance are enrolled in some type of health maintenance organization, this shift affects a formidable group. In the United Kingdom, the desire to achieve cost savings, decrease patient waiting times, and improve the national health system's efficiency has also driven a shift toward same-day surgery (Jarrett, 1995).

Beyond reducing costs, other factors have fueled the movement toward outpatient surgery. These factors include technology development, improvements in pain medication and anesthesia, and patient-related factors.

Advances in Surgical Technology

In the past 25 years, a multitude of surgeries, including those done on the spine, have become easier and safer to perform as technological advances have decreased their invasiveness. Imaging techniques, such as magnetic resonance imaging and computed tomography, increase physicians' ability to identify problem areas preoperatively, making the surgery process much more efficient. A number of advances in spine surgery techniques, including microscopic and arthroscopic surgeries and the use of lasers and fluoroscopy, have greatly decreased the invasiveness and level of tissue damage during the operation. Thus, a number of spine procedures and operations can now be done on an outpatient basis, including epidurals with or without fluoroscopy, nerve root blocks, percutaneous discectomy, intradiscal electrothermal therapy, and microdiscectomy.

Improved Pain Medication and Anesthesia

Until relatively recently, a patient had to stay in the hospital to be carefully monitored for postanesthesia nausea and vomiting. Advances in general anesthesia over the past several years have decreased risk overall and diminished these types of side effects. Newer, faster acting agents do not cause vomiting and have a much shorter recovery time. Also, longer acting local anesthetics can be injected directly into the incision sites, resulting in improved acute postoperative pain control. Once the patient is discharged from the outpatient surgery center, improvements in pain medications (both oral and via other methods of delivery, such as the transdermal patch) have made them more effective, safer, and more easily monitored on an outpatient basis.

Improved Patient Control and Satisfaction

All other things being equal, most patients would choose to undergo an outpatient rather than an inpatient operation because hospital stays can be disruptive in so many ways (e.g., they take one away from family and entail more time lost from school or work). Outpatient surgery offers at least three other benefits, including: (a) a shorter waiting time prior to surgery, decreasing preoperative anxiety; (b) the ability to recuperate at home, which most patients prefer; and (c) decreased probability of postoperative infections, likely due to lowered exposure to bacteria normally present in the hospital (Benson, 1996; M. Cohen, 1995).

The Challenges of Outpatient Surgery

Notwithstanding its positive aspects, outpatient surgery involves many potentially negative factors that must be addressed in preparation for surgery. In the past, health care providers closely supervised patients in the hospital setting; with outpatient surgery, the patient and his or her family must assume a significant portion of the presurgical and postsurgical care (Eddy & Coslow, 1991). Spine surgery preparation must help the patient acquire the information he or she needs about postoperative responsibilities, such as medication regimens and physical activity requirements and restrictions, and how to fulfill them properly. Exhibit 8.1 provides a sample list of postoperative patient requirements after an outpatient spine surgery.

PREPARATION FOR SURGERY: CONCEPTUAL MODELS

A preparation for surgery program often involves multiple components; many use a combination of cognitive behavioral techniques, such as information gathering, cognitive restructuring, and various types of relaxation training. Early research studies attempted to partial out the active components of a surgery preparation program by comparing one technique against another or a combination of techniques with a single approach (Deardorff, 2000; Horne et al., 1994; Prokop et al., 1991). Generally, a combination of approaches is most effective when compared to a unilateral intervention. An

EXHIBIT 8.1
Example of Postdischarge Instructions for Spinal Fusion Patients

Care of your incision:
- If your sutures or staples have not been removed before discharge, please call the office and schedule a time for this to be done.
- You must sponge bathe until at least 10 days following surgery.
- You may leave the wound uncovered; however, most people find a light 4 × 4 gauze covering more comfortable.
- Do not swim or sit in a spa until cleared by the doctor, usually after a minimum of 3 months when the fusion is well healed.
- Do not expose your wound to direct sunlight for 3 to 4 months following surgery. Sun block or a Band-Aid covering is recommended.
- You will be returning to the surgeon at 1, 2, and 3-month intervals following your operation. At each visit a radiograph will be taken to check the fusion.

Activity:
- You must wear your brace at all times unless otherwise instructed.
- Let pain be your guide with activity. If you experience discomfort, you should rest. Never take pain medication to allow you to complete an activity that is making you uncomfortable.
- You must maintain good alignment, taking special care when getting up or down from a lying or sitting position. Absolutely no bending, twisting, or lifting is permitted.
- After discharge, you should continue the same types of activities and rest periods as you have had in the hospital.
- Do not resume any exercise or activity other than gentle walking until cleared by the surgeon.
- You may drive a car approximately 1 month following surgery; however, it is recommended that you do so only when necessary for short trips.
- Your surgeon will discuss with you your return to work.
- It is normal to have good days and bad days. Listen to your body and rest accordingly if you experience back or leg pain.
- Sexual activities can recommence approximately 1 month following discharge provided you take a passive role and your back is supported.
- Always use good judgment. Be aware of good body mechanics as you recover and get stronger.
- Take only the medications your doctor has prescribed for you and only when needed. Wean yourself from pain medications as soon as possible.

When to call the office:
- Call any time you need to discuss your activity level or other concerns that are not covered in this handout.
- If you experience the following, contact the office: pain, weakness, or numbness persisting for more than 2 or 3 days with no improvement despite bed rest.

understanding of the conceptual models informing psychological preparation for surgery allows the psychologist to individualize patient assessment and treatment.

Psychological preparation for surgery programs have been based on a variety of different and often overlapping "models," including informative preparations, preoperative education, cognitive–behavioral approaches, self-efficacy and empowerment, individual and social self-regulation, and a biopsychosocial model. This list progresses from the least to the most comprehensive interventions

Informative Preparations

The idea that providing patients with realistic information about their surgery will improve outcome can be traced to Janis (1958, 1971). Subsequent studies have generally demonstrated a positive correlation between preoperative surgical knowledge and postoperative outcome (for reviews, see Prokop et al., 1991; Shuldham, 1999). Studies have identified two different types of information that might be provided: procedural and sensory. *Procedural information* consists of basic information about the surgery experience, including preoperative activities, events that will occur during the hospital stay, and postoperative recommendations. Sensory information has often been added to the procedural information in an attempt to enhance the outcome. *Sensory information* describes what sensations the patient can expect throughout the surgery experience, including what he or she will feel, hear, taste, and see.

Although the provision of procedural and sensory information has usually been found to enhance surgical outcome, this finding has not been consistent. Researchers have speculated that these inconsistencies may be due to the patients' individual coping styles in response to the stressor of impending surgery. Studies have focused on a coping dimension of information seekers (also called "sensitizers," "copers," or "monitors") versus information avoiders (also called "repressors," "avoiders," or "blunters"). Information seekers typically respond to a stressful situation by gathering detailed information about it, whereas information avoiders will do just the opposite (for reviews, see S. M. Miller, 1987, 1992; Miro & Raich, 1999; Prokop et al., 1991).

A number of studies have investigated how a patient's coping style (information seeking vs. information avoiding) affects preparation for surgery (see Miro & Raich, 1999, for a review). It has generally been found that patients do best when the amount and detail of presurgical information provided matches their individual coping style. There is some indication that providing information in a manner that is inconsistent with the patient's coping style (e.g., providing detailed information to an information avoider) can actually have deleterious effects (see Prokop et al., 1991, for a review).

Preoperative Education

Preoperative education is an expansion of the simple information provision approach to surgery preparation. Devine and Cook (1986) defined *preoperative education* or *teaching* as providing the patient with health-related information, psychosocial support, and the opportunity to learn specific skills in preparation for surgery. Preoperative education programs might include a number of components: provision of information, interactive education done either individually or in groups, inclusion of family members, and teaching of specific skills helpful for recovery. Several meta-analytic reviews have demonstrated the beneficial effects of preoperative education on surgery outcome (Devine, 1992; Devine & Cook, 1986; Hathaway, 1986; Shuldham, 1999).

Cognitive–Behavioral Approaches

Depending on the definition used, preoperative education approaches may or may not include cognitive–behavioral techniques. For the purposes of this discussion, cognitive–behavioral approaches will be treated separately and formulated as an expansion of preoperative education techniques. Cognitive–behavioral preparation for surgery programs are designed primarily to teach patients self-control strategies that will decrease the stress, anxiety, and pain associated with the surgery experience (for reviews, see Contrada et al., 1994; Prokop et al., 1991). Cognitive–behavioral approaches use a variety of techniques such as cognitive restructuring and deep relaxation training. The cognitive interventions are based on the premise that a patient's beliefs about the surgery will determine the amount of emotional and physical stress he or she experiences. Changing a patient's "maladaptive" thoughts is one means of reducing stress. *Cognitive restructuring* is a means of helping patients identify "unhealthy" or "irrational" thoughts and to combat or substitute these with "coping" or "healthy" thoughts. It is based on the early work of Ellis (1975), Beck (1979), and Meichenbaum (1977). Cognitive restructuring is also referred to as changing an individual's "self-talk." The details of a cognitive restructuring approach to preparing patients for spine surgery are discussed in chapter 9.

The behavioral component of cognitive–behavioral approaches focuses primarily on teaching patients self-regulating techniques that induce a state of deep relaxation. The specifics of these methods, reviewed in detail in chapter 9, include breathing exercises, hypnosis, progressive muscle relaxation, and other techniques to induce a physiological state of deep relaxation. The relaxation response is associated with positive physiological results that can enhance wound healing and surgical outcome. A variety of studies have found that a cognitive–behavioral surgery preparation program can provide numerous positive outcomes (for reviews, see Devine, 1992; Horne et al., 1994; Johnston & Vogele, 1993; Prokop et al., 1991).

Self-Efficacy and Empowerment

Although extensive research has demonstrated the benefits of preoperative education and cognitive–behavioral programs, the psychological mechanisms by which these effects occur are not exactly clear (Oetker-Black & Taunton, 1994; Pellino et al., 1998). The theoretical concept of self-efficacy (and the related idea of empowerment) has been applied to the area of surgical preparation in an effort to explain positive outcomes. These concepts have also guided the expansion of the preoperative education and cognitive–behavioral approaches.

Self-Efficacy

Self-efficacy has been researched in the psychological literature for quite some time since Bandura (1977) originally formulated the concept. According to this theory, "expectations of personal efficacy determine whether coping behavior will be initiated, how much effort will be expended, and how long it will be sustained in the face of obstacles and aversive experiences" (Bandura, 1977, p. 191). Self-efficacy is a belief that one can effectively perform a given behavior and that the behavior will result in desired outcomes. Motivation and perseverance in performing specific behaviors are dependent on the individual's evaluation of his or her self-efficacy. If the individual does not believe that he or she can perform the behavior, motivation and perseverance decrease. Thus, self-efficacy mediates the relationship between knowledge and action. In the simplest terms, there are three basic tenets of self-efficacy theory: (a) Self-efficacy is situation specific; (b) self-efficacy can be altered through various means such as education, practice, and role modeling; and (c) increased self-efficacy can improve outcomes relative to specific behaviors.

Bandura (1977) postulated that an individual's self-efficacy in a situation comes from four sources of information. *Performance accomplishments* are behaviors that the individual has actually performed or practiced. This source of information is the most influential for self-efficacy because it is based on personal mastery experiences. *Verbal persuasion* occurs when an individual is guided by suggestion into believing that he or she can perform the activity. Verbal persuasion is usually provided by someone who is perceived as an authority or expert in the area. *Vicarious experience*, or modeling, is obtained by seeing others similar to oneself perform the activity. *Physiological states* is information the individual receives from his or her level of arousal in response to the specific situation. For instance, individuals who experience a high level of physical arousal (e.g., anxiety) when thinking about an upcoming stressful situation (e.g., the spine surgery process) may believe that their ability to cope with the situation is low; they are considered to have diminished self-efficacy.

A substantial body of research demonstrates that enhancing self-efficacy (e.g., through educational programs) is related to improved health outcomes (for reviews, see Bandura, 1991; Oetker-Black & Taunton, 1994; Pellino et al., 1998). Perceived self-efficacy has specifically been found to improve coping with pain (Pellino & Ward, 1998) and compliance with recommendations after surgery (Bastone & Kerns, 1995; Mahler & Kulik, 1998). It has been hypothesized that many of the benefits of psychological preparation for surgery programs stem from participants' enhanced self-efficacy (Mahler & Kulik, 1998; Oetker-Black & Taunton, 1994; Pellino et al., 1998).

Empowerment

Although patient education programs for surgery have been investigated and implemented for many years, there has been a recent shift from the traditional medical model of patient education to more of an empowerment model (Pellino et al., 1998). Early preparation for surgery programs were based on a medical or "disease-based" model in which the health care provider is the expert who decides the content, amount, and detail of the information he or she provides to the patient about the surgery. In this model, the provider is the primary decision-maker and problem solver (see Pellino et al., 1998, for a review).

The empowerment model of patient education is based on the idea that the role of health educators is to assist patients in gaining knowledge, developing skills, and identifying resources relative to the surgery experience. *Empowerment* has been described as a process of enabling others to take control of their own lives (Pellino et al., 1998). In promoting empowerment, psychologists help patients actively reassess various issues in an ongoing manner and modify their coping strategies accordingly. Thus, the role of the health care provider is to assist the patient in taking appropriate charge of his or her own care on a daily basis (Anderson, 1991). In the empowerment approach to surgery preparation, the teaching is interactive, and the patient helps to determine the content of the surgery preparation program.

The concept of empowerment is closely related to that of self-efficacy, and the differences are subtle. Self-efficacy is a belief that one can effectively perform a behavior and that the behavior will result in the designated outcome. However, someone other than the patient might determine the designated outcome or goal. In contrast, empowerment encourages the patient to become an active participant in identifying and choosing health care goals. Once the patient has established these goals, enhancing self-efficacy will increase the probability that he or she will achieve them. As portrayed by Pellino et al. (1998), empowerment directly influences self-efficacy, which in turn affects outcome.

Individual and Social Self-Regulation

Contrada et al. (1994) discussed two interrelated sets of theoretical principles involving self-regulation derived from research in the areas of psychological stress (Lazarus, 1966; Lazarus & Folkman, 1984), illness cognition (Leventhal & Johnson, 1983), and social support (S. Cohen, 1988). These theoretical principles, called individual self-regulation and social self-regulation, provide a conceptual framework for understanding how psychological interventions enhance surgical outcome.

Individual Self-Regulation

The principle of individual self-regulation involves "cognitive and behavioral activity whereby the patient influences the course of surgical recovery" (Contrada et al., 1994, p. 221). Individual self-regulation is an intrapersonal coping process including cognitive (e.g., appraisal and coping) and emotional (e.g., level of arousal) components. This coping process occurs in response to the many different stressors that occur throughout the different phases of the surgery experience and postoperative recovery.

For most patients, surgery is a significant stressor that can be perceived as a threat because of the potential for severely negative consequences (Contrada et al., 1994; Lazarus & Folkman, 1984). This sense of threat is reflected in the content and extent of patients' worries about the surgery process (see Exhibit 9.1 for a list of common fears). When first informed of the need for an operation, a patient develops an internal "problem representation" of the surgical stressor. This problem representation defines the dimensions, features, and implications of the perceived threat of the impending surgery. A patient's problem representation has objective and subjective elements. The *objective problem representation* includes the patient's perception of the "facts" about the surgery experience such as the mechanics of the operation itself, its effects on physical functioning, the projected recovery time, and behaviors that will be required for postoperative rehabilitation. The *subjective problem representation* is the patient's emotional response to his or her objective problem representation. Subjective problem representation might include worry about being able to cope with the surgery, anxiety over the loss of function, and depression in response to perceived long-term deficits postoperatively.

The amount of threat a patient perceives is related not only to his or her appraisal of the danger implications of the surgery, but also to how much the threat is buffered "by the perceived availability of personal and social resources to mitigate these dangers" (Contrada et al., 1994, p. 229). When the patient appraises the danger as outweighing his or her buffering resources, the result is a stress response. The self-regulation model has two important postulates related to surgery preparation interventions. First, it is the patient's formulation of the surgical threat, and not the health care professional's, that needs to be understood and modified. Second, if the clinician can help the patient formulate an accurate mental representation of the surgery experience, then the patient will have a reality-based framework to guide self-regulation (Contrada et al., 1994; Leventhal, Diefenbach, & Leventhal, 1992).

Contrada et al. (1994) also reviewed patient coping activities. Patients select coping activities on the basis of their problem representation of the threat posed by surgery. Coping involves two different types of individual self-regulation that correspond to the objective and subjective components of the problem representations. *Problem-focused* coping consists of efforts designed to deal with objective elements of the problem. Relative to surgery, problem-focused coping might include patient behaviors that enhance physical recovery and decrease the probability of complications, behaviors such as engaging in range of motion exercises and breathing procedures and, ultimately, returning to usual activities of daily living. Later on in the surgery recovery process, problem-focused coping may include resuming social, family, and occupational roles. *Emotion-focused* coping refers to techniques for decreasing distress and other subjective responses. Preoperatively, such coping might include controlling anticipatory anxiety and distress. Immediately following surgery, this might encompass such things as cognitive–behavioral methods to diminish suffering and encourage emotional acceptance of temporary physical and social limitations. A preparation for spine surgery program should include components that teach patients both problem- and emotion-focused coping skills.

As the patient proceeds through the surgery experience, he or she modifies the problem representation and coping activities on the basis of ongoing appraisal. In other words, the patient's perceived ability to cope with the surgery and its effects constantly changes. *Appraisal* is the process of modifying and updating the problem representation based on new information from external sources, perceived changes in physical and psychological well-being, and evaluation of the effectiveness of coping procedures (Contrada et al., 1994). In *adaptive appraisal*, after the various coping behaviors are completed, the patient assesses their effectiveness and outcome as compared to his or her own goals. *Outcome appraisal* is the patient's evaluation of his or her progress (usually most salient postoperatively) as influenced by social comparison processes. It is important to note that social psychology research suggests that patients generally compare themselves to other patients who are recovering at a faster rate (termed "upward comparison"; Contrada et al., 1994; Festinger, 1954).

Although it is possible that upward comparison could result in the patient emulating successful coping strategies, it seems that negative consequences are more likely. Patients and their family members may tend to select unrealistically successful models for comparison, such as those who are younger, have had a less serious surgery, or have a less significant medical history (S. E. Taylor, 1983). Upward comparison may lead the patient and family members to set unrealistic criteria for evaluating coping efforts and overall progress. Clinically, we have certainly seen this phenomenon in the area of postoperative spine rehabilitation. It is not uncommon for patients to begin making comparisons once they are released to begin postoperative physical therapy. In the spine rehabilitation setting, there are ample opportunities for upward comparison, and the negative effects are not infrequent.

Contrada et al. (1994) identified four different phases of the surgical experience, each of which has its own unique challenges and coping issues that affect individual self-regulation (Figure 8.1). The four phases include

Phases of the Surgery Experience

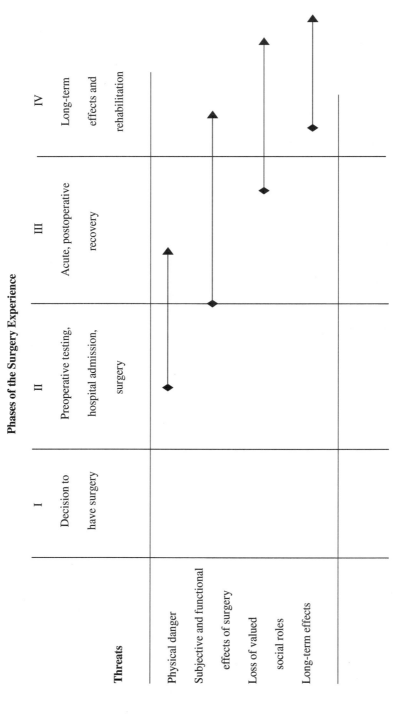

Figure 8.1. Salience of the four primary threats to patient adaptation across the four phases of the surgery experience. From "Psychological Preparation for Surgery: Marshaling Individual and Social Resources to Optimize Self-Regulation," by R. J. Contrada, E. A. Leventhal, and J. R. Anderson, 1994, p. 230, in S. Maes, H. Leventhal, and M. Johnston (Eds.), *International Review of Health Psychology*, Vol. 3, New York: Wiley. Adapted with permission of the authors.

phase I, or the decision to have the surgery; phase II, or preoperative testing, admission to the hospital, and surgery; phase III, or acute recovery, either in the hospital or immediately postoperative at home; and phase IV, or longer term postoperative rehabilitation issues. Across these four phases, the patient confronts four major issues related to adaptation to the surgical experience (Contrada et al., 1994, p. 230):

1. the immediate physical danger represented by the surgery itself: general anesthesia, incision, resection, reconstruction, catheterization, and immediate postoperative complications. As can be seen in Figure 8.1, this threat is most significant in phases II and III.
2. the aftereffects of the surgical procedures: pain, discomfort, disorientation, fatigue, and reduced capacity for physical activity and ambulation. These threats involve the subjective and functional effects of the surgery itself on the patient, beginning just after surgery (the middle of phase II) and decreasing through phases III and IV.
3. the patient's potential inability to enact valued social roles: family, occupational, and leisure activities. The threat to social roles begins or worsens in phase III and increases through phase IV.
4. the long-term management of a possibly chronic medical condition: diet control, exercise, medication regimens, follow-up visits, management of chronic pain, limitations in function. This threat occurs in phase IV.

These issues vary in relative salience through the surgery experience. The physical danger and subjective and functional effects dominate during the period immediately surrounding the surgery, whereas social role issues and long-term management issues become increasingly salient after the acute phase of postoperative recovery and over the long term. A psychological preparation for surgery program can help prepare patients to confront each of these issues within each of these phases.

Social Self-Regulation

The interpersonal aspect of self-regulation, called *social self-regulation*, departs from the premise that the social context in which the individual functions significantly determines the impact of a life stressor. *Social self-regulation* involves exchanges between the patient and members of his or her social network (family, friends, and co-workers; Contrada et al., 1994). Individual self-regulation is intrapersonal, whereas social self-regulation is interpersonal.

Although a patient's social network may consist of several levels, the primary support person (spouse, significant other, or close family member) is often considered the most important potential source of support, and clinical research has frequently investigated the role of this support person. However, some patients do not have a support person in the home to help with surgical recovery, and support from friends and others may be critical. Social self-regulation has two main components. *Task-focused* social self-regulation is the interaction between the patient and caregiver that evolves around the task of understanding and coping with the surgery. *Role-focused* social self-regulation involves the social roles enacted by the patient and his or her significant others.

The literature has identified a set of *adaptive goals* for the support person, and these are related to, but somewhat different than, those of the patient. Even though both patient and partner share the goal of optimizing the patient's recovery from surgery, the task focus differs for each due to their own specific mental representations of the problem. The support person does not have access to the patient's internal experience related to the surgery process (e.g., level of pain and discomfort, thoughts about the surgery, worries), but he or she is in a unique position to either enhance or diminish the patient's overall coping ability. A support person who has an accurate view of the surgery experience can help the patient develop a similar representation that will, in turn, aid the patient's overall coping and achievement of adaptive goals. However, a support person who has inaccurate and unrealistic beliefs (e.g., that spine surgery is a "cure" for back pain, that spine surgery will forever limit certain activities) will increase the chances that the patient will also adopt a maladaptive view. In addition, discrepancies in beliefs about the postoperative pain experience may prevent the patient and support person from developing a cooperative approach to coping with the surgery and can produce conflict in other areas of the relationship. As Contrada et al. (1994) observed,

> In effect, the partner is a mirror in which the patient may see an image that exaggerates, minimizes, or more or less accurately reflects his or her medical status and emotional state. If these reflections bias the patient's self-appraisal in either direction, before surgery, or at any stage of recovery, there is a risk of negative consequences including over/under-utilization of pain medication, too slow/rapid resumption of daily activities, and non-optimal timing in returning to work. (p. 240)

A patient's support person can provide assistance in a variety of ways, including tangible assistance, emotional support, and informational support (see Contrada et al., 1994, for a review). *Tangible assistance* includes direct efforts to assist the patient in such areas as health behaviors, activities of daily living, and work-related endeavors. *Emotional support* includes any efforts directed at reducing the patient's worries and elevating his or her spirits. *Informational support* is the provision of suggestions that will help the patient cope more effectively with recovery tasks such as managing pain, doing prescribed exercises, and resuming social roles and functions.

The manner in which the support person provides these different types of support can either enhance or inhibit recovery. The degree of discrepancy between the patient's and support person's mental representation of the problem determines whether the type of support provided is appropriate or not. For example, if the patient seeks informational support about how to manage an acute pain flare-up, providing emotional support instead could actually cause the support person to worsen the patient's situation by highlighting the patient's lack of ability to control his or her pain.

The surgery episode may significantly alter the patient's and support person's customary social roles. The surgical patient often faces significant disruption in a number of valued role areas: work function and career, family life, community involvement, recreational activities, and gender identity; in addition, he or she must at least temporarily relinquish the role of "well person." Loss of role function may lead to depression and lowered self-esteem in the patient, placing additional strain on support persons trying to cope with the surgery process itself. Further, in taking care of the patient and performing responsibilities that he or she cannot, the support person may also experience loss in such roles as employee, parent, spouse, community member, and recreational participant. Support persons who experience role loss over the long term can also develop low self-esteem, anger, depression, and resentment toward the patient for "causing the loss" (Contrada et al., 1994). For a complete and detailed discussion of psychosocial role adjustment, see S. Cohen (1988); Contrada et al. (1994); Coyne and DeLongis (1986); and Pearlin, Mullan, Semple, and Skaff (1990).

During the surgical recovery process, the support person is likely to relinquish or modify various normal responsibilities to assume the caregiver role. For a variety of reasons (see Contrada et al., 1994; Coyne & DeLongis, 1986), the support person may become either under- or overinvolved in the patient's recovery, either of which can have negative consequences. In the case of underinvolvement, the support person's goals for caregiving are less than what is appropriate and required. The support person fails to facilitate the patient's recovery, requiring the patient to draw more on the support of others or his or her own efforts. Overinvolvement results from inappropriately low goals for the patient's recovery based on the support person's mental representation of the problem. Overinvolved support persons can impede the patient's recovery by being less than encouraging about the patient's progress, slowing the patient's resumption of activities by continuing to perform them, and reinforcing the "sick role" by inappropriate nurturing. Further, the patient may perceive a well-intended but overzealous support person as intrusive, controlling, and critical, which may strain the relationship (Contrada et al., 1994). In some cases, a negative cycle may develop in which the support person alternates between underinvolvement and overinvolvement depending on interactions with the patient.

Consistency between the patient's and support person's mental representations of the surgical problem and efforts towards concordant, adaptive goals is a critical element in recovery. Social self-regulation expands the concept of surgery preparation beyond the individual to include family, friends, co-workers, health care professionals, and others as appropriate. The model also underscores the importance of considering a patient's social relationships as a target of intervention for spine surgery preparation.

Biopsychosocial Model of Surgery Preparation

As with many medical treatment programs, there has been a move from a strictly medical model to a biopsychosocial model of surgery preparation in recent years. A biopsychosocial model takes into account not only the physical aspects of the medical problem and surgery, but also the patient's individual psychological makeup, coping resources, and social issues.

Any physical problem and treatment (such as surgery) can be conceptualized from a biopsychosocial perspective (Engel, 1977). Biopsychosocial concepts related to pain began with the formulation that the pain experience is influenced by higher order processes in the brain (Chapman, Nakamura, & Flores, 1999; Melzack & Casey, 1968; Melzack & Wall, 1965, 1982; Sternbach, 1966). This conceptual model requires that the psychologist investigate and understand the biological, psychological, and family-social factors related to the problem. The biopsychosocial approach can be thought of as an open systems model of relationships that contains multiple feedback loops (see Figure 8.2). Interactions can occur in an almost endless number of ways among the following influences on surgical outcome:

- the patient's health status, health habits, medical condition, and type of surgery;
- the patient's psychological status and coping resources;
- the health care professionals and others involved in the patient's treatment;
- family members' behavior toward the patient and among themselves in response to the surgery; and
- the patient's and family's interaction with extrafamilial systems such as relatives, friends, and co-workers.

The open systems model describes how changes in any of the subsystems (e.g., the relationship between the patient and support person) may reverberate throughout all other subsystems (e.g., the patient's own health status, the emotional status and behavior of family members).

A biopsychosocial model of surgery preparation dictates that all aspects of the surgery and recovery experience are appropriate targets for intervention. The open model of systems and subsystems also shows that any subsystem has the potential to exert a negative influence on the entire surgical

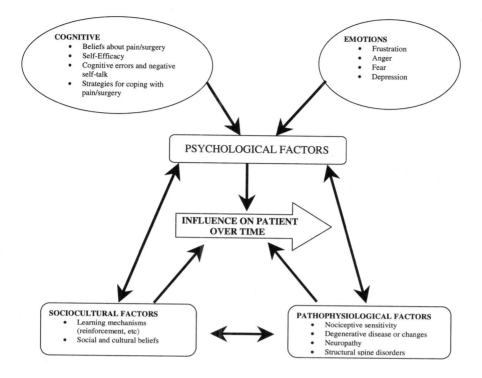

Figure 8.2. The biopsychosocial conceptual model of the surgery experience. From "Chronic Pain and Consciousness: A Constructivist Perspective," by C. R. Chapman, Y. Nakamura, and L. Y. Flores, 1999, p. 43, in R. J. Gatchel and D. C. Turk (Eds.), *Psychosocial Factors in Pain: Critical Perspectives,* New York: Guilford Press. Adapted with permission of the authors.

recovery if appropriate intervention is not provided. For example, a spine surgery patient may successfully complete a surgery preparation program that focuses on cognitive–behavioral techniques (an intrapersonal treatment focus), only to face recovery in a family environment that is nonsupportive, dysfunctional, and unhealthy. If the surgery preparation program does not assess the family environment and intervene as appropriate, the cognitive–behavioral techniques will likely fail, as would any other program that missed an important source of intervention and preparation.

CONCLUSION

The literature provides valuable models of psychological preparation for surgery programs developed using a variety of surgical experiences. These models can easily be adjusted to take into account the different coping and recovery challenges of spine surgery. Many of the preparation for surgery studies we have reviewed in this chapter involved general orthopedic patients, including those with back pain, whose population characteristics, surgery experience, and rehabilitation issues are very similar to those of candidates for spine surgery.

Some recent research has addressed the issues spine patients confront more directly. Hueppe, Uhlig, Vogelsang, and Schmucker (2000) investigated the personality traits, coping styles, and mood states of patients with lumbar disc disorders. In two different studies, patients expecting lumbar disc surgery were compared to patients awaiting another kind of surgery. Patients completed self-rating questionnaires, and their anesthesiologists completed questionnaires that rated the patient's mood. The authors concluded, "the results characterize lumbar disc patients as a subgroup that is not different from other surgery patients and, therefore, does not need a specific form of psychological management prior to surgery" (p. 119). The authors stated that earlier studies had demonstrated higher depression and anxiety scores in lumbar disc patients prior to surgery relative to healthy control participants.

The conceptual models discussed in this chapter provide a variety of perspectives from which to view and approach the surgical preparation process. The models emphasize that specific skills and behaviors (e.g., relaxation training, healthy diet, exercise, pain management) can lead to broader emotional and psychosocial changes. Self-efficacy, realistic expectations about surgical recovery, and improved mood are only some of the positive effects that psychological preparation procedures can provide. In turn, these emotional improvements and coping skills interact and provide additional energy and motivation for the postoperative recovery process.

The models reviewed in this chapter emphasize that recovery does not take place in a vacuum—the patient's support person, friends, relatives, and even co-workers can exert positive or negative influences on recovery. By incorporating the multiple perspectives of these conceptual models, the psychologist is in the best possible position help the patient build on the surgeon's expertise and turn the corner on pain.

9

PREPARING FOR SPINE SURGERY: COGNITIVE–BEHAVIORAL INTERVENTIONS

Patients being considered for spine surgery develop many ideas about their injuries and about potential medical treatments. Some of these beliefs are realistic and appropriate—the patient may have a good idea of what is wrong and how to fix it. However, other beliefs and thoughts arise out of fear, desperation, uncertainty, and many months or years of demoralizing, ineffective medical treatments. Preparing patients for surgery means identifying and helping them alter such negative beliefs so that they avoid becoming their own worst enemies during the recovery and rehabilitation process.

Just as there are many conceptual models of psychological preparation for surgery interventions, there are also a variety of methods for developing such programs. Differences occur across programs both in the structure (e.g., individualized, group, or combination) and content or specific components (e.g., cognitive–behavioral techniques, relaxation training, music therapy). In individualized surgery preparation programs, the patient works one-on-one with a health care professional (usually a psychologist, social worker, nurse, or health educator) in customizing and constantly modifying program content on the basis of the issues the patient presents. Although this can be a very effective approach, often it is not feasible due to cost, time, and staffing constraints. Therefore, most surgery preparation programs offer a blend of individualized content and group treatment with preformatted, structured components. We were unable to locate research studies that have investigated whether one approach works better than another.

Most psychological preparation for spine surgery programs have at their core a set of cognitive–behavioral interventions. These techniques teach the patient to recognize and modify a number internal processes such as thoughts, emotions, and physiological sensations. Cognitive–behavioral interventions, the topic of this chapter, have great power in influencing the process of recovery from and rehabilitation after spine surgery.

ASSESSING BELIEFS AND FEARS

When the patient enters the preparation for spine surgery program, a psychologist should assess his or her fears and concerns about the surgery and recovery. Much of this information can be obtained from the presurgical psychological screening (PPS) report, if one has been completed. Some of the most common fears and concerns are listed in Exhibit 9.1 (see also Johnston, 1988; Trousdale, McGrory, Berry, Becker, & Harmsen, 1999). In addition, the psychologist should obtain the following types of information about the patient:

- beliefs about what is going to happen;
- beliefs about why the operation is necessary and anticipated outcome;
- knowledge about the operation and postoperative recovery;
- previous experience with surgery;
- understanding about the psychological preparation for surgery program;
- home, work, and family environments; and
- motivation for participating in treatment (Block, 1996; Deardorff & Reeves, 1997; Horne et al., 1994).

These very general, initial categories of patient assessment will help the psychologist target interventions to the patient's needs. Over the course of the preparation for surgery intervention, assessment and adjustment of intervention strategies are ongoing, as dictated by the biopsychosocial model.

FOSTERING INFORMED PATIENTS

One of the first steps the health psychologist undertakes in preparing the patient for spine surgery involves helping him or her become better in-

EXHIBIT 9.1
Patients' Main Worries About Surgery

- whether the operation will be a success
- how long it will be before life returns to normal
- feeling unwell after the surgery
- whether the patient will be able to walk as much as he or she wishes
- being away from home
- how one's spouse will cope
- how one's children will cope
- getting an infection
- getting AIDS or hepatitis from a transfusion
- dying during the operation
- what is physically wrong
- pain after the operation; that the operation won't take the pain away
- being unconscious
- family's worries
- doctors explaining the procedure
- waking up during the operation
- whether the doctor will make a mistake during the operation

Note. This list is based on Johnston, 1988, and Trousdale et al., 1999.

formed about the surgery process. The desire for adequately informed patients was behind the passage of informed consent legislation, and inadequate informed consent has been the basis for successful lawsuits in spine surgery. Patients have made the case that if they had been adequately informed, they would have not undergone the spine surgery or would have chosen some other treatment option (Benton, 2001; Benzel & Benton, 2001). These cases were successful even though the patients had signed the usual consent forms. As Benzel and Benton concluded,

> One of the main problems with the consent process is that it is just that—a process. Usually, it does not take place only during the final counseling of the patient regarding risks, benefits and alternatives of an operation. To one degree or another, it takes place during each physician–patient encounter that precedes an operation. (p. 33)

Making sure a patient acquires accurate and understandable medical information is important to all areas of spine surgery practice.

The type and level of information gathering most valuable to an individual patient depend on the patient's information coping style and ability to understand and remember important medical information. Once the psychologist has assessed the patient's style of gathering information, he or she can recommend sources of information for the patient to explore.

Information Coping Style

Providing detailed information about the surgery has generally been found to enhance surgical outcome, but how much information is beneficial

EXHIBIT 9.2
Assessing Information Coping Style

Does the patient tend to agree or disagree with the following statements?

1. Investigating books, magazines, and television programs about medical conditions and surgeries makes me feel more comfortable, confident, and in control.
2. I prefer to gather very specific and detailed information about my health condition.
3. Detailed medical information does not bother me.

Patients who tend to agree with these statements are information seekers and do better with more specific and detailed information. Those who disagree with the above statements do better with very general information.

depends on the patient's coping style. For information seekers, the general rule is, the more information the better (Contrada et al., 1994; Horne et al., 1994; Prokop et al., 1991; Shuldham, 1999). Conversely, information avoiders prefer only general information and may even respond negatively to too much detail. A very simple way to assess a patient's coping style relative to information gathering can be found in Exhibit 9.2. In addition, S. M. Miller (1987) developed measures that assess an individual's information-seeking style. Before providing medical information, the psychologist should assess the patient's coping style in some manner.

Ability to Understand and Remember Medical Information

Research has consistently demonstrated that surgical patients are dissatisfied with the amount of preoperative information they receive (for reviews, see Deardorff & Reeves, 1997; Webber, 1990). Even when information is provided, the patient's ability to use it is dependent on the "readability" of the written information and on the patient's level of understanding and recall of medical information.

The quality of written information provided to patients has improved somewhat in recent years. However, surgical consent forms even now often contain medical language at the level of a scientific journal or specialized academic magazine that is incomprehensible to most laypersons facing a spine surgery (Deardorff, 1986; Webber, 1990). About 40% or fewer of patients actually read surgical informed consent forms carefully (Deardorff & Reeves, 1997). As Webber (1990) concluded, "written materials are desired and appreciated by patients; however, more attention needs to be given to producing them at a reading level appropriate to their intended audience" (p. 1095).

Research also has indicated that patients generally remember very little of the information presented to them regarding their surgery, and this is true whether the information is provided in written or verbal form (for reviews, see Deardorff, 1986; Ferguson, 1993; Shuldham, 1999; Webber, 1990). The reason remains unclear; the quality of the information being presented and the distractions of the surgical experience process likely contribute. Thus, even when understandable and appropriate information is provided to spine surgery patients, many have difficulty recalling it.

Sources of Information About Surgery

Many patients are reluctant to request information from their surgeon, family doctor, or other health care professionals involved in the presurgical process. Teaching patients how to ask questions and where to go for answers is an important part of a spine surgery preparation program. Chapter 10 reviews simple assertiveness training techniques that may be used in a psychological preparation for surgery program. Also, the psychologist should inform patients that they can get information from many sources, not just their doctor's office, although that is the best place to start. Other sources might include the hospital, the library, government agencies such as the National Institutes of Health, and the Internet. Another good source of information is specialized professional and lay public societies such as the following, many of which have patient education divisions that can provide excellent information:

- The North American Spine Society
- The American Pain Society
- Society for the Study of the Lumbar Spine
- International Association for the Study of Pain
- The American Chronic Pain Association.

To help surgery patients with the information gathering process, the psychologist could provide the list of questions in Exhibit 9.3 as the starting point for a more self-guided preparation for surgery program (Deardorff & Reeves, 1997). Patients can be encouraged to get these questions answered preoperatively as necessary for their particular spine surgery and from the appropriate information source (which may not always be the doctor's office).

The Internet can be a powerful tool for patients gathering medical information related to spine surgery, and preparation for surgery programs should address this issue specifically. A strong caveat is in order relative to the Internet as information resource: A great deal of misinformation is promulgated through this media, and patients should be warned. Incorrect information, because it can lead to unrealistic and inaccurate patient expectations, can compromise surgery outcome. Patients should be encouraged to compare the information they gather from the Internet with that provided by their health care professionals and to question any discrepancies.

Judicious use of the Internet for information gathering is appropriate. However, when a patient becomes obsessed with gathering information about surgical options from all the different sources and viewpoints, it may be ap-

EXHIBIT 9.3
Questions Patient Often Ask About Surgery

About the condition and surgery:
- What is wrong with me? What is my diagnosis?
- Why do I need the surgery?
- How will the surgery improve my condition?
- What other treatment options are available? Have these been adequately tested?
- What will happen if I don't have the surgery or delay it until a later date? How long can I delay the surgery if I decide to do so?
- What are the risks of the surgery? Do the benefits of the surgery outweigh the risks?
- If the surgery is successful, what results can I expect? If it is not successful (or only partially successful), then what remaining symptoms can I expect?
- Can you describe the surgery to me in simple language?
- Do you have a brochure or information sheet that describes the surgery?
- How will I feel after the surgery (in the recovery room, the following day, and so forth)?
- How can I expect to feel each day in the hospital after the surgery? What will I be able to do, and what should I try to do, each day in the hospital after the surgery?
- What complications might arise after surgery or after I am discharged from the hospital? What is the best way to manage these complications if they arise? With whom should I discuss these issues?
- Will I need assistance at home after I am discharged from the hospital? Should I arrange for that now? Will I go directly home after discharge, or should I go to a rehabilitation or transitional care facility?
- Once I go home, what will my level of functioning be, and for how long?

About blood transfusion:
- Is it possible that I may need a blood transfusion during the surgery?
- Can I give blood in advance in case I need it during the surgery? Where should I go to give blood before my operation? (The psychologist should record the address, phone number, and name of the contact person at the blood collection center.)
- Is there enough time before surgery to give the blood that I may need?
- What are the risks involved in giving and receiving my own blood?

About what to do before the surgery:
- What presurgical tests or evaluations are necessary? Who will be doing these, and when should they be done?
- Should I make sure my family physician knows about the surgery?
- Will my family doctor be involved in my postoperative care? Does he or she need any special medical records?
- Do I need to be on a special diet before or after the surgery? If so, can you explain it in detail?
- Will this operation be done on an outpatient or inpatient basis?
- In what hospital will the operation be done?
- Are the surgery and hospitalization preapproved by the insurance company? Has the hospitalization approval letter been received from insurance company?
- How many hospitalization days has the insurance company preapproved? What if the surgeon recommends more days? How do I get approval, and who is responsible for making the request?
- What doctors can I expect to see in the hospital, and why?
- When will I first see my surgeon in the hospital after the surgery?
- Will my surgeon be in town and managing my case the entire time I am in the hospital?

propriate to discourage Internet use. The multiple conflicting messages available on different Web sites, like those one would receive in getting five or ten surgical opinions, can confuse and disorient the patient.

The psychologist should guide interested patients to Web sites that are known to contain accurate information. Most Web sites that are associated with university medical centers (sites ending in .edu) and those maintained by government institutions (e.g., the National Institutes of Health and sites ending in .gov) can be trusted as reliable sources of information.

COGNITIVE–BEHAVIORAL TECHNIQUES

Cognitive–behavioral approaches used in preparation for spine surgery programs generally revolve around cognitive restructuring and deep relaxation training. For the purposes of this discussion, we will also place hypnosis in the cognitive–behavioral category. This section will provide a brief overview of these techniques, with a special emphasis on their applicability to the spine surgery patient.

Cognitive Restructuring

The philosophy of cognitive restructuring is guided by observations that have been made since the very remote past. For instance, William Shakespeare, in *Hamlet*, stated that "there is nothing either good or bad, but thinking makes it so." Centuries before the time of Shakespeare, the philosopher Epictetus wrote in *The Enchiridion* in the 1st century, "men feel disturbed not by things, but by the views which they take of them." These principles have recently been rediscovered and refined (Beck, 1979; Ellis, 1975; Meichenbaum, 1977). The cognitive restructuring approach is guided by several basic tenets:

1. It is not the situation that causes a specific emotional response, but rather an individual's thoughts or cognitions about the situation.
2. Thoughts influence how people behave, including what they choose to do or not do and the quality of their performance.
3. Thoughts can be considered "behaviors" that are susceptible to change.
4. Changing cognitions to be more positive or "coping oriented" can improve the surgical patient's coping abilities and, therefore, enhance outcome.

Self-Talk

People are constantly judging and interpreting things that occur in the environment around them. These thoughts and judgments occur both consciously and unconsciously, and they have been labeled *self-talk* because they are analogous to internal dialogues. Cognitive researchers have found that this self-talk can occur very quickly, almost in an automatic fashion, to the point that its exact content goes unnoticed. When these messages are unhealthy, they are termed *automatic negative thoughts*. Most often, the first indicator of unhealthy self-talk is the experience of negative emotions (e.g., depression, anxiety, fear, hopelessness), as well as concomitant physical stress reactions.

One of the first tasks of cognitive restructuring therapy is to enable people to identify negative thoughts that may be occurring, often through the use of a *thoughts and feelings diary*. The details of this procedure can be found elsewhere (Deardorff & Reeves, 1997), but it basically entails having the patient keep a journal of his or her thoughts and emotions, especially in response to specific situations. Of particular interest in preparing for surgery is the identification of negative automatic thoughts as they relate to the surgical experience. Having the patient identify this type of thinking provides the basis for cognitive restructuring intervention. Negative automatic thoughts often contain certain terms, such as *what if, always, should, must,* and *never*. Self-talk can influence an individual's emotional status, as illustrated in the first two columns of Table 9.1.

Styles of Negative Self-Talk

Over the years, cognitive researchers have identified a variety of *irrational*, or negative, styles of thinking. Although many negative styles have been identified, we will review only those most applicable to the spine surgery patient. (For further details regarding negative styles of thinking, see Beck, 1979; Ellis, 1975; McKay & Fanning, 1991; Meichenbaum, 1977).

Catastrophizing. *Catastrophizing* is imagining the worst possible scenario and then acting as if that will actually happen. This type of negative thinking often includes a series of *what ifs*, such as

- What if I never get better?
- What if I get worse?
- What if the spine surgery doesn't work?

In catastrophic thinking, the dire predictions are based not on facts, but rather on pessimistic beliefs.

Filtering. *Filtering* involves focusing on only the negative aspects of a situation to the exclusion of any positive elements or options. This type of negative self-talk has also been termed *tunnel vision* because it causes the patient to look at only one element of a situation and to disregard everything else. This style commonly includes a search for evidence of "how bad things really are" and the discounting of any positive or coping focus. Examples of filtering self-talk statements include the following:

TABLE 9.1
Examples of Negative and Coping Self-Talk and Corresponding
Emotional Responses for Spine Surgery Patients

Negative Self-Talk	Emotional Response	Coping Thought	Alternative Response
My spine is weak and fragile. It will never be the same.	Fear	I can strengthen my back muscles after surgery. I will strive to become as functional as possible.	Less fear and more confidence
My pain is going to get worse and worse.	Anxiety and hopelessness	There are techniques I can use to help with the pain. No one can predict the future.	More sense of control
I can't handle this surgery. I hate the hospital.	Fear and anxiety	I can get through this. I can look forward to discharge and working on recovery.	Less anxiety, less hospital stress
My family is going to leave me.	Depression and hopelessness	My family will help me, especially if I help myself.	More feeling of comfort and support
I should be better by now. The surgery didn't work. I should never have allowed this to happen.	Frustration, anger, guilt, and helplessness	I will continue to work on getting better. It's not my fault this happened.	Less helplessness, more hopefulness
If I move the wrong way, I'll do myself in. I'll wait until the pain is gone, then I'll exercise.	Helplessness and fear	I will begin to move and exercise slowly. Small steps will lead to bigger ones.	More sense of control and less fear
There is nothing I can do during the surgery and recovery. It's up to my doctor.	Helplessness and apathy	I can participate in my own recovery.	More confidence
What if the surgery doesn't work? I bet it won't. Either I'm cured or I'm not.	Anger and hopelessness	No one can predict the future. I'll get out of this treatment what I put into it.	Less anger and more control
I feel worthless. The future looks awful.	Hopelessness	There are things I can do to lead a quality life.	More hopeful

- There is nothing that will help my situation.
- This situation is awful.
- Everything in my life is rotten due to this spine condition.
- Nobody really cares.

- I can't stand it.
- The doctors and surgeons have nothing to offer.
- I've tried everything, and nothing has helped at all.

This style of negative thinking is often characterized by discounting and *yes-buting*. No matter what positive option or coping method is suggested, the person engaging in filtering will discount it saying, "yes, but . . . ." For instance, a person requires a surgical procedure that will cause a limitation in certain activities but improve the person's overall health and quality of life. When the health care professional presents this as being very positive overall, the person retorts, "Yes, but I will have these limitations." This type of thinking fosters helplessness, hopelessness, and depression.

Black-and-White Thinking. *Black-and-white thinking*, which has also been termed "*all-or-nothing*" thinking, amounts to seeing things either one way or the other, with no middle ground or shades of gray. People and things are either good or bad. Events and situations are either great or horrible. This type of thinking is typified by such statements as

- I'm either cured, or I'm not.
- I either have pain, or I don't.
- The surgery either works, or it doesn't.
- This doctor is either good or bad.
- My family is supportive, or they're not.

This type of thinking undermines any small steps towards improvement, severely limits one's options, and filters out any positive aspects of a situation.

Overgeneralization. *Overgeneralization* is the process of taking one aspect of a situation and applying it to all other situations. It involves generalizing reactions to situations in which such reactions are not appropriate. The following are examples of overgeneralizing self-talk:

- With this pain, I'll never be able to have any fun.
- People don't want to be around me.
- My wife told me to try and do something about the pain. She must be ready to leave me.
- I will always be sad.
- I will never be able to get beyond this medical problem.

This style of negative self-talk applies an aspect of one incident to another, which results in the person reaching an incorrect conclusion. Overgeneralization is often indicated by such key words as *all, every, none, never, always, everybody,* and *nobody*.

Mind Reading. The negative self-talk "trap" of mind reading involves making assumptions about what other people are thinking without actually knowing. The person then acts on these assumptions, which are usually erroneous, without checking them out for accuracy. Examples of mind reading self-talk include the following:

- I know my wife thinks I'm less of a man due to my condition.
- I know my husband thinks I'm exaggerating my back pain.
- My doctor doesn't really think I'll get better, even though she tells me I will.
- They're not telling me everything about my problem.

If the patient accepts these assumptions as facts, then his or her behavior will follow accordingly and will be likely to create a self-fulfilling prophecy. For example, a patient's spouse might ask, "How do you feel today?" Instead of taking his or her comment at face value, the patient believes he or she really means, "Are you still letting that problem bother you?" So the patient responds, "How do think I feel today? The same as always, that's how." Mind-reading self-talk can thus lead to interpersonal conflict, weakening the patient's support network.

Should statements. When making *should statements,* the patient operates from a list of inflexible and unrealistic rules about his or her own actions as well as those of others. Examples of such thinking include the following:

- I should be getting better.
- I should never have allowed this to happen.
- I should have known not to have that procedure (or surgery).
- My employer should have protected me.
- I should be tougher.
- My family should be more helpful.

Should statements also include terms like *ought, must, always,* and *never.* Should thinking is judgmental and often involves an individual measuring his or her performance against some irrational perfect standard. It has the effect of making the patient feel worthless, useless, and inadequate. When directed at others, should thinking can cause angry and resentful interactions in those relationships. The phenomenon of upward comparison in social self-regulation (i.e., the tendency to compare oneself with other spine patients who are "doing better") often involves should thinking (e.g., "I should be recovering as fast as he is.").

Blaming. In *blaming,* the person makes something or someone else responsible for a problem or situation. There is some comfort in being able to attach responsibility for one's suffering to someone else. Unfortunately, blaming can often cause a person to avoid taking responsibility for his or her own choices and opportunities for improvement. This type of negative thinking is very often seen in cases of industrial injury, automobile accidents, and other such trauma. Examples include

- My boss is to blame for my injury.
- They should have mopped up that water I slipped on. It's all their fault.

- That guy who hit me owes me everything for the pain I'm suffering.
- I'm to blame for this lousy medical problem.

Blaming as a form of negative self-talk can be focused either externally or internally. Internally focused blaming (self-blame) often takes the form of "It's all my fault." Self-blame is often an excuse for not taking responsibility and can lead to depression, hopelessness, and helplessness. Blaming can be very destructive when it keeps the patient's focus on whom or what is to blame instead of what he or she needs to do to get better.

Challenging Negative Self-Talk and Thought Reframing

As the patient practices identifying negative automatic thoughts, certain patterns will usually emerge. Most often, individuals tend toward a certain style of negative automatic thinking, and identifying this style can help them be alert to such thoughts as they occur. Once patients have identified their negative automatic thoughts, cognitive preparation for surgery involves helping them challenge and reframe these thoughts by asking themselves the following questions:

- What is the evidence for that conclusion?
- Is this statement always true?
- What is the evidence for that conclusion being false?
- Among all possibilities, is this belief the most healthy one to adopt?
- Am I looking at the entire picture?
- Am I being fully objective?

Having the patient subject his or her self-talk to these questions will help the patient identify negative versus positive (or *coping*) messages. After identifying and challenging negative self-talk, the patient must then substitute positive, realistic, or coping self-talk. The patient writes coping thoughts in his or her thoughts and feelings diary and then practices through rehearsal. Bourne (1995) developed the following rules to help patients write positive coping self-talk statements:

- *Avoid negatives*. When patients write positive coping statements, they should avoid using negatives. For instance, instead of saying, "I can't be nervous about going to the hospital," a patient can say, "I will be confident and calm about going to the hospital." The first type of statement can be anxiety producing in and of itself, which will defeat the purpose of the coping thought.
- *Keep coping thoughts in the present tense*. Because most negative self-talk occurs in the here and now, it should be countered by coping thoughts that are in the present tense. Instead of saying, "I will be happy when this surgery is over," the patient might

say, "I am happy about _____ right now." Beginning self-statements with "I am learning to . . ." and "I can . . ." is very beneficial for cognitive restructuring.

- *Keep coping thoughts in the first person.* Whenever possible, patients should write their coping thoughts in the first person by beginning them with *I* or ensuring that *I* occurs somewhere in the sentence.
- *Make coping thoughts believable.* Coping thoughts should be based in reality to ensure that the patient will have some belief in his or her own coping self-talk. As a patient practices the positive self-talk, it becomes more and more believable to him or her. A person's coping thoughts should not be broadly positive, Pollyannaish, and unrealistic; otherwise, the patient will discount them as untrue. For instance, the coping thought "I can't wait to have spine surgery. I'm sure I will have no problems" is unrealistic and not convincing. Rather, the thought "I will be able make the surgery experience as positive as possible, and I look forward to beginning the recovery process" is much more tenable.

Coping self-talk can challenge each of the negative styles. The health care professional can review the following examples with patients to help them understand how the thought reframing process works. Also, Table 9.1 provides examples of coping thoughts that directly combat negative self-talk.

Catastrophizing. In intervening with the patient who engages in catastrophizing, the psychologist should remind the patient that no one can predict the future. He or she can tell the patient that it is in his or her best interest to predict a realistic or positive outcome, rather than a catastrophic, *what if* outcome, and that acting "as if" things will turn out OK is usually the best course of action. The patient should repeat the following to himself or herself:

- No one can predict the future.
- If I'm going to engage in *what ifs*, I might as well choose healthy ones.
- If I believe in myself, I'll be able to handle any situation, including this spine surgery.

Filtering. If a patient is filtering out everything except the most negative aspects of a situation, he or she needs to learn to shift focus. First, the psychologist should teach the patient to redirect his or her attention to active strategies for making the situation more manageable. The intervention should help the patient look at the situation realistically rather than magnify the negative aspects. Then, the patient can focus on the positive aspects of the situation. Patients should be encouraged to avoid the negative thought "I can't stand it" and to substitute this thought with a more positive one, such as

- I can handle this situation (surgery).
- I've developed a number of resources to make this surgery turn out as positive as possible.
- I am doing this spine surgery for the positive reasons of ____.
- I'm looking forward to getting beyond the surgery and beginning to heal and recover.
- I've had the spine surgery, and now I can focus on getting better.

Black-and-White Thinking. Thinking in black and white will always set the patient up for disappointment, because he or she will make no allowance for gradual improvement. The first step in changing black-and-white thinking is to help the patient identify when he or she is using absolute words like *all, every, always, never,* and *none.* The second step is to have the patient focus on how the situation may be changing in gradual steps. Finally, the psychologist can remind the patient there are always different options, not just the two extremes of black and white. The following self-talk can be useful:

- I am making progress in the following areas: ____
- My ultimate goal is ____ and I'm moving toward it in the following ways: ____

Overgeneralizing. A patient can learn to stop overgeneralizing by learning to evaluate each aspect of a situation realistically and independently. Examples of appropriate self-talk are as follows:

- I've been able to get through a lot of situations, and I'll get through this one.
- Just because my last hospitalization was unpleasant, this one doesn't have to be.

Mind Reading. Individuals who attribute thoughts to another person often act and feel toward others on the basis of inaccurate conclusions. For instance, a patient might think, "I know my doctor doesn't like me." The psychologist should remind patients that nobody can read another person's mind and that the way to handle this type of thought is to "check it out." The patient should rehearse the following self-talk:

- I can't be sure about what he or she thinks unless I check it out.
- I need to act based on the facts, not on what I assume.

Should statements. If a patient has a propensity to use the words *should, ought,* or *must,* he or she is judging self or others by standards that are unrealistic. This type of statement lowers a patient's self-confidence and self-esteem. When patients use this type of self-talk, they can learn to ask themselves, "Is this standard realistic?" "Is this standard flexible?" and "Does this standard make my life and situation better?" The following self-talk statements can help combat should statements:

- I do not have to be perfect.
- Forget the shoulds, oughts, and musts.
- I am doing the best I can.
- I am doing what I can to get better, and I will reward myself for that.

Blaming. If patients tend toward self-blame, the psychologist should remind them that they have always tried to make the best choices and can continue to make healthy choices from now on. If patients blame others, they can be helped to assess realistically how they made their choices and reminded of the aspects of the situation that are in their control and realm of responsibility. The following self-talk can help:

- They are doing the best they can.
- I did the best I could.
- From now on, I will _____.

Deep Relaxation Training

A frequently used component of preparation for surgery programs is training to achieve the relaxation response. It is important to distinguish the relaxation response from simple relaxation. Engaging in an enjoyable and sedentary activity may be relaxing, but this does not necessarily induce what researchers have termed the relaxation response. The relaxation response, first described in the early 1970s (Benson, 1975), is a physiological state that counteracts the stress response, as shown in Table 9.2. The relaxation response promotes healing by counteracting the adverse physiological effect of stress, and it can help with pain control. Thus, teaching patients to elicit the relaxation response is a powerful tool in preparation for spine surgery that the patient can use both pre- and postoperatively.

The relaxation response can be achieved only through regular practice of one of the many types of relaxation exercise, which include breathing techniques, progressive muscle relaxation, visualization, and meditation, among others. It is beyond the scope of this chapter to review the various types of relaxation exercises, and the reader is referred elsewhere for more details (M. Davis, Eshelman, & McKay, 1995; Deardorff & Reeves, 1997; Goleman & Gurin, 1993). In choosing relaxation techniques for a spine surgery preparation program, the psychologist should keep a few guidelines in mind. First, because there is often not much time to complete a preparation for surgery program before the scheduled operation, breathing techniques

TABLE 9.2
Comparison of the Stress Response and the Relaxation Response

Physiologic Criterion	Stress Response	Relaxation Response
Metabolism	Increases	Decreases
Blood pressure	Increases	Decreases
Heart rate	Increases	Decreases
Rate of breathing	Increases	Decreases
Blood flowing to the muscles of the arms and legs	Increases	Stable
Muscle tension	Increases	Decreases
Slow brain waves	Decrease	Increase

Note. From H. Benson, 1996, *The Relaxation Response,* New York: Morrow, p. 131. Adapted with permission from the author.

can be especially helpful because they are easy to learn and practice. Second, progressive muscle relaxation (in which the patient tenses and relaxes the muscle groups one after the other) may not be feasible after a major spine surgery.

Deep Breathing

One of the most straightforward and simple-to-learn relaxation exercises is deep breathing. The deep breathing exercise can easily be recorded on audiotape to enable patients to practice at home. Exhibit 9.4 provides an example of a deep breathing exercise.

Patients must be aware that learning the relaxation response is similar to acquiring any other skill: It takes practice. It is not uncommon for patients to attain deep relaxation when they do the exercise but to have trouble making practicing it a priority. Regular practice is essential to firmly establish the relaxation response as a skill that can be used efficiently at any time. When first learning the skill, the patient may need 20 to 30 min to achieve deep relaxation, whereas after practice it may take only a few deep breaths to accomplish the same result. Deardorff and Reeves (1997) provided the following guidelines to help patients structure their relaxation practice and ensure that the skill is acquired in a timely manner:

- *Practice once or twice a day.* Practicing at least once per day is the minimum necessary to learn to elicit the relaxation response. As patients practice regularly, they will find that the amount of time required to elicit the relaxation response decreases.
- *Practice in a quiet location.* The patient should connect the answering machine, turn the ringer off the telephone, and block outside distracting noises using a fan or air conditioner.
- *Give a 5-min warning.* The patient should give family members a 5-min warning before beginning breathing exercises and explain that he or she will be unavailable for the next 20 minutes. The patient can use this period to tie up loose ends before prac-

EXHIBIT 9.4
Example of a Deep Breathing Exercise

1. Lie down on your back. Bend your knees and move your feet about 8 in apart, with your toes turned slightly outward. This will help straighten your spine and keep you comfortable as you practice the breathing exercise. If you have back pain, you may want to place a pillow under your knees for extra support.
2. Mentally scan your body for any tension.
3. Place one hand on your abdomen and one hand on your chest.
4. Inhale slowly and deeply through your nose into your abdomen, so that your hand rises as much as feels comfortable. Your chest should move only a little and should begin to rise slightly after your abdomen begins to rise.
5. When you feel at ease with step 4, you can practice the deep breathing cycle. In the deep breathing cycle, inhale deeply and diaphragmatically through your nose while smiling slightly, then exhale through your mouth by gently blowing the air out of your lungs and making a whooshing sound like the wind. Making this whooshing sound will help relax the muscles of your mouth, tongue, and jaw.
6. Take long slow deep breaths that raise and lower your abdomen. Focus on the sound and feeling of breathing as you become more and more relaxed.
7. Continue this deep breathing pattern for 5 or 10 min at a time, once or twice a day. Once you have done this daily for a week, you might extend your deep breathing exercise period to 15 or 20 min.
8. At the end of each deep breathing session, take time to once again scan your body for tension. Compare the tension you feel at the conclusion of the exercise with the tension you felt at the beginning of the exercise.
9. As you become more proficient at deep breathing (you quickly achieve the deep relaxation response through deep breathing), you can practice it any time during the day, in addition to your regularly scheduled sessions. Simply concentrate on your abdomen moving up and down and the air moving in and out of your lungs.
10. Once you have learned to use the deep breathing technique to elicit the relaxation response, you can practice it whenever you feel the need.

ticing the deep breathing. For instance, if a patient tends to be distracted during the relaxation exercise by things he or she has to do, making a short list before beginning the exercise will increase concentration.

- *Practice at regular times.* Making deep breathing exercises part of a routine will increase the likelihood that the patient will practice regularly. Patients should select a time when they will have no scheduling conflicts and when they feel able to concentrate; for instance, just before bedtime the patient will be too tired and likely to fall asleep.
- *Practice on an empty stomach.* Practicing deep relaxation after a big meal increases the likelihood that a patient will fall asleep in the middle of trying to relax. Also, the process of digestion after meals can disrupt deep relaxation. Therefore, it is recommended that patients eat nothing for at least 2 hours before exercising if possible.
- *Assume a comfortable position.* A commonly used position is flat on one's back with the legs extended and arms comfortably at the sides. If the patient's spine condition and surgery make this

posture impossible, other recommended positions are lying on the back with knees supported by a pillow, sitting, or even standing. Sitting up rather than lying down can prevent a patient from falling asleep during relaxation exercises.

- *Loosen clothing.* Patients should loosen any tight clothing and take off shoes, watch, glasses, jewelry, and other constrictive apparel when practicing relaxation. Again, the object is to have the patient be as comfortable as possible while practicing.

- *Assume a passive attitude.* It is important for patients to adopt an attitude of "allowing" the relaxation response to happen. The patient should not think of "trying" to relax or "control" his or her body.

Cue-Controlled Relaxation

Cue-controlled relaxation can help facilitate the relaxation response by teaching the patient to use a specific "cue" to signal the relaxation response. The relaxation cue could basically be anything, but common cues are a phrase (saying "relax"), a visual reminder, or a muscular signal. Deardorff and Reeves (1997) discussed the simple cue of having the patient touch his or her thumb and index finger while thinking about relaxing. This type of cue can help the patient invoke the relaxation response in almost any situation, refocus concentration on relaxing and coping, engage in cognitive restructuring, manage acute pain, and control nausea and vomiting (Deardorff & Reeves, 1997).

Cue-controlled relaxation is based on classical conditioning principles originally developed by Pavlov. In Pavlov's famous experiment in the early 1900s, dogs salivated in response to a bell or a light if the stimulus had previously been paired with the provision of food. Cue-controlled relaxation training works on the same principle. The critical component of cue-controlled relaxation is that, as with Pavlov's dogs, the cue must be repeatedly paired with the relaxation response before the patient will be able to use the technique effectively. To pair a cue with the relaxation response, a patient would practice deep breathing exercises for a week or to the point of being able to reliably elicit the relaxation response. Then, he or she can pair the relaxation response to a specific cue by practicing the cue while in a state of deep relaxation.

Obstacles to Practicing the Relaxation Exercises

Relaxation training is a critical component of a preparation for spine surgery program. Therefore, it is important to make every effort to ensure that patients practice and master this skill. Many obstacles may prevent patients from practicing, and the presurgical intervention must try to address these problems. The following are some of the more common obstacles to practicing relaxation exercises and suggestions for helping patients overcome them.

- *There is no time to relax.* Not having enough time is one of the most common obstacles encountered in practicing relaxation exercises. This obstacle is especially salient before surgery; patients often feel overwhelmed by the number of issues they have to address prior to the operation. The psychologist should help the patient prioritize the relaxation exercises and schedule a specific time for practice. After all, relaxation practice takes less than 30 min to complete, and even less time after regular practice.
- *It is boring.* Some patients have trouble completing the relaxation exercises because they are "boring." These patients typically deal with stress by becoming quite busy and, in general, have trouble being still as a personality style. When the patient complains of boredom, it is important to remind him or her that the relaxation response skill is critical to the success of the preparation for spine surgery program. These patients often need to be convinced that relaxing is valuable and not simply a waste of time. In more extreme cases, patients could benefit from a more "active" type of relaxation exercise including imagery or another procedure that requires the patient to "do something" during the relaxation exercise. Also, for such patients, relaxation exercises following physical therapy exercises may be helpful; the natural deceleration in arousal that occurs at the end of therapy can augment the effects of the relaxation and provide a more active form of relaxation practice.
- *No place to relax.* Patients sometimes complain that they don't have any quiet place to practice the relaxation exercises on a regular basis. Thorough exploration of this issue often indicates that the patient has not made relaxation practice a priority. Deardorff and Reeves (1997) recommended closing the door to the room in which the patient is going to practice and placing a "do not disturb" sign on the door knob. If there is not room enough for the patient to get away from distractions, he or she might have to practice when the other people in the household are out of the house.

Hypnosis

Hypnosis has been extensively used as a component of preparation for surgery programs (Blankfield, 1991; Kessler & Dane, 1996; Lynch, 1999; Wood & Hirschberg, 1994). In fact, one of the earliest known uses of hypnosis was as an anesthetic agent with a surgery patient in the United States in 1836 (Wood & Hirschberg, 1994). Reviews of the literature show that hypnosis training for surgical patients might include a single session or multiple presurgical consultations (see Wood & Hirschberg, 1994, for a review). The patient can practice audiotaped hypnosis exercises on his or her own, which can be very cost effective.

The content of hypnotic suggestions for spine surgery patients can vary considerably, from inducing simple relaxation to enhancing wound healing (Deardorff & Reeves, 1997; Wood & Hirschberg, 1994). As with the relaxation response, patients must practice the hypnotic exercises before using them to cope with surgical process, but once the patient has mastered these exercises, the hypnotic state can be induced quite rapidly and in almost any stressful situation related to the surgery.

If hypnosis is to be part of the preparation for spine surgery program, the psychologist should discuss misconceptions about hypnosis with the patient. Deardorff and Reeves (1997) addressed the most common erroneous beliefs as follows:

- *Hypnosis is not a state of deep sleep or unconsciousness.* A person is not asleep when under hypnosis. In reality, hypnosis is a state of relaxed attention in which the person is able to hear, speak, move around, and think independently. The brain waves of a hypnotized person are similar to those of someone who is awake, and reflexes, such as the knee jerk, which are absent in the sleeping person are present when hypnotized.
- *Hypnosis does not allow someone else to control the patient's mind.* Books, movies, and stage hypnotists have capitalized on perpetuating this myth, and it is perhaps the biggest misconception that keeps people from pursuing and benefiting from hypnosis. A patient cannot be hypnotized against his or her will, and once hypnotized, a person cannot be forced or coerced into doing something he or she finds objectionable or does not want to do.
- *A hypnotized person is always able to come out of a trance.* It is actually easier to slip out of hypnosis than it is to become hypnotized. Patients frequently become alert when the hypnotherapist stops talking, inadvertently says something inconsistent with the person's beliefs, leaves the room, or is otherwise distracted. If left alone when hypnotized, most people reorient, alert themselves, and awaken naturally.
- *A hypnotized person will not give away secrets.* When hypnotized, a person is aware of everything that happens both during and after hypnosis, unless he or she wants to accept and follow specific suggestions for amnesia. Thus, secrets cannot be forced from a person unwilling to divulge them.
- *Some people are more responsive than others to hypnosis.* Nearly everyone, however, can achieve some level of hypnosis and can

benefit from it with practice. Stumbling blocks to hypnosis include trying too hard, fears or misconceptions about hypnosis, and unconscious desires to hang on to troublesome symptoms. A licensed psychologist, physician, or dentist experienced in hypnosis can help a person overcome these stumbling blocks.

CONCLUSION

Many forces militate against the patient's achieving an appropriate understanding of the surgery process and of realistic outcomes. The information the surgeon and the treatment team present must be compatible with the patient's intellectual abilities and coping style. Unrealistic outcome expectations, fears of the hospital and of postoperative pain, and uncertainty about abilities to persist through rehabilitation are obstacles to recovery. Thus, the psychologist in a preparation for surgery program has a large role to play in helping shape the patient's conceptions about the surgical and recovery processes.

Cognitive–behavioral therapy provides the framework for restructuring irrational or maladaptive beliefs about the surgery into ones that facilitate surgical outcome. On the basis of the initial assessment, the psychologist and patient work together in designing and individualizing cognitive–behavioral interventions and establishing a regular practice regimen and individual or group program sessions. The end result is that, with cognitive–behavioral therapy as its backdrop, a psychological program of preparation for spine surgery helps patients acquire the skills, knowledge, and adaptive beliefs that will allow them to maximize the improvements that can result from spine surgery.

10

PREPARING FOR SPINE SURGERY: PSYCHOSOCIAL INTERVENTIONS

Throughout this book we have referred to ways in which the patient's emotional state, motivation, and thoughts are greatly influenced by their interactions with others. Employers, for example, can be supportive in a way that encourages the patient's recovery and return to work—or they can provoke so much anger that the patient would rather suffer and be disabled so the employer has to pay disability and worry about litigation. Similarly, in chapter 4, we described how the responses of the spouse or other support person can support or inhibit the patient's efforts toward recovery. It appears that almost anyone of significance to the patient has the potential to create positive or negative effects on the patient's ability to overcome pain. In recognition of this fact, this chapter focuses on the social context of spine surgery preparation and in particular on improving communication with health care professionals, strengthening patients' psychosocial environments, nurturing patients' spirituality, and empowering patients to manage postoperative pain control.

171

IMPROVING COMMUNICATION WITH
HEALTH CARE PROFESSIONALS

Closing the Doctor–Patient Communication Gap

Communication between the surgical patient and the professionals involved in his or her medical care is of the utmost importance; likewise, information gathering is a critical component of any preparation for spine surgery program. In an ideal world, patients could attain accurate and understandable information from their health care providers as well as from other sources. Unfortunately, research indicates that this is simply not the case as evidenced by the following statistics collected by the American Medical Association (see Deardorff & Reeves, 1997; Ferguson, 1993). Recent studies have found that

- 58% of patients felt that their physicians did not provide adequate explanations about their condition,
- 69% felt that their physician did not spend enough time with them,
- 60% did not read complex consent and hospital forms,
- patients retained only about 30% to 50% of the surgical information provided them, and
- a majority of complaints against health maintenance organization physicians involved communication issues.

Research has also found that effective communication between doctor and patient enhances patient recall of information, compliance with treatment recommendations, satisfaction with care, psychological well-being, and overall treatment outcomes (for reviews, see Levinson & Chaumeton, 1999; Stewart, 1995).

Certainly, research indicates that patient concerns about obtaining appropriate information are not unfounded. For instance, one study found that general practice physicians and surgeons spend an average of between 7 min and 13 min per patient visit and that doctors were likely to interrupt a patient within the first 18 sec of their explanation of symptoms (Beckman & Frankel, 1984). However, responsibility for problems in doctor–patient communication cannot be placed entirely with the physicians; patients share this responsibility. For instance, Kaplan, Greenfield, and Ware (1989) determined that the average patient asked fewer than four questions in a 15-min visit with their doctors, one of the more frequent being, "Will you validate my parking?"

A preparation for spine surgery program should teach patients how to work effectively with their doctors, including their surgeons. Treatment is most effective when patients and health care professionals work in a partnership. Such a partnership allows for efficient gathering of information and accurate communication of needs, leading to improved patient satisfaction and enhanced outcome overall. The social self-regulation model of surgery preparation suggests that interactions between the patient and health care providers are primarily task focused. Discordance between the surgeon and patient's perceptions and goals arising from ineffective physician–patient communication can compromise compliance, health status, and patient satisfaction (Stewart, 1995; Temple et al., 1998).

Levinson and Chaumeton (1999) investigated communication between a mix of general and orthopedic surgeons and their patients during the course of routine office visits. The average office visit was 13 minutes, and the surgeons talked more than the patients. The typical surgical consultation consisted of "relatively high amounts of patient education and counseling," but consultations had a narrow biomedical focus with little discussion of the psychological aspects of patient problems. Surgeons infrequently expressed empathy toward patients, and social conversation was brief. The authors observed that the results are "consistent with the work of physicians in this setting, because they often see patients referred to them for a surgical intervention" (p. 132).

Some might argue that it is not the role of the spine surgeon to address emotional or psychosocial issues. Even so, the importance of these findings for a surgery preparation program is to give the patient appropriate expectations regarding visits with his or her spine surgeon. Patients should expect that the office visit will be relatively brief, that a great deal of information will be provided, and that emotional and psychosocial issues will not be addressed. If patients go in with expectations that are different than these, they are likely to be dissatisfied with the visit and possibly with overall care.

Beyond giving patients appropriate expectations about interactions with their spine surgeon, the preparation for surgery program can teach them how to effectively work with all members of their health care treatment team. The following recommendations are adapted from Deardorff and Reeves (1997) and Ferguson (1993).

Help patients plan their doctor visits in advance. An important component of a preparation for spine surgery program is patient information gathering. Patients should learn to develop a list of questions and concerns to address with their spine surgeons during their office visits. These questions should be very specific and reasonable in scope and length; a patient who develops a list of 20 questions will be extremely frustrated if only two or three of them are addressed during the office visit. Therefore, program staff can help patients be realistic about the number of questions to try to get answered during the course of an office visit.

Teach patients to be assertive. Teaching patients basic assertiveness skills (discussed later in this chapter) can enhance their overall surgery experience and outcome. These skills can be useful in gathering information during office visits, as well as getting other needs and concerns addressed. Once again, program staff can help patients to be reasonable in using the assertiveness skills. If patients are seen as aggressive and overly demanding by their health care team, the health care providers will often react in a passive-aggressive manner without even realizing it, setting up a negative interaction that may affect spine surgery outcome.

Help patients direct their questions to the appropriate person. Health care professionals often take for granted that patients understand the medical system. Most patients do not, and they are often confused about where to get the information they need. Thus, patients often attempt to obtain information from their spine surgeon, for example, when the most appropriate person is a physician's assistant or nurse. As with other inaccurate patient expectations, this one will likely to lead to dissatisfaction.

Remind patients to bring someone else to doctor visits. Patients are often quite nervous and preoccupied during visits with their spine surgeon. They may miss the opportunity to ask important questions, and they may have difficulty remembering medical information they are given. Ferguson (1993) and Deardorff and Reeves (1997) advocated bringing another individual to the doctor's appointment to help calm the patient, ensure that various concerns are addressed, and assist the patient in recalling medical information.

Avoiding Medical Errors

Unfortunately, medical errors are more common than is generally realized. Medical errors range from mistakes in hospital meals to blatant surgical mistakes. One of the more common mistakes in hospitals is the medication error (Leape et al., 1995). The *Journal of the American Medical Association* estimated that doctor- or hospital-related mistakes could be at least partially responsible for 180,000 deaths annually (Leape, 1994). In addition, a hospital stay carries a significant risk of infection. According to the Centers for Disease Control and Prevention (CDC), 5% to 10% of hospitalized patients—between 1.75 and 3.50 million people per year—pick up an infection (see Benson, 1996; M. Cohen, 1995). CDC officials estimated that health care professionals' failure to follow standardized infection control practices cause at least one third of hospital-acquired infections. These procedures include such simple tasks as washing hands before any type of physical contact with the patient. A comprehensive review of 37 studies on hand washing found that doctors and nurses typically washed their hands only 40% of the time prior to physical contact with patients (Griffin, 1996). In addition, hospital settings may harbor antibiotic-resistant bacteria, or "super bugs" (M. Cohen, 1995).

Because medical errors are so frequent, the Agency for Healthcare Research and Quality developed 20 Tips to Help Prevent Medical Errors. Exhibit 10.1 summarizes these tips, and many are discussed in the following

EXHIBIT 10.1
Patient Handout: Avoiding Medical Errors

1. The single most important way you can help to prevent errors is to be an active member of your health care team.
2. Make sure that all of your doctors know about every medication you are taking, including prescription and over-the-counter medicines and dietary supplements such as vitamins and herbs.
3. Make sure your doctor knows about any allergies and adverse reactions you have had to medicines.
4. When your doctor writes you a prescription, be sure you can read it.
5. Ask for information about your medicines in terms you can understand—both when your medicines are prescribed and when you receive them.
6. When you pick up your medicine from the pharmacy, ask, "Is this the medicine that my doctor prescribed?"
7. If you have questions about the directions on your medicine labels, ask.
8. Ask your pharmacist for the best device to measure your liquid medicine. Also, ask questions if you're not sure how to use it.
9. Ask for written information about the side effects your medicine could cause.
10. If you have a choice, choose a hospital at which many patients have had the procedure or surgery you need.
11. If you are in the hospital, consider asking all health care workers who have direct contact with you whether they have washed their hands.
12. When you are being discharged from the hospital, ask your doctor to explain the treatment plan you will use at home.
13. If you are having surgery, make sure that you, your doctor, and your surgeon all agree and are clear on exactly what will be done.
14. Speak up if you have questions or concerns.
15. Make sure that someone, such as your personal doctor, is in charge of your care.
16. Make sure that all health care professionals involved in your care have all important health information about you.
17. Ask a family member or friend to be there with you and to be your advocate (someone who can help you get things done and speak up for you if you can't).
18. Know that more is not always better.
19. If you have a test, don't assume that no news is good news. Call in for the results.
20. Learn about your condition and treatment by asking your doctor and nurse and by using other reliable sources.

Note. From Spine Line (March/April, 2001) and Agency for Healthcare Research and Quality (Publication No. 00-PO38, February 2000, AHRQ, Rockville, MD, http://www.ahrq.gov/consumer/20tips.htm)

---

section. This list should be provided to patients participating in a spine surgery preparation program.

Because a myriad of health care professionals are usually involved in the spine surgery process, having patients complete a "medical fact sheet" as part of a spine surgery preparation program can help avoid treatment errors by ensuring that everyone has the same information about the factors that might influence the patient's surgical experience. Use of a medical fact sheet is becoming more and more critical given changes in the health care system that place much more responsibility on the patientfor managing their own care, and such a tool can give patients a sense of control over their treatment. A useable medical fact-gathering sheet is available in Deardorff and Reeves (1997).

Assertiveness Training

Consistent with several models of surgery preparation (e.g., biopsychosocial, self-efficacy, empowerment, social self-regulation), assertiveness skills are necessary for a patient to implement many of the preparation for surgery recommendations. Being appropriately assertive can help spine surgery patients obtain the necessary information preoperatively and protect them from medical errors.

Many patients have difficulty dealing assertively with health care providers. They may feel intimidated or do not want to appear foolish. Others, feeling that physicians are condescending or resenting physicians' power, may be aggressive, threatening, or obnoxious in their interactions with health care providers. There are four types of communication styles:

1. *Nonassertive or submissive communication* is characterized by giving in to another person's preferences while discounting one's own rights and needs. The people around a person with this communication style may not even be aware that the patient is being nonassertive or submissive, because the individual never expresses his or her needs. Surgical patients who communicate in this way may leave themselves open to the mistakes of others and are usually less engaged in their own treatment.

2. In *aggressive communication*, the patient expresses his or her wants and desires in a hostile or attacking manner. Aggressive communication often accompanies insensitivity to the rights and feelings of others and may involve attempts to coerce and intimidate health care professionals. Typically, aggressive communication increases the level of conflict in any situation. In the context of a surgery preparation program, health care professionals who respond to aggressive communication by withdrawing from the patient (being passive-aggressive) or responding in a similarly aggressive manner will likely lose an opportunity to help improve surgery outcome.

3. *Passive-aggressive communication* is a way of expressing anger in a passive manner. This communication style is often seen when the spine injury resulted from a work-related or other accident. Patients angry at an employer or other party for "causing" the spinal injury may, either consciously or unconsciously, use the pain behaviors to get back at the perceived perpetrator. Often, patients engaging in passive-aggressive communication have no insight into their behavior.

4. *Assertive communication* enables an individual to express his or her wants and desires while respecting the rights of others.

Such communication is simple and direct and does not attack, manipulate, or discount others (Alberti & Emmons, 1974; Bourne, 1995; Bower & Bower, 1991; Deardorff & Reeves, 1997). As Deardorff and Reeves observed, "Communicating in an assertive fashion allows you to express your needs and desires while keeping those around you comfortable and non-defensive" (p. 175).

For patients who have difficulty communicating with health care providers and others involved in their care, discussion and training in assertiveness can play a large role in improving their spine surgery experience. The following is a brief outline of assertiveness skills as they relate to the spine surgery patient. The reader is referred to other sources for more detailed information (Alberti & Emmons, 1974; Bourne, 1995; Bower & Bower, 1991; Deardorff & Reeves, 1997; McKay, Davis, & Fanning, 1983).

Instruction in assertive communication should be included as part of a spine surgery preparation program for several reasons: It helps the patient take greater responsibility for his or her own care. It creates a greater bond between the patient and the health care team, which can foster compliance and motivation. Assertive communication helps the patient obtain more information and helps the health care team avoid treatment errors and problems. The following suggestions can promote assertive communication in spine surgery patients.

Use assertive nonverbal behavior. Body language can communicate a great deal. Assertive behavior includes staying calm, establishing eye contact, and maintaining an open posture. Alternatively, nonassertive behavior includes looking down at the floor while communicating, avoiding eye contact, speaking softly, and turning slightly away from the person with whom one is talking. A component of assertiveness training related to surgery preparation would involve teaching the patient nonverbal assertiveness skills.

Keep requests simple. An effective, assertive request is delivered in a simple, direct, and straightforward fashion. A good rule of thumb is to ask for only one thing at a time in an easy-to-understand format.

Be specific. Being specific means being clear and concrete about one's wants, needs, and feelings in expressing them to health care professionals and others. An example of a nonspecific request is, "I would like to get more help from your office staff regarding my spine surgery." A more specific version of the same request would be, "I would appreciate it if your office staff could help me with getting insurance preapproval and scheduling my blood donation and give me information about postoperative pain control." The latter example is specific, direct, and nonaggressive.

Use I statements. Assertive communication often begins with I statements: for example, "I need to," "I would appreciate it if," or "I would like to." Teaching patients to use *I* statements in their communication is one of the primary components of assertiveness training. Patients should also avoid *you* statements, which often sound threatening and put the other person on the defensive.

Address behaviors, not personalities. Patients must learn to address the behavior, rather than the personality, of the other person when making requests. For instance, if a spine surgery patient needs help with housework postoperatively, he or she will get better results by saying, "I would like you to take over the heavy household chores while I am recovering from my spine surgery," rather than "I know you tend to be careless about housekeeping, but would you help me with the chores while I am recovering from my spine surgery?" This guideline also applies to requesting behaviors from health care professionals.

Do not apologize for making requests. Patients who tend to be submissive or nonassertive often make requests in an apologetic manner. They might ask, "I am really sorry to have to ask, but is it possible for you to help me understand the spine surgery I am going to have?" Such requests may go unacknowledged and communicate that the person making the request does not feel deserving or has no right to ask.

Learn to say no. Learning to say no will help the patient set important limits on the demands of family, friends, work, and others. Often submissive and nonassertive individuals have trouble saying no because they "feel guilty." Teaching patients to set appropriate limits is extremely important, especially during the postoperative recovery phase, when pacing is essential for enhanced recovery from spine surgery.

Use the "broken record" technique. To use the broken record technique, the patient simply makes a request or says no repeatedly until the communication is acknowledged. People just learning assertiveness skills may tend to make a request and then back down if they encounter any resistance. Or the patient might try to come up with more and more reasons why his or her request is justified; every time the patient expresses another reason for the request, the other person may further doubt that the request has merit. The broken record technique can help patients feel comfortable making their request and then following through. In the following example, a postoperative spine surgery patient wants to make sure his doctor washes her hands before she examines him:

> *Patient:* I would appreciate it if you would wash your hands before . . .
> *Doctor:* Don't worry about it. It will be fine. I really am in a hurry.
> *Patient:* I understand you're in a hurry, but I would like you to wash your hands.
> *Doctor:* You really need not be concerned. I just need to take a quick look.
> *Patient:* I still would like you to wash your hands.

STRENGTHENING PATIENTS' PSYCHOSOCIAL ENVIRONMENTS

A spine surgery preparation program should help the patient strengthen his or her psychosocial environment. When the patient and his or her family have similar adaptive goals, treatment outcomes are enhanced. Further, the family can facilitate surgical outcome by providing appropriate tangible assistance and emotional and informational support. A preparation for spine surgery program should contain a component of work with the patient's family. There is evidence that including the patient's family in the preparation for surgery program will enhance results (Raliegh, Lepczyk, & Rowley, 1990).

Most surgery preparation interventions for the patient can also be applied to family members, including those involving information gathering, cognitive–behavioral training, and interaction with the medical system. Family members must have appropriate and realistic expectations regarding the course of the patient's recovery from spine surgery, because if they expect too much, or too little, the patient is less likely to do well. In addition, preparing the home environment for the postoperative recovery period is an important program component; the family might benefit from assistance in organizing the patient's living space for surgery recovery, obtaining any necessary assistive devices beforehand, and arranging home health care if necessary, among other things.

The primary support person may benefit in particular from participation in a preparation for surgery program. This person has been called the "partner in pain" (Engel, 1959; Szasz, 1968; Waddell, 1998) or the "associate victim" (Halmosh & Israeli, 1984; Waddell, 1998). The primary support person provides most of the social support throughout the illness and recovery, although other members of the patient's family and friends often assist. This relationship, which is essential to recovery from spine surgery, entails risks for both parties. As Waddell described it,

> Chronic pain patients and their partners play active, mutually supporting roles, and the pain may become a major focus in their whole relationship. Their whole social milieu may become pervaded by pain and disability, medical values and health care. Chronic pain and caring may become almost full-time careers, with both partners equally committed. In extreme cases, this may actually provide a more satisfying emotional relationship for both of them. (p. 208–209)

If presurgical screening has indicated that caregiver solicitousness is an issue (see chapter 4), the surgery preparation program can provide the necessary interventions to avoid the negative effects of inappropriate care.

One of the most valued aspects of an individual's psychosocial environment is his or her work. Work provides such values as income, activity, occupation and structure of time, creativity and mastery, social interaction, a sense of identity, and a sense of purpose (Waddell, 1998). Given the pervasive importance of work values, surgery preparation programs should address how the operation will affect a patient's work abilities. Issues for discussion include how long the patient will be disabled from work, how he or she will survive financially, and whether he or she will ever be able to return to full-time and unrestricted work.

The preparation for surgery program should help patients develop strategies for dealing with the work and financial issues that surround surgery and disability. Unfortunately, many spine surgery patients are so concerned with and distracted by the approaching surgery that they forget to deal with the work and financial issues until negative consequences occur. When this happens, usually postoperatively, the stress it generates can interfere with recovery.

NURTURING PATIENTS' SPIRITUALITY

The medical system rarely addresses spiritual issues. For instance, a review of more than 1,000 articles in primary care physician journals revealed that only 11 studies (1.1 percent) examined religious considerations. Another review found that in the past 200 years, only about 200 studies, out of hundreds of thousands of English medical journal articles, investigated some aspect of spiritual faith. Benson (1996) concluded that these findings show how taboo the topic of religion and spirituality have become in the recent history of Western medicine.

Even though Western medicine rarely incorporates spirituality into the treatment and healing process, it is often an important part of patients' lives. In a Gallup poll conducted in 1990, 95% of Americans said they believed in God, and 76% said they prayed on a regular basis (Gallup, 1990). In addition, spiritual beliefs have been found to correlate with health benefits, including surgery outcome (for reviews, see Deardorff & Reeves, 1997; Larson, 1993; Levin, 1994; D. A. Matthews, Larson, & Barry, 1994; Oxman, Freeman, & Manheimer, 1995; Pressman, Lyons, Larson, & Strain, 1990). The following examples of findings are applicable to spine surgery patients:

- Levin reviewed hundreds of epidemiologic studies and concluded that belief in God lowers death rates and increases health.
- A study completed at Dartmouth Medical School found that of 232 patients who had undergone elective open heart surgery for either coronary artery or aortic valve disease, those who were "very religious" were three times more likely to recover than those who were not religious (Oxman et al., 1995).
- In a study of hospitalized male patients, 20% reported that religion was "the most important thing that keeps me going," and almost 50% rated religion as very helpful in coping with their illness (Larson, 1993). Religious coping helped these men to be significantly less depressed.

- A 7-year study of older adults revealed that religious involvement was associated with less physical disability and less depression (Larson, 1993).
- In various research studies, church attenders had nearly half the risk of heart attack and lower blood pressure, even after taking into account the effects of smoking and socioeconomic status (for reviews, see Larson, 1993; D. A. Matthews et al., 1994).
- Of 300 studies on spirituality in scientific journals, the National Institute for Health Care Research found that nearly three fourths showed that religion had a positive effect on health (Larson, 1993).
- Pressman et al. (1990) studied 30 elderly women recovering from surgical correction of a broken hip to determine relationships between religious beliefs and health. At comparable times postoperatively, those with strong religious beliefs were able to walk significantly further and were less likely to be depressed than those who had no religious beliefs.

These findings indicate that religious and spiritual beliefs form a vital part of the way most people view and cope with life and are associated with health benefits. These beliefs provide the following elements that can enhance spine surgery outcome:

- *a sense of meaning and purpose*. Spiritual beliefs can give an individual a sense of meaning and purpose that can help him or her rise above, or cope more effectively with, the stress related to surgery.
- *healthy priorities*. Spirituality can provide a framework for setting priorities and placing stressors in perspective. Healthy priorities can support patients in carrying out actions that foster healing process, such as reducing anxiety, promoting proper exercise and diet, and allowing oneself to be cared for during the immediate postoperative phase.
- *security, safety, and peace of mind*. The sense of security, safety, and peace of mind religion and spirituality can provide are especially important when approaching a major life stressor such as surgery. Patients with spiritual beliefs know that their higher power is close by, and they find peace of mind in "letting go" and "turning over" their anxiety and fear about the surgical procedure and recovery process.
- *self-confidence*. Self-confidence is often enhanced in individuals with spiritual beliefs; such individuals feel that they were created worthy of love and respect.

- *guidance*. In most belief systems the higher power is all knowing, and many patients draw on spirituality when seeking wisdom and guidance in dealing with the surgical process.

A preparation for spine surgery program may or may not specifically include a spiritual component. However, program staff should at least acknowledge these issues and give patients specific opportunities and encouragement to discuss how this aspect of their lives relates to the spine surgery. If spirituality is important to an individual patient, program staff can help him or her use those beliefs in preparing for surgery by incorporating them into coping self-talk statements and making prayer part of deep relaxation exercise, which can greatly enhance the patient's commitment to practice (see Benson, 1996; Deardorff & Reeves, 1997). In addition, the preparation for surgery program can help patients call on appropriate psychosocial spiritual support relative to their surgery from their church or synagogue, family members, friends, or others. A visit or two with the hospital chaplain can also be of great value in preparing for surgery.

EMPOWERING PATIENTS TO MANAGE POSTOPERATIVE PAIN CONTROL

Postoperative pain control is one of the primary concerns of spine surgery patients. Unfortunately, research indicates that fears about how effective it will be are frequently justified, as pain is often not well regulated by physicians and hospital staff. In fact, many studies have found that postoperative pain control is grossly inadequate, even though this need not be the case (American Pain Society, 2001; Peebles & Schneiderman, 1991; Warfield & Kahn, 1995). As discussed in chapter 7, psychoneuroimmunology research has demonstrated that pain leads to negative bodily responses that can impede wound healing, suppress immune system function, and delay recovery from surgery. Therefore, a critical component of a preparation for spine surgery program is to help the patient ensure that adequate postoperative pain control will be achieved.

We discuss pain control in this chapter because the patient will need to interact with a number of other individuals (e.g., doctors, nurses, family members) to ensure that adequate pain control postoperatively takes place. Although many hospitals have established pain services that specifically manage postoperative pain, such services are not available in all hospitals. Excellent information about pain control issues can be found at a number of Web sites. See Additional Resources section after the references in this volume.

Patient Care Standards and Guidelines

According to the American Pain Foundation (2001a), pain is a major health care crisis, as evidenced by estimates that more than 50 million Americans suffer from chronic pain and another 25 million experience acute pain as a result of injury or surgery. Recognition of the widespread inadequacy of acute pain control prompted Congress, through the Agency for Health Care Policy and Research (AHCPR), to commission a multidisciplinary panel of experts to develop guidelines for the management of acute postoperative pain. This mandate led to the publication and distribution of the Practice Guidelines for Acute Pain Management (AHCPR, 1992). Other professional groups also published acute pain treatment guidelines at that time (American Pain Society, 1992; Ready & Edwards, 1992).

The specific problem of acute pain management in hospitals was addressed shortly thereafter. The Joint Commission on Accreditation of Healthcare Organizations (JCAHO) established "new" standards for the assessment and management of pain in accredited hospitals and other health care settings (JCAHO, 2000). These standards require that JCAHO-accredited hospitals maintain specific functions and activities related to pain assessment and management for patients. These standards can be summarized as follows (Chapman, 2000):

- Recognize the right of patients to appropriate pain assessment and management.
- Screen for pain in a variety of ways, document the results, and perform regular follow-up assessments.
- Ensure that the staff is competent in pain assessment and management.
- Establish policies and procedures related to appropriate use of pain medications.
- Educate patients and their families about pain management.
- Address patient needs for pain management as part of discharge planning.
- Maintain a pain control improvement plan.

In addition to the new JCAHO standards, the American Pain Foundation (2001b) recently developed the *Pain Care Bill of Rights* (see Exhibit 10.2). The *Pain Care Bill of Rights* can be given to spine surgery patients as part of the preparation for surgery program. A list of these rights, along with a *Pain Action Guide*, can be downloaded from the American Pain Foundation Web site for free (www.painfoundation.org). Exhibit 10.3 lists the topic headings covered in the *Pain Action Guide*.

Similar to the *Pain Action Guide*, but more detailed, Deardorff and Reeves's (1997) pain control plan was developed as part of a surgery preparation program. This plan encourages patients to do the following:

Determine if there is a hospital-based surgical pain service. Hospitals that have placed a high priority on pain relief by establishing a surgical pain service provide the most effective pain management. If a patient's spine surgeon operates in more than one hospital, and if there are no other medical

EXHIBIT 10.2
Pain Care Bill of Rights

As a person with pain, you have:

- The right to have your report of pain taken seriously and to be treated with dignity and respect by doctors, nurses, pharmacists, and other health care professionals.
- The right to have your pain thoroughly assessed and promptly treated.
- The right to be informed by your doctor about what may be causing your pain; possible treatments; and the benefits, risks, and costs of each.
- The right to participate actively in decisions about how to manage your pain.
- The right to have your pain reassessed regularly and your treatment adjusted if your pain has not been eased.
- The right to be referred to a pain specialist if your pain persists.
- The right to get clear and prompt answers to your questions, to take time to make decisions, and to refuse a particular type of treatment if you choose.

Although not always required by law, these are the rights you should expect, and if necessary demand, for your pain care.

Note. From American Pain Foundation, 2001, *Pain Care Bill of Rights,* Baltimore, MD: Author. Reprinted with permission from the author.

factors related to hospital choice, patients should use the hospital with the established pain service. Also, the surgical patient should have only one individual or service in charge of pain control, both during hospitalization and while recovering at home, to avoid confusion.

Talk to doctors about pain control. In helping patients develop a pain control plan with their surgeon and surgical team, program staff should encourage them to talk with doctors and nurses about

- pain control methods and medications that have been effective and ineffective in the past,
- concerns related to pain medicine,
- any allergies to medicines (these should have been recorded on the patient's medical fact sheet), and
- medicines being taken for other health problems.

Find out what to expect relative to pain. Research has suggested that surgeons, doctors, and other health care professionals tend to minimize discussions about what the patient may feel following the surgery. This lack of discussion frequently increases the patient's anxiety and distress. To enhance their sense of control, security, and self-efficacy, patients should obtain answers to the following questions as part of their surgery preparation program:

- Will there be much pain after surgery?
- What will the pain likely feel like?
- Where will the pain occur?
- How long is the pain likely to last?
- How long will it be before I am able to be active?
- Will there be any side effects to the treatment (such as nausea)? How long will these last?

EXHIBIT 10.3
Summary of the Pain Action Guide

How do I talk with my doctor or nurse about pain?

- Speak up! Tell your doctor or nurse that you're in pain.
- Tell your doctor or nurse where it hurts.
- Describe how much your pain hurts.
- Describe what makes your pain better or worse.
- Describe what your pain feels like.
- Explain how the pain affects your daily life.
- Tell your doctor or nurse about past treatments for pain.

How can I get the best results possible?

- Take control.
- Set goals.
- Work with your doctor or nurse to develop a pain management plan.
- Keep a pain diary.
- Ask your doctor or nurse about nondrug, nonsurgical treatments.
- Ask your doctor or nurse about ways to relax and cope with pain.
- If you have questions or concerns, speak up.
- If you're going to have surgery, ask your doctor for a complete pain management plan beforehand.
- If you're a patient in a hospital or other facility and you're in pain, speak up.
- Pace yourself.
- If you're not satisfied with your pain care, don't give up.

Note. From American Pain Foundation, 2001, *Pain Action Guide,* Baltimore, MD: Author. Adapted with permission from the author.

Discuss pain medication options. There are many pain management options available to patients. Some of these involve the use of pain medications, and others do not. It is important for patients to understand these options prior to surgery. The preparation for surgery program staff can inform patients about the different types of pain medication and modes of delivery (e.g., oral, injection, patient-controlled analgesia) using a simple informational handout.

Understand time-contingent scheduling and patient-controlled analgesia (PCA). As most health care professionals are aware, two major advances in the way pain medications are scheduled have resulted in significant improvements in postoperative control of pain: time-contingent scheduling and patient-controlled analgesia. Program staff should teach these concepts to patients as part of a surgery preparation program.

Time-contingent scheduling involves giving the pain medication at set times, whether or not the pain is severe. Instead of waiting until the pain gets worse or "breaks through," the patient is given the medicine at set times during the day to keep the pain under control. Thus, time, rather than severity of the pain (as in prn, or as-needed, dosing), determines when the medication is delivered. By giving medications in a time-contingent manner, a steady-state level of pain medication in the blood can be achieved by adjusting the doses. Time-contingent dosing avoids the peaks and valleys of pain that are characteristic of as-needed dosing and is one of the most important advances in the effective use of pain medications. This type of dosing is commonly used when the patient is in the hospital, and it should be maintained during the acute recovery phase.

The second major advance in medication scheduling and delivery is patient-controlled analgesia (PCA). PCA involves the use of special medication pump that allows the patient to deliver predetermined amounts of pain medication through a catheter into a vein by pushing a button. PCA puts the patient in charge of pain management by providing him or her with increased control over pain medicine delivery. Built-in safety measures prevent the patient from administering too much medication. The results for the patient are immediate; he or she does not have to wait for the nursing staff to respond to requests for medication. In addition, PCA can be programmed to deliver medication through the night automatically to ensure that pain control is achieved around the clock.

PCA is the method of choice for controlling pain following most major surgeries. A great many research studies have found that patients using PCA are much more comfortable, use less pain medication overall, can be discharged from the hospital earlier, and are generally more satisfied with their care (for reviews, see Carron, 1989; Ferrante, Ostheimer, & Covino, 1990; Warfield & Kahn, 1995; Williams, 1996, 1997). However, recent research has found that a patient's use of PCA is influenced by psychological variables such as anxiey, fear of pain medication, stoicism, a lack of readiness to take control of the pain, and not wanting to be seen as a complainer (Gil, Ginsberg, Muir, Sykes, & Williams, 1990; Perry, Parker, White, & Clifford, 1994; Wilder-Smith & Schuler, 1992; Williams, 1996, 1997). Program staff should discuss these psychological and emotional influences on the use of PCA with patients as part of the preparation program, so that patients will feel comfortable with PCA and use it appropriately.

Talk to the surgeon or anesthesiologist about anesthesia. Many advances have been made in anesthesia options, and patients should discuss these with the appropriate physician. Many surgery preparation programs recommend that patients meet with their anesthesiologist before the surgery. The patient should discuss his or her previous experience with anesthesia and whether any problems occurred.

Investigate nonmedication approaches to pain control. There are several nonmedication techniques that can be very effective for pain control and that, even though they are readily available, are rarely suggested. Most pain is best treated with a combination of medications and nonmedication approaches. The non-medication approaches discussed here are readily available, easy to use, low risk, and inexpensive. Patients can easily learn these techniques as part of a spine surgery preparation program and use them both pre- and postoperatively.

- *patient education.* Patients can be instructed on aspects of surgical recovery that may help with pain control, including coughing exercises, deep breathing, proper body mechanics, and physical restrictions. Patients given such instruction prior to surgery report less pain, require fewer pain medications, and have shorter hospital stays (Contrada et al., 1994; Deardorff, 2000; Deardorff & Reeves, 1997; Johnston & Vogele, 1993).
- *cognitive–behavioral techniques.* These techniques, reviewed in chapter 9, can help not only with overall surgical recovery and outcome, but also with pain control.
- *heat and cold.* The application of heat and cold is used to reduce pain sensitivity, reduce muscle spasms, and decrease congestion in an injured area (e.g., the site of surgery). The initial application of cold decreases tissue injury response, and heat is then used to promote clearance of tissue toxins and accumulated fluids.
- *massage and exercise.* Massage and exercise are used to stretch and regain muscle and tendon length and range of motion. With spinal surgeries, these techniques can be especially important to recovery of previous functioning.
- *transcutaneous electrical nerve stimulation (TENS).* TENS involves placing adhesive pads containing electrodes in specific locations related to the pain following surgery or injury. The electrodes are connected by thin wires to a small battery-operated stimulator that produces electrical current that the patient can adjust. The electrical current, which produces a tingling sensation, is thought to decrease pain by raising the threshold of the nerves in the spinal cord that respond to injury. TENS may also promote healing by reducing inflammation and increasing mobilization following surgery.

Learn to stay ahead of the pain. The most important thing for patients to learn about effective pain management is to stay ahead of the pain by taking medications and using nonmedication techniques when the pain first begins or before it starts. If the pain escalates and gets to be too much to bear, it is more difficult to bring under control.

Inquire about postdischarge pain control. Patients who are experiencing pain at the time of discharge from the hospital are generally given oral medications to take with them. These are usually to be taken using a strict time-contingent scheduling with a gradual tapering as pain subsides. If patients are taking too much pain medication before the surgery, it may put them at risk for inadequate pain control or side effects following surgery. In this case, part of the surgery preparation program might be a time-contingent tapering or modification of pain medications prior to the surgery. A target level of acceptable preoperative pain medication use is established, and patients are taught to modulate their pain using some of the nonmedication techniques described previously while reducing the medications to achieve the target level.

Understand key concepts in pain medication management. Patients should understand that a large body of research has demonstrated that if pain medication is given for a legitimate reason (e.g., related to surgery), addiction to analgesics is very unlikely (Cleary & Backonja, 1996; Portenoy, 1994; Porter & Jick, 1980; Zenz, Strumpf, & Tryba, 1992). The fear of addiction is prevalent among individuals facing spine surgery and may cause the patient to be reluctant to take appropriate doses of medication for adequate pain control. To help ease patient fears, program staff must help them (and sometimes other health care professionals) understand important pain medication concepts: tolerance, pseudotolerance, physical dependence, addiction, and pseudoaddiction (American Academy of Pain Medicine, American Pain Society, & American Society of Addiction Medicine, 2001):

- *Tolerance*, a well-known property of all narcotics, is the need for an increased dosage of a drug to produce the same level of analgesia that was previously obtained. Tolerance also occurs when a reduced effect is observed with a constant dose. Analgesic tolerance is not always evident during opioid treatment and is not addiction.
- *Pseudotolerance* is the need to increase dosage not because of physical tolerance but because of other factors such as changes in the disease, inadequate pain relief, change in medication, increased physical activity, drug interactions, and lack of compliance. Patient behavior indicative of pseudotolerance may include drug seeking, "clock watching" for dosing, and even illicit drug use in an effort to obtain relief. Pseudotolerance can be distinguished from addiction in that the behaviors resolve once the pain is effectively treated.
- *Physical dependence* is also a well-known and understood physical process. It is a state of adaptation that is manifested by a drug class-specific withdrawal syndrome that can be produced by abrupt cessation, rapid dose reduction, decreasing blood level of the drug, or administration of an antagonist. Physical dependence is not a problem if patients are warned to avoid abrupt discontinuation of the drug, a tapering regimen is used, and opioid antagonist (including agonist-antagonist) drugs are avoided.
- *Addiction* is a psychological dependence on the medication for its psychic effects and is characterized by compulsive use. The

medication is sought after and used even when it is not needed for pain relief. Addiction includes both tolerance and dependence as well.

- *Pseudoaddiction* is drug-seeking behavior that is similar to addiction but is due to unrelieved pain. The behavior stops once the pain is relieved, often through an increase in pain medication. If the patient complains of unrelieved pain and shows drug-seeking behavior, careful assessment is required to distinguish between addiction and pseudoaddiction.

Patients (and health care professionals) often confuse these concepts. Both tolerance and dependence commonly occur in pain medication use and can be readily managed by a physician specializing in this area. Tolerance can be managed by adding other nonaddictive medicines that help the narcotics work better and by emphasizing nonmedication pain control techniques. Dependence is addressed by slowly tapering the pain medication and, possibly, adding other medication to control withdrawal symptoms, as appropriate.

CONCLUSION

Most surgery preparation programs focus primarily on self-regulation techniques. Although these approaches are certainly important, a great deal is missed if psychosocial factors are not taken into account. A comprehensive surgery preparation program will intervene both with the individual surgery patient and with others in the social network.

Figure 10.1 illustrates the process of putting together a preparation for spine surgery program. The program begins with assessment of patient needs and proceeds to assembling program components, implementing the intervention, and following up postoperatively to enhance outcome. The preparation for spine surgery program must be flexible. It can be modified based on individual patient's needs, the program structure (individual, group, or combination) required, and the time available before the operation. The health psychologist must take care to include program components that address all unmet patient needs and to avoid overloading the patient with excessive, superfluous, or unnecessary information. Emphasizing patient self-guidance can be especially valuable if time is short and the patient has demonstrated a strong desire and ability to direct his or her own care.

Surgery preparation programs often end with the surgery, and this is a mistake. Follow-up after spine surgery increases the probability that the patient will continue to use the information, skills, and pain management techniques throughout the postoperative period. Follow-up might include postoperative visits in the hospital, outpatient sessions after the patient is discharged and ambulatory, or simple telephone calls.

```
┌─────────────────────────────────────────────────────────┐
│                   Assess Patient Needs                     │
│   •  Obtain information from PPS, if completed             │
│   •  Assess the following areas:                          │
│        o  cognitive                                        │
│        o  affective/emotional                              │
│        o  behavioral                                       │
│        o  psychosocial                                     │
└─────────────────────────────────────────────────────────┘
```

```
┌─────────────────────────────────────────────────────────┐
│          Assemble Appropriate Program Components           │
│   •  Cognitive-behavioral components                      │
│        o  Information gathering                            │
│        o  Cognitive restructuring                          │
│        o  Relaxation exercises and cue-controlled relaxation│
│   •  Psychosocial components                              │
│        o  Communication and assertiveness                  │
│        o  Family, friends, and work                        │
│        o  Spirituality                                     │
│        o  Pain control plan                                │
└─────────────────────────────────────────────────────────┘
```

```
┌─────────────────────────────────────────────────────────┐
│              Select Implementation Strategy                │
│        •  Self-guided                                      │
│        •  Individual                                       │
│        •  Group                                            │
│        •  Blended                                          │
└─────────────────────────────────────────────────────────┘
```

```
┌─────────────────────────────────────────────────────────┐
│               Provide Postoperative Follow-up             │
│   •  Assess implementation of the treatment plan.         │
│   •  Encourage the patient to use the various             │
│      program skills.                                       │
│   •  Facilitate family involvement, as appropriate.       │
│   •  Assess and facilitate the postoperative              │
│      recovery process, as appropriate.                     │
└─────────────────────────────────────────────────────────┘
```

Figure 10.1. Components of a spine surgery preparation program. PPS = presurgical psychological screening.

IV

BIOPSYCHOSOCIAL ASPECTS OF POSTSURGICAL REHABILITATION

11

POSTSURGICAL DECONDITIONING AND RECONDITIONING

With a jolt, the patient awakens from the chemically induced slumber of anesthesia. The clearing of consciousness brings with it the initial reaction of body and mind to a medically controlled assault on the spine. Inchoate physical sensations become concrete hints of surgical outcome. The almost inevitable pain at the incision site brings doubts about the wisdom of undergoing surgery. Some even experience disheartening new pains; for example, a patient who has undergone a spinal fusion using bone harvested from the iliac crest may add hip pain to his or her experience. On the other hand, for some fortunate patients, the recovery room is a place of joy, as when the patient awakens with a great reduction in leg pain from relief of pressure on peripheral nerves. No matter the subjective experience, some facts remain certain: The patient's recovery, although under way, is far from over and is fraught with difficulties.

Rehabilitation after spine surgery is necessary to achieve maximum results. However, rehabilitation methods vary widely between surgeons, because many questions have uncertain answers. For example, it is not always clear which types of physical exercises are necessary. Further, the role of pain in guiding the intensity of rehabilitation is often a matter of conjecture: Should the patient exercise only to the point of pain increasing, or should pain be only a barrier through which the patient must break? And although it is clear that motivation, incentives, and expectations greatly influence patients' efforts, often providers do little to address these issues.

Surgery represents a new stage in recovery from an injury. Prior to the surgery, a noxious kind of steady state exists. Patients know how they will feel if they engage in certain activities, such as sitting or lifting. They know how to use pain medication effectively. Significant others, too, know pretty much what each day will bring. Pain, unfortunately, often acts as a familiar guide and definer of life. Surgery changes all that. Surgery heals by causing damage, through the repair or removal of pathological tissue. In other words, the surgery itself is a kind of controlled injury! Thus, the meaning of pain changes. Postoperative pain can be a sign of healing, recovery, and tissue regrowth. Once the patient overcomes the initial effects of surgery, with guidance from the rehabilitation team pain no longer causes fear and cessation of activity. Rather, a new and final phase begins wherein overcoming the pain through an aggressive set of physical and mental exercises is the best route to recovering from this medically induced insult to the body.

Because surgery damages the body, the postoperative rehabilitation process is concerned with healing, regrowth, and restoration of function at both the physical and psychological levels. Physiologically, in order to fully recover tissues must repair, muscles must strengthen, flexibility must be achieved, and, in the case of spinal fusion, bone mass must consolidate. This means replacing inactivity and avoidance of pain with physical exercises and conditioning that necessitate a temporary increase in pain. Emotionally, patients must learn to resume living and to replace the role of invalid with a measured return to normalcy, while mentally fortifying not only themselves but significant others as well. The health psychologist who understands the physical and emotional processes underlying recovery is in the best position to help patients successfully navigate the murky course of recovery.

PHYSICAL DECONDITIONING

Physiological Principles

Mayer, Gatchel, and Evans (2001) pointed out that the predominant initial effect of surgery is to produce trauma on the spine (see chapter 7 for a discussion of this process). Inflammation occurs, followed by either effective repair of tissue or, when there are large defects, replacement with collagenous scars. Often the key element in determining which of these occurs is timing of rehabilitation. Postsurgical rehabilitation is often a matter of charge and retreat—attacking the damaged and recovering tissues through aggressive rehabilitation, then allowing periods of rest and rebuilding. If, as some-

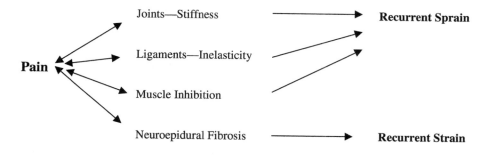

Figure 11.1. Negative effects of pain on strength, flexibility, and endurance.

times occurs, the patient is immobilized for long periods after surgery, the result can be to unnecessarily increase joint stiffness and hasten muscle atrophy.

A postoperative *deconditioning syndrome* (Mayer & Gatchel, 1988) then follows that involves a loss of physical capacity, measured by deterioration in a variety of basic elements of musculoskeletal performance such as motion, strength, endurance, and agility (e.g., Kondraske, 1986, in press), as well as decreased cardiovascular performance and muscle and tendon shortening. Pain perception is also enhanced during such deconditioning, and learned protective mechanisms, such as bracing and fear of reinjury, can lead to a dynamic vicious cycle of inactivity and loss of capacity. As physical capacity decreases, the likelihood increases of fresh sprains and strains to unprotected joints, muscles, ligaments, and discs (see Figure 11.1). On the other hand, overly aggressive therapy can have many ill effects, including damage to recovering tissues, reherniation of repaired discs, or such greatly increased pain that the patient is unable to progress through exercise. In either case, failure to find the balance between aggressive activity and therapeutic rest may lead to a cascade of biopsychosocial factors that will often impede effective rehabilitation.

Sports Medicine Principles

Sports medicine principles provide some general guidance in the rehabilitation of spine surgery patients. The following summary, previously presented by Gatchel (1991a, 1996), will focus on some of the basic principles of sports medicine deconditioning concepts and rehabilitation techniques that have been used in the extremities and are applicable to the spine.

The initial phase of most injuries is characterized by hemorrhage and edema. During the first few days, dead tissues are cleared. In the next phase healing begins, with its timing and duration related primarily to the quality of the blood supply to the area. In instances where there is a small amount of tissue injury, with relatively good nutrition and low-grade stresses (such as a wrist sprain or muscle contusion), one proceeds through this process quite quickly. However, for many spine areas, extremely high stresses, large musculoskeletal ligamentous structures, and poor blood supply usually make for considerably delayed healing.

At the end of the healing process, the injured area is left with a scar, either visible or hidden, that has matured to fill the injured area but lacks the resilience, strength, and durability of the original tissue. After spine surgery, asymmetric scars, produced by the initial injury, degeneration, or surgical intervention, may then produce significant disturbances of biomechanical performance in the critical spine joints. Most injured individuals have a natural tendency to *splint*, or protect the injured area, the first of a series of events that, in the end, leads to the deconditioning syndrome. Mental deconditioning follows as a natural consequence of the initial physical deconditioning.

As Mayer (1991) noted, the process of inactivity and disuse leading to physical deconditioning has been seen in both human and experimental animal models. Immobilization studies have consistently shown the negative effects of immobilization on soft tissue homeostasis (e.g., Akeson, Amiel, & Woo, 1980; Woo & Buckwalter, 1988). Healing tissue that has been immobilized has a great tendency to produce an amorphous, nonfunctional scar with low strength unless it has been subjected to adequate physiologic stress. Similar adverse effects of inactivity and disuse have been documented for every organ system. Bortz (1984), in reviewing the literature, found that bed rest results in protein loss of approximately 8 g per day and calcium loss of up to 1.54 g per week. Moreover, such inactivity results in a great loss in cardiovascular functioning, including decreases in stroke volume and cardiac output and increases in peripheral resistance and systolic blood pressure. Thus, physical deconditioning effects are widespread and decrease strength, flexibility, and endurance factors associated with performance. Physical deconditioning can have a significantly negative effect on the recovery of function in postsurgical patients if it is not addressed in a timely manner.

MENTAL DECONDITIONING

Mental deconditioning, initially described by Gatchel (1991a), refers to the development of a layer of psychosocial and behavioral problems that occur in response to the stress of pain and the patient's attempts to cope with it. Such psychosocial problems prevent the person from resuming a productive life style, prompting additional cessation or reduction of normal functioning. Also, the person expends psychological resources dealing with the stress, pain, and disability. In a sense, the atrophy of normal psychosocial and behavioral functioning parallels its physical counterpart.

In an elaboration of the mental deconditioning model, Gatchel (1996) presented a broad conceptual framework of three stages involved in the tran-

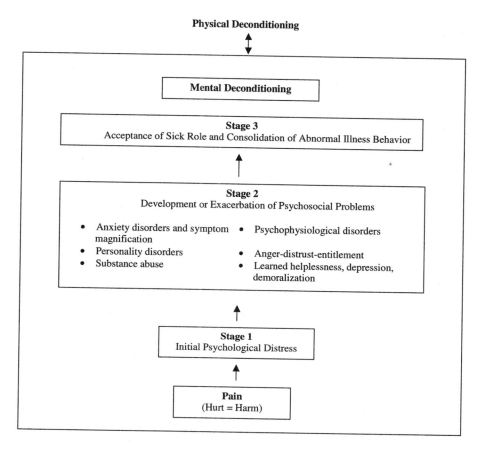

Figure 11.2. Progression of the mental deconditioning process.

sition from acute low back pain into chronic low back pain disability and accompanying psychosocial distress. This model has significant applicability to postoperative rehabilitation, as it identifies processes that can transform effective recovery into a surgically induced descent into invalidism. As presented in Figure 11.2, stage 1 of the mental deconditioning model is associated with normal emotional reactions such as anxiety, fear, and worry in response to the perception of pain and possible harm during the acute phase of an injury. Pain or hurt is usually associated with harm, and so there is a natural emotional reaction to the potential for such physical harm.

Pain that persists past a reasonable acute period of natural healing time leads to stage 2. At this stage a wider array of behavioral and psychosocial reactions and problems, such as learned helplessness, depression, somatization, anger, and distress, result from the now chronic suffering of pain and associated stress in attempting to deal with it. This model proposes that the form these problems takes depends primarily on the premorbid or pre-existing personality and psychological characteristics of the patient, as well as current socioeconomic and other environmental conditions. Thus, for example, for an individual with premorbid depression who is seriously affected economically by loss of employment due to the pain and disability, the depressive symptomatology will be greatly exacerbated during stage 2. Likewise, a person with premorbid tendencies toward high levels of pain sensitivity, especially if there are significant incentives for remaining disabled, will most likely display a great deal of pain behavior and experience excessive pain.

It should be clearly noted that this model does *not* propose that there is one primary pre-existing "pain personality." It assumes that there is a general nonspecificity in terms of the relationship between personality and psychological problems and pain, in keeping with the great deal of research that has not found any consistent personality syndrome (Gatchel, 2000; Gatchel & Turk, 1996.

Finally, this conceptual model proposes that as the layer of behavioral and psychosocial problems persists, the patient progresses to stage 3, which can be viewed as the acceptance or adoption of the sick role, during which patients are excused from their normal responsibilities and social obligations. Indeed, this may become a potent reinforcer for not becoming healthy. Medical and psychological disabilities or abnormal illness behaviors (e.g., Pilowsky, 1978) are consolidated during this phase. If compensation issues are present, these can also serve as disincentives for becoming well again.

There is usually a reciprocal pathway between the physical deconditioning and the stages of mental deconditioning. Research has demonstrated that physical deconditioning can feed back and negatively affect the emotional well-being and self-esteem of individuals (Baum, Gatchel, & Krantz, 1997). This, in turn, can lead to further psychosocial sequelae. Likewise, negative emotional reactions such as depression can significantly feed back to physical functioning by, for example, decreasing motivation to get involved in work or recreational activities, thereby contributing further to physical deconditioning. Effective rehabilitation requires breaking into this downward spiral and gradually allowing the patient to experience, recognize, and build on experiences of recovery rather than degeneration.

POST-SURGICAL REHABILITATION

The Evidence on Intensive Rehabilitation

The key to effective rehabilitation is the recognition of the potentially devastating effects of physical and mental deconditioning. Recent research supports the importance of building up to the level of intensive exercise necessary to prevent such deconditioning. For example, Manniche, Skall, et al. (1993) reported an investigation that examined the effects of dynamic back exercises on 96 patients following lumbar discectomy surgery. Patients were randomly assigned to one of two groups: The first group underwent traditional, nonaggressive rehabilitation, and the second group received an intensive rehabilitation program using heavy exercises driven by the philosophy to work "without regard for the pain." These rehabilitation programs were initiated 5 weeks after surgery and included 14 hours of exercises over a 6-week period. The intensive exercise group demonstrated much greater work capabilities and lower disability indices at 26 weeks than the traditionally rehabilitated group. In addition, these gains were maintained at the 52-week interval. Although this study did not find differences in self-report of pain or impairment, the investigators concluded that the length of treatment was inadequate to achieve better results, and they suggested a longer period of aggressive rehabilitation.

Subsequently, a similar study evaluated the intensive exercise rehabilitation approach but used a longer rehabilitation period (Manniche, Asmussen, Lauritsen, et al., 1993). The investigators found improvements in back pain and disability following the intensive exercise approach and concluded that intensive rehabilitation, which begins within a 4- to 5-week period following surgery and continues for a significant length of time, is more likely to lead to functional improvements and reduction of chronic pain. Such studies, therefore, have demonstrated that aggressive rehabilitation following shortly after surgery (5 weeks) is a practical and effective means of increasing the positive effects of surgical intervention.

Until recently, except for the above two investigations of discectomy surgery, the evaluation of aggressive postoperative rehabilitation following other forms of surgery (such as fusion surgery) had been largely neglected. This shortcoming was somewhat remedied by a study conducted by Mayer et al. (1998) that prospectively evaluated a cohort of patients who were carefully administered a functional restoration program combining aggressive rehabilitation with objective measurement of progress ($N = 1,202$). Two surgical groups—a discectomy group ($n = 123$) and a fusion group ($n = 101$)— were carefully matched to two groups of unoperated comparison patients (selected from the same patient cohort with chronic spinal disorders) on the basis of age, gender, race, length and severity of disability, diagnosis, and workers' compensation status. At 12-month follow-up, the two surgery groups had work, health care utilization, and recurrent injury outcomes comparable to those for unoperated comparison patients. Thus, in spite of the common assumption that spine surgery patients fare poorly in a workers' compensation environment, the results of this study clearly demonstrated that both fusion and discectomy patients can show remarkably successful objective outcomes at 1 year if provided effective rehabilitation.

Another study, reported by Haider, Kishino, Gray, Tomlin, and Daubert (1998), evaluated whether chronic low back pain patients who underwent surgery would demonstrate comparable gains in functional capacity relative to patients who had not undergone surgery after completing an aggressive functional restoration program. The types of surgical cases included noninstrumented fusions, laminectomies, discectomies, and decompression. A subset (n = 350) of demographically matched patients from a larger cohort (n = 483) of consecutive chronically disabled patients who had undergone functional restoration was evaluated. The findings of this study revealed that the surgical and nonsurgical groups displayed comparable levels of strength measures and improvement from pretreatment to posttreatment evaluation. Such findings imply that various functional capacity measures in surgery patients would be comparable to unoperated comparison patients when undergoing functional restoration immediately following surgery. Thus, in marked contrast to earlier studies demonstrating poor outcomes of lumbar spine surgery (e.g., Deyo, Cherkin, Loeser, Bigos, & Cociol, 1992; Turner et al., 1992), results of this study, as well as those of Mayer et al. (1998), clearly suggest that spine surgery patients can demonstrate comparably successful physical and socioeconomic outcomes relative to nonsurgical spinal patients if surgery is followed by effective functional restoration. These results are in keeping with successful outcomes of knee surgery when followed by effective and high quality postsurgical rehabilitation.

Finally, in a follow-up of Haider et al.'s (1998) study, Kishino, Polatin, Brewer, and Hoffman (2000) conducted a prospective study of the long-term (1-year) effectiveness of combined spine surgery and functional restoration. This represented the first investigation of patients who underwent spinal surgery followed immediately by a comprehensive functional restoration program. Two groups of patients were compared: One group of patients underwent surgery followed by functional restoration, and a second group did not require surgery but underwent functional restoration. At 1-year follow-up, the two groups were comparable in return-to-work rates, satisfaction, and perceived helpfulness of the treatment program.

Although the aforementioned studies found similar results, they differed in terms of when patients began the functional restoration program. Whereas one group of patients had a long delay before beginning (approximately 1 year; Mayer et. al, 1998), the other group began functional restoration almost immediately (Kishino et al., 2000). Thus, functional restoration has been found to be beneficial even if it begins quickly after surgery.

The Interdisciplinary Team

The complex phenomenon of pain involves an intimate interaction of physical and psychosocial events. It follows, then, that postoperative rehabilitation, to be effective, must recognize and make effective use of this interaction. Thus, the rehabilitation team must be interdisciplinary. The optimal team includes the treating physician, a psychologist, a physical therapist, and an occupational therapist.

The treating physician assumes a direct role in the medical management of the patient's pain and disability. The physician also should have a strong educational role with each patient; he or she should discuss expected progress, potential obstacles, and the anticipated timeline for return to activities of daily living.

The psychologist plays a major role in dealing with the day-to-day supervision of the psychosocial aspects of the patient's care. He or she assesses for and treats anxiety and fear of reinjury, depression, pain sensitivity, potential secondary gain issues (e.g., the bonus of being home with the children because of the back injury), and other psychosocial issues.

The physical therapist interacts daily with the patient to promote his or her physical progression toward recovery. The therapist needs to work with the psychologist in helping the patient overcome potential psychosocial barriers to recovery, such as exaggerated pain sensitivity and noncompliance during participation in physical therapy. The physical therapist will also need to help educate the patient by addressing the physiological basis of pain and by teaching ways to reduce the severity of intermittent pain episodes through the use of appropriate body mechanics. Also, he or she will need to underscore the importance of regaining and maintaining adequate physical conditioning to reduce the risk of reinjury and to function adequately in daily home, occupational, and recreational activities.

An occupational therapist may need to be involved in both the physical and vocational aspects of the patient's treatment. The patient may need to learn techniques for managing any residual pain on the job in ways that do not jeopardize employment status. The patient may have also become pessimistic about the prospect of returning to work and may have some financial difficulties related to a temporary inability to earn an income. The occupational therapist may also play an important role as a case worker in the following areas: contacting the employer to obtain job descriptions and other information that would be beneficial in helping the patient to set goals for rehabilitation, contacting the employer near the time of discharge to help facilitate a smooth return-to-work transition process, and helping the patient deal with any child care issues that are potential barriers to recovery.

Regularly scheduled team staff meetings are essential to ensure that all team members are "on the same page" in terms of the overall goals of the treatment program for each patient and to present a unified treatment philosophy to the patient. Any modifications to the overall treatment plan can also be made at this time, as well as a summary report of progress.

Expected Recovery Time After Spine Surgery

Recovery time refers to the expected duration of healing and convalescence after a surgical procedure, following which the patient is expected to resume normal activities of daily living. Of course, recovery may be prolonged by extenuating medical factors such as age, concomitant medical disease, postoperative complications, and psychosocial factors such as emotional distress, fear of reinjury, and secondary gain issues. In general, an uncomplicated recovery time from spine surgery varies from 6 weeks to 6 months, depending on the extent of the operative procedure. For example, a simple removal of instrumentation may result in very little down time, whereas a more complicated procedure (e.g., a two-level lumbar laminectomy/discectomy with posterior or posterior-lateral fusion) may require 24 weeks or longer for recovery.

Of course, recovery from surgery does not occur in a vacuum. Any prolonged postoperative bed rest increases the risk of complications, such as urinary tract infections, muscle atrophy, and thrombophlebitis (Polatin, Rainville, Haider, & Kishino, 2000). In general, most patients tolerate well the progression to early ambulation and independence in self-care activities. Mobilization can be initiated in the immediate postoperative period, except in arthrodesis patients. A systematic progression of activation will ensure the most optimal recovery for patients following spine surgery.

Patients Who Fail to Progress

As Polatin and colleagues (2000) noted, a postoperative patient who reports very elevated pain and who is reluctant to initiate physical activities may be difficult to initially evaluate during the first few months following surgery. Imaging technology may be misleading; normal postoperative healing may "confuse" the differentiation of scar from deformity, or it may mask indications of complicating or recurring disease. Moreover, distortion of imaging from surgical hardware may add to assessment problems.

After all efforts have been made to rule out anatomic reasons for pain complaints, the focus should shift toward correcting the patient's pain behaviors in a two-step process. First, the rehabilitation team must reassure the patient that the surgery was successful and clearly state the expectation that function will improve in spite of the pain. Second, the team should provide a systematic reinforcement of progressive physical activation, even in the face of the patient's reluctance to do so, under the direction of therapists who are comfortable with the active treatment philosophy. Backing down from active rehabilitation because of subjective pain or distress complaints, if there are no strong clinical data indicating any potential additional underlying structural pathology, will lead to the reinforcing of the patients' pain behaviors and may jeopardize successful recovery.

Indeed, rehabilitation personnel must be alert to potential incentives for disability, whether psychosocial, legal, financial, job related, or familial. This awareness allows rehabilitation members not only to better understand and serve the patient, but also to be more effective in problem solving when the patient is not progressing as expected. Failure to progress physically often

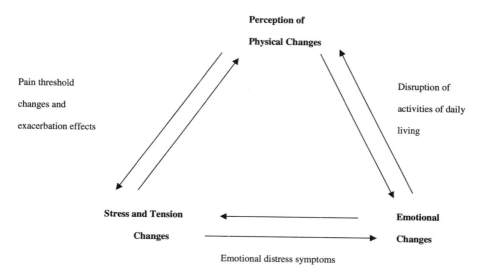

Perception of

Physical Changes

Pain threshold

changes and

exacerbation effects

Disruption of

activities of daily

living

Stress and Tension

Changes

Emotional

Changes

Emotional distress symptoms

Figure 11.3. Diagram that can be shown to patients describing the various factors that can affect the cycle of stress and pain. The therapist explains that a worsening in one area of emotion, stress, or physical difficulties can worsen problems in other areas. As reconditioning is successful, improvements in all of these areas are reciprocal.

results from psychosocial barriers to recovery; muscles and joints will not fail to respond if they are being exercised and trained as planned.

Patient education is the key to addressing barrier-to-recovery issues. The team must impress on the patient that psychosocial and emotional factors are involved in his or her pain and disability. The diagram presented in Figure 11.3 can help team members explain this relationship. Physical changes and their effects on the patient's various roles can lead to emotional changes, such as anxiety, depression, and frustration. Such emotional changes, in turn, can lead to increased stress and tension, which exacerbates the pain. Once this cycle is completed, it can begin at any new point in the cycle and start the whole process again. Educating the patient about this cycle is a very important part of the entire rehabilitation process.

THE RECONDITIONING PROCESS

Pacing

To avoid the physical and mental deconditioning syndromes and improve the outcome of surgical procedures, rehabilitation should begin to address, as early as possible, potential mobility, strength, endurance, and cardiovascular deficits resulting from inactivity following surgery. Of course, rehabilitation must be done under close medical supervision. The exercises prescribed must progress to involve simulation of customary physical activity to restore task-specific endurance, coordination, and agility. Appropriate pacing of reconditioning must be carefully monitored to avoid damage to the surgical results and to minimize pain exacerbation.

Patients should also be educated about pacing as they become more functional after surgery. Because some patients are overly and prematurely motivated to perform presurgical activities of daily living too soon, significant pain often forces them to stop and rest and may produce increased fear of activity, muscle fatigue and tension, and subsequent avoidance of activity. Gil, Ross, and Keefe (1988) suggested training patients in activity-rest cycling so that activity levels become contingent on time and not on pain. They proposed four steps in this approach:

1. Patients are helped to set a goal (in minutes or hours) for engaging in a moderate amount of activity (defined as a level of activity a patient can safely maintain without increasing pain to a very high level).
2. Patients are helped to set a goal for engaging in a limited rest period, which they take after completing their moderate-activity goal.
3. Patients are instructed to repeat this cycle frequently throughout the day.
4. After a period of days or weeks, patients are helped to gradually increase their goal for moderate activity and to decrease their goal for limited rest.

Gil et al. (1988) suggested that the ultimate goal of this process is for patients to be able to tolerate approximately 1½ to 2 hours of activity, followed by a 5- to 10-min rest period.

A mental reconditioning program, including a return to the activities of daily living characteristic of productivity, must also be initiated as early as possible. Effectively dealing with the psychosocial and behavioral problems that develop during different stages of mental deconditioning requires as much attention as dealing with the physical issues. One cannot deal with one without simultaneously dealing with the other.

GOALS

As the research reviewed in this chapter indicates, physical reconditioning can be initiated soon after surgery. Strength must be restored in a variety of modes. Initially, during the period of immobilization following surgery, the patient may be able to perform only isometric exercises. Dynamic muscle training, which has been shown to be the most efficient method of muscle training, begins later.

A reconditioning program has critically important secondary effects, including a specific beneficial effect on pain, prevention of scarring and adhesions, and improvement of cartilage nutrition (Gelberman et al., 1986). In addition, the goal of developing above-normal strength and endurance may be beneficial in protecting the damaged or unstable area that required surgery, particularly when a complete return of normal architecture can no longer be anticipated.

This active, sports-medicine approach involves a graduated progression of physical activity. Mayer (1991) summarized the important issues involved in managing physical progression so that pain complaints are minimized and tissue response is sufficient to produce increased joint mobility and muscle strength and endurance. The critical aspect of progression is that it cannot be permitted to occur in a haphazard manner. As Gatchel (1991a) observed, the rehabilitation specialist must recognize the limitations of relying solely on patient complaints and visual and palpation skills in making judgments. The therapist must also rely on the available technology for objective assessment of functional capacity for mobility, strength, and endurance and must use these tests at multiple intervals throughout the treatment process. Furthermore, a generic program designed for all patients is inappropriate, because the type and degree of deficits vary greatly from one patient to the next. Thus, rehabilitation programs must be individualized from the beginning and modified as necessary based on the progression the patient displays.

As in any training regimen, progressive resistance above the patient's current capabilities may produce a painful episode that the patient interprets as a new injury or recurrence. In actuality, the patient has merely exceeded his or her pain threshold, which has generally been reduced to a low level by disuse, emotional distress, or medication. Such episodes are common, and the treatment staff must explain their mechanisms to the patient promptly and effectively if the patient's willingness to participate in rehabilitation is to be maintained. In other words, both the patient and the health care team must understand, as well as possible, the bases for increased pain complaints during rehabilitation. Rehabilitation staff may need to investigate and rule out anatomic reasons for such pain complaints, especially if the patient experiences pain in new areas. Generally, a new or recurrent injury during rehabilitation is quite rare. Most often medical diagnostic tests at this point yield negative results, so active methods for reducing pain behaviors and pain sensitivity through aggressive physical and psychological therapies can continue.

The need for the physical therapist to constantly educate the patient regarding the progression procedures cannot be overemphasized. Thus, there must be a close alliance between the patient and the rehabilitation specialist throughout the therapy process. Like the psychologist, the therapist must be aware of the often-paradoxical interrelationship between pain and progression. The physical therapist should reiterate to the patient the procedures that were involved in the surgery and the physical basis for continued pain and elaborate the rationale for aggressive rehabilitation. When flare-ups occur, the therapist can teach the patient how to avoid misinterpreting these as a sign of failure to progress, thereby avoiding discouragement and resistance to training regimens. The therapist must be diligent in educating the patient in pain relief maneuvers and prepared to perform physical quantification tests if pain increases. When the patient is able to observe progress in physical capacity in spite of pain, he or she develops a sense of mastery over fear and pain and begins seeing himself or herself as more functional and on the road to recovery.

CONCLUSION

The process of postsurgical rehabilitation is most effective when conducted by a highly experienced interdisciplinary team. Following months or years of pain-limited activity, most patients begin the surgical process hampered by physical and mental deconditioning. Further, the surgery most often produces pain that can, if not properly addressed, exacerbate the deconditioning process. The rehabilitation process, therefore, should begin quickly after surgery. Its primary goal is to improve functioning through the use of aggressive physical therapy reconditioning exercises combined with psychological treatment.

12

PSYCHOLOGICAL ASPECTS OF POSTSURGICAL REHABILITATION: THE FUNCTIONAL RESTORATION APPROACH

Recovery from spine surgery is a slow, confusing process. Periods of soaring hopefulness may alternate with desperation. Small gains in functional ability or reduction in pain may seem almost inconsequential in comparison to the patient's state before injury, limiting motivation for rehabilitation. Patients often become quite skeptical. If pain persists, they may doubt the surgeon's ability. They may even come to question the validity of their own pain experience, wondering whether the pain is real or psychosomatic. They are frequently angry about the past, distressed about the present, and terrified about the future.

Recovery from spine surgery involves significant, unique stresses and concerns. The psychologist can become a partner in helping the patient identify and deal with these problems to achieve the best possible outcome of surgery. This chapter has two purposes. First, we describe a well-established functional restoration approach to postoperative rehabilitation of the surgery patient, give general time frames for rehabilitation following different types of surgeries, and describe general exercise programs. The *functional restoration approach* combines careful timing of progress with objective outcome measurement to provide the most effective postsurgical rehabilitation possible.

Later in the chapter we focus on some special psychosocial issues involved in postoperative rehabilitation. Unfortunately, there has been little research on these particular topics; therefore, this section draws more on the clinical experience of the authors than on a research base. In our experience, these psychosocial issues are the most frequently encountered, and adequately addressing them is critical to the patient's recovery and return to a more functional lifestyle and a more sanguine outlook.

OVERVIEW OF A FUNCTIONAL RESTORATION PROGRAM

Our functional restoration approach to rehabilitation after spine surgery is based on the concepts of physical and mental deconditioning discussed in chapter 11. Exhibit 12.1 presents its major components. This interdisciplinary approach begins with the basic assumption that postsurgical patients are stiff, weak, and lacking in physical endurance. They must be mobilized and exercised to improve their physical and functional capacities so that they can successfully return to activities of daily living. Dysfunctional pain behaviors, symptomatic emotional distress, and behavioral issues are recognized as potential psychosocial barriers to recovery, which are listed in Exhibit 12.2. A rehabilitation team member defines such barriers for each patient during an initial evaluation soon after surgery. It is then the responsibility of the team to overcome these recovery barriers so that rehabilitation may proceed to the end point of return to productivity and activities of daily living.

Polatin et al. (2000) provided an excellent description of the postsurgical functional restoration program offered at the West Coast Spine Restoration Center (WCSRC) in Riverside, California. This is a therapist-directed

EXHIBIT 12.2
Barriers to Recovery in the Postsurgical Rehabilitation Process

- Financial and other disincentives to recovery
- Compliance and resistance issues
- Excessive pain sensitivity and poor pain coping skills
- Emotional distress: Anxiety, fear, anger, depression
- Employer issues: Anger, uncertainty about return to work
- Substance abuse
- Personality disorders
- Malingering

rehabilitation center that treats a large volume of postsurgical patients each year. Referring physicians may dictate their own preferences for rehabilitation progression for particular patients, and they receive direct feedback from the rehabilitation team. The postsurgical program is divided into preprogram and program phases and has separate tracks for younger and older patients, who may differ in the intensity of reconditioning required. Table 12.1 describes the timetables associated with the different types of spine surgery.

Before rehabilitation begins, the team holds a conference to formulate recommendations for the interdisciplinary rehabilitation effort, including physical and occupational therapy. The psychologist presents the data from the psychological evaluation, makes treatment recommendations, and discusses potential obstacles to improvement. Once the team's recommendations are finalized, it reviews the treatment plan with the patient.

The postsurgical preprogram is initiated anywhere between 8 and 16 weeks after surgery, depending on the surgical procedure. The preprogram consists primarily of stretching for 2 to 6 weeks, as dictated by the particular patient's response during this preprogram phase. Supervised mobilization, including range of motion exercises, begins as a 1-hour session twice weekly, and then progresses to three times a week. During this period, the patient undergoes range-of-motion measurements before starting and then at regular intervals thereafter. Swiss ball stretches are used to initiate the mobilization process, with progression to light stabilization exercises. Usually, manual stretches are not initiated until the next phase, but cardiovascular training on a treadmill or stationary bike is a standard part of the preprogram phase. In addition, mobilization and walking in a therapy pool may also be offered depending on the readiness of the patient.

Subsequent progression to the postsurgical program is dictated by the patient's degree of response in the preprogram phase but normally occurs within 6 weeks. This phase, in turn, lasts from 6 to 8 weeks, although typically it lasts longer for fusion patients. At the start of this phase, the patient undergoes quantification testing, which objectively measures the physical capabilities that are targets for rehabilitation. Such testing includes the following: a submaximal effort treadmill test and upper body extremity (UBE)

TABLE 12.1
Timetable for Progression of Postsurgical Care at the West Coast Spine Restoration Center

Activity	Approximate Time Following Surgery		
	Lumbar Laminectomy/Discectomy	Anterior Cervical Fusion	Lumbar Fusion
Postoperative hospitalization	1–2 days	2–3 days	4–5 days
Program for activities of daily living	Day 1	Day 1	Day 1
Stretching preprogram	6–8 weeks	14 weeks	12 weeks
Rehabilitation program	8–10 weeks	16 weeks	14 weeks
Discharge	5 months	6 months	6 months

Note. From P. B. Polatin, J. Rainville, T. T. Haider, and N. D. Kishino, 2000, "Postoperative Treatment: Outpatient Medical Rehabilitation," in T. G. Mayer, R. J. Gatchel, and P. B. Polatin (Eds.), *Occupational Musculoskeletal Disorders*, Philadelphia: Lippincott, Williams & Wilkins, p. 541. Adapted with permission from the authors.

protocol, a lifting test, and material-handling tests. Trunk extension testing is not yet performed in this phase.

The patient then attends the program 5 days a week, for 2 hours per day, during which period he or she performs regular restorative exercises. In addition, the patient participates in physical therapy three times per week, which consists of treadmill, stationary bike, UBE training to tolerance, aerobic and manual stretching sessions, and strength training on weight machines. The team monitors the strengthening program very closely. Patients begin at low weights and progress slowly under careful supervision. Additionally, they perform lumbar stabilization exercises. Occupational therapy, provided twice a week, consists of functional activities training, particularly directed at lifting drills, material handling, and positional activities related to subsequent work requirements. Finally, an educational "back school" provided once a week covers various relevant topics such as anatomy, body mechanics, nutrition, communication skills, lumbar stabilization exercises, stress management, benefits of exercise, exercise pacing, and job readiness.

When the patient has completed the postsurgical program, he or she is typically given work restrictions, initially with limited lifting and no repetitive bending or stooping. At this point, the patient may return to the job or go through vocational rehabilitation, which is offered to almost every injured worker in most states. The patient continues to make regular follow-up visits to the initial referring surgeon for up to 2 years postoperatively and is also encouraged to maintain a home fitness program based on the exercise routines learned during the formal rehabilitation at WCSRC.

Of course, an important part of all rehabilitation programs is weekly staff meetings to discuss the status and progression of each patient and any modifications that need to be made. In addition, a psychologist is always available to provide help in dealing with any psychosocial and barriers-to-recovery issues that may be negatively affecting rehabilitation progress. Many of these issues will have been identified during the presurgery or postoperative psychological evaluation.

The psychologist may provide individual psychological treatment, group therapy, or marital or family therapy to help patients cope more adaptively with psychosocial barriers. Cognitive–behavioral interventions are used to address pain-related depression, anger, anxiety, and fear. The number of sessions provided is dictated by the particular demands of the patient. Typically, for patients with a moderate level of psychosocial distress, 10 to 16 individual treatment sessions, 10 group therapy sessions, or one or two marital or family therapy sessions are sufficient to reduce interference with rehabilitation.

Psychological barriers to recovery, as well as negative emotional reactions during the postrehabilitation process, need to be addressed for the rehabilitation progress to occur smoothly. When the patient fails to progress in physical rehabilitation or when compliance is a problem, the barriers to recovery and emotional issues need to be immediately addressed. The multimodal disability management program (MDMP; Gatchel, 1991b) provides a framework for addressing these issues.

MDMP is based on a cognitive–behavioral approach to crisis intervention, and it focuses on overcoming psychosocial difficulties that may significantly interfere with returning a patient to a productive, functional lifestyle. Treatment focuses on events in the present or the recent past, and the psychologist helps patients better understand thoughts that contribute to feelings and behaviors. It is often helpful for the therapist to explore with the patient any early learning experiences or long-standing psychological issues that may be affecting his or her reactions to recent life experiences. For example, a patient from a family background involving significant emotional deprivation may experience chronic feelings of anger, depression, and low self-esteem. Such issues, along with the distress and emotions that accompany them, may be rekindled quickly when the patient finds himself or herself in a medical-compensation-disability system that fosters dependency.

MDMP encompasses four areas of treatment:

1. individual and group counseling (e.g., on coping with family or work problems).
2. family counseling, during which family members may be encouraged to take an active part in the rehabilitation process and are provided information about the philosophy and specific details of MDMP.
3. stress management training that involves initial training in muscle relaxation, followed by exercises in guided imagery or hypnotherapy (or both) in which patients practice relaxation while imagining themselves in various stressful situations.

Patients also receive biofeedback sessions in which they refine their relaxation skills, with the understanding that these skills will help them cope more effectively with any residual pain and discomfort.

4. cognitive–behavior skills training, including instruction in rational versus irrational thinking and the use of positive coping statements to manage stress.

The final component of the MDMP approach is to help patients maintain their rehabilitation gains. Marlatt and Gordon (1985) originally developed a relapse-prevention model to address the potential problems in long-term maintenance of new health behaviors. This model focuses on helping patients acquire new coping strategies that will reduce the risk of an initial relapse and prevent any relapse from escalating into a total relapse. Keefe and Van Horn (1993) subsequently modified this model for use with pain patients and delineated various relapse prevention methods. Some methods that we have found to be effective are the following:

- Caution patients during the rehabilitation program that setbacks may occur and that, when they do , the patient should contact a health care professional and not become alarmed.
- Remind patients to maintain their exercise program, and help them establish an exercise program for use at home or at a local health club.
- Remind patients to continue to practice their pain coping skills (such as relaxation and stress management) on a regular basis.
- Contact patients on a regular basis during the year following rehabilitation to be certain that treatment goals are being maintained; patients may need to come back to the facility for refresher courses.

It is often useful to include this information, along with any other advice and recommendations, in a written booklet the patient can take home.

Although a functional restoration approach is essentially interdisciplinary, its success rests, to a large extent, on the effectiveness of psychological intervention. The health psychologist must be, at once, both supportive and challenging. At times the psychologist may have to add emotional pain to the physical pain already being experienced. For example, helping a very active, highly physical individual to accept that he or she may have significant long-term limitations or may be unable to work at a physically demanding job may mean taking the patient through a significant process of grieving. Spine surgery patients often need to express anger, depression, and fear in psychotherapy before they achieve acceptance. Because such emotions are frequently then expressed outside the psychologist's office in physical or occupational therapy or to the physician, the psychologist must regularly communicate psychotherapy issues to other members of the interdisciplinary team.

PSYCHOTHERAPY TOPICS IN POSTSURGICAL REHABILITATION

Expectations

Most patients see surgery as a life-changing event, an aggressive attempt to regain control of their lives, eliminate pain, and return to preinjury levels of functioning. In other words, most patients have very high expectations for the results spine surgery can achieve. The reality of spine surgery, however, is often at great variance with these expectations. Although a few lucky patients can eventually become pain free and have unrestricted activity levels, it is more often the case that recovery is only partial and that postoperative rehabilitation is both slow and difficult. As noted in the Introduction, spine surgery on average achieves only about a 50% reduction in perceived pain and moderate improvement in functioning. When expectations crash against the rocky reality of postoperative symptoms and limitations, the psychological results can be debilitating. Even a successful surgery can seem like a total failure if the patient's excessively high hopes are not met.

One of the most important rehabilitation tasks of the psychologist, then, is to help the patient reconcile his or her surgical outcome expectations with the new reality. Setting expectations should begin in the preoperative period; during presurgical psychological screening (PPS) or in a preparation for surgery program surgery patients are informed about the usual course of recovery, including average recovery time, pain experience, pacing of postoperative activities, and the expected ultimate outcome of the surgery. However, many patients are quietly but certainly overly optimistic, despite the efforts of the health care team to educate them about the surgical results they should expect. During the postoperative period, therefore, expectations warrant a great deal of discussion.

One effective approach to discussing expectations during postoperative rehabilitation is to help the patient perform an "outcome projection" (see Exhibit 12.3). This projection is analogous to the budget projections accountants perform. The projection divides outcome into its key parts: pain, function, medication, emotional state, and personal goals (e.g., improvement in sleep, weight loss). Patients identify what they would consider excellent, good, and fair results at specific points in time. We suggest that patients complete projections at 1, 3, and 6 months and at 1 year after surgery. The psychologist and patient discuss the projections in a therapy session, with the psychologist helping the patient adjust projections so that they are realistic—not overly optimistic or pessimistic.

EXHIBIT 12.3
Worksheet for Patient Outcome Projections

Patient's name: _____

Time after surgery: _____

Instructions: Provide ratings of the following experiences and abilities, on a scale of 1 to 10, that you feel would constitute a fair outcome, a good outcome, and an excellent outcome.

Outcome Criterion	What would be a *fair* outcome?	What would be a *good* outcome?	What would be an *excellent* outcome?
Worst pain level experienced			
Least pain level experienced			
Average pain level experienced			
Need to take medications: _____ _____ _____			
Ability to participate in recreational activities: _____ _____ _____			
Ability to perform work activities: _____ _____			
Ability to participate in family caretaking activities: _____ _____			
Depression level experienced			
Anger level experienced			
Tension experienced			
Ability to achieve other goals: _____ _____			

Besides providing a realistic guideline to acceptable improvement, the outcome projections accomplish one other important task—they help patients recognize small but essential gains. When patients have experienced such immense losses in function and emotional stability that they are willing to undergo surgery, it is sometimes difficult for them to recognize incremental daily and weekly improvements if they constantly compare their state at any one point in time to their abilities prior to the injury. The distance between the two can be overwhelming, and frustration can draw away all the energy needed for rehabilitation. By reminding patients of their projections, psychologists can help them focus on the gains they are making rather than the losses they have sustained. These gains can also be made concrete through a record of progress in physical therapy exercises.

Pain and Pain Control

Most patients undergo surgery to get relief from pain. Although they are distressed by loss of function, inability to work, decreased sexual activity, and the many other changes resulting from their injuries, it is the experience of pain that is most noxious and from which they most desire escape. Unfortunately, surgery often causes pain, by virtue of harming the body in order to repair it. Further, postoperative rehabilitation exercises often induce more pain as tissues build and strengthen. These increases and variations in pain can be both disheartening and confusing to postoperative patients. Further, the role of pain changes as rehabilitation proceeds. Early after surgery, when tissues are most inflamed and healing begins, pain acts as a natural braking mechanism. Properly used, it can help the patient recognize the upper limits of acceptable activity. However, after an initial recovery phase (usually about 6 weeks), pain is more an obstacle—a sensation through which the patient must push rather than a barrier at which the patient must stop.

The vagaries of pain and its course during the rehabilitation process point to a very significant component of postoperative psychotherapy: Treatment involves a large degree of education. It is not that patients simply need to identify and discuss problems they are having. Rather, for rehabilitation to be effective, the patient must understand the reasons for the changes he or she is experiencing. In no area is this more important than in the perception of and response to pain. The following six points need to be conveyed to and discussed with patients:

1. Pain is an inevitable part of the rehabilitation process.
2. During the initial phases after surgery (usually up to 6 weeks), pain must act as a guide to limit activity. During this initial phase, patients should not push activity to the point of experiencing a significant increase in pain. Patients should discuss with their physician when it is safe to "push through" the pain.
3. During the initial phases of recovery, medication must be used carefully. Pain medication greatly reduces pain perception, and if the patient engages in excessive activity, recovery may be set back.

4. Pain does not necessarily signal new injury, and patients should not be afraid of pain. They should be concerned about a new injury only when they experience pain in new body areas or when the pain has a new quality (e.g., burning or shooting). An increase in intensity of already existing pain is normal.

5. Strengthening muscles always creates pain, and this is to be expected. Once the patient has passed the initial phase of recovery, pain increases are acceptable and in fact may indicate that the patient is increasing muscle strength sufficiently to recover.

6. Setbacks in the pain experience occur frequently. Patients will feel as though the pain is resolving, then suddenly it reappears. These setbacks need to be viewed from the broad perspective of overall improvement. A sports analogy may be helpful: A team that wins the championship does not win every game. Losses do not mean total defeat, and they identify areas needing further improvement.

Hypnotherapy, biofeedback, relaxation, and the other techniques for reducing the pain experience discussed in chapter 9 can be of great value during the rehabilitation process in reducing muscle tension, distraction from pain, and alteration of the processing of pain signals. Learning proper body mechanics minimizes the stress on healing tissues, reducing spine pain. Involving oneself in pleasurable activities—reading, studying, watching movies—also promotes pain control. In some cases, patients may need to accept medication as a necessary component of life.

Medications

Patients are almost inevitably placed on a number of medications after spine surgery. Most patients are discharged from the hospital on opioid pain medications. If they were depressed or anxious before the surgery, they usually continue on psychotropic medications during the postoperative phase. Therefore, the integration of pharmacotherapy into the rehabilitation process is essential.

A general goal of postsurgical rehabilitation is to ultimately reduce medication use to as low a level as possible. Initially, however, as Polatin and Gajraj (2002) noted, when used in a multidisciplinary setting pain-relieving medication can be quite beneficial. It can reduce emotional distress and increase the patient's ability to engage in an exercise program. As noted in chapter 4 (see Merskey & Moulin, 1999), the likelihood of becoming addicted to pain medication is quite low. In fact, most patients typically plateau at a particular dose, beyond which further increases are not required to control the immediate pain. However, as the patient progresses in rehabilitation, the psychologist should discuss with him or her the desirability of eliminating the use of opioids. Although pain may increase somewhat during the withdrawal process, the following will likely eventually occur:

- Pain will be less than when the patient was taking opioids.
- The patient will not have to struggle with opioid side effects, such as constipation or cognitive impairment.
- The patient will not run the long-term health risks associated with opioid medications (e.g., liver damage from acetaminophen-containing hydrocodone preparations such as Lortab or Vicodin).

To facilitate opioid reduction, a trial with a nonsteroidal anti-inflammatory (NSAID) can be introduced. This NSAID can be maintained as the patient is systematically weaned from the opioid. Then the NSAID can be reduced. As opioids are withdrawn, the patient should use self-regulation strategies such as hypnotherapy or pain-control imagery to both reduce noxious sensations and counteract the increase in arousal that may occur. If the patient experiences sleep problems during the process (which is typical), relaxation exercises can be supplemented with a traditional sedative such as Ambien® or Sonata®. An anxiolytic, such as a benzodiazepine like Ativan®, may also prove useful. Such medications are used only short term, as they carry with them the likelihood of habituation or dependency. In the end, even after the struggles of withdrawal, most patients who have discontinued the use of opioid medications are quite pleased.

Although the elimination of medications is desirable, it is not the most important goal for most patients, and it may be counterproductive in some cases. Certainly, antidepressant medications may need to be maintained long after discharge from the rehabilitation program; it may take a year or even longer to reverse the biochemical basis of depression. Withdrawing antidepressant medication too early can send a patient into a downward emotional spiral, often accompanied by a return of or increase in pain. More controversial, however, is the long-term use of opioid medications such as Oxycontin, MS Contin, Kadian, or Duragesic patches. For some patients, chronic use of these extended release products is critical to maintaining a productive lifestyle. We have frequently seen postoperative patients taking no opioids who are depressed to the point of being suicidal or unable to function at all. Maintaining such patients on a stable level of chronic opioid therapy often reduces their emotional distress and allows them a much greater quality of life. Two notes of caution about chronic opioid therapy are in order. First, patients must sign a medication contract stating the exact amount of medication they will be given and the consequences (usually discharge) if they call in early to receive more medicine or make excuses for losing it. Second, chronic opioid therapy should be used only if it achieves its goals of reducing emotional distress and improving function. If these do not occur, alternative pain control techniques, such as spinal cord stimulation, should be considered.

Acceptance of Limitations

Most patients have to accept something less than complete recovery following spine surgery. Patients may have to give up strenuous recreational activities, such as skiing or skating, that put the spine at risk for further injury. Most other activities, although still possible, need to be altered significantly. Patients may need to modify their golf swings and take more breaks when mowing the yard. The need to maintain a physical therapy exercise routine may alter the pattern of leisure and work activities.

There are three areas where the most fundamental long-term limitations are experienced. First, patients will experience periods of stiffness, pain, and limitations in movement perhaps for the rest of their lives, and they need to develop a set of skills for dealing with these episodes. Second, spontaneity in activities is problematic. Patients must remember to move correctly, avoid certain movements, and even find ways to halt certain actions that are almost reflexive. For example, the mother of a toddler may have to learn not to lift the child, even when it is crying or hurt (except in emergencies), lest an already weakened back suffer a recurrence of injury. Finally, patients may have to change jobs, especially if their vocation prior to the surgery involved heavy labor. This change may mean earning a reduced income, retraining, and accepting positions they may have thought were impossible. For example, a construction worker who abhorred the idea of working behind a desk may need to find just such a position to earn a living.

One of the key elements of psychotherapy with postoperative patients involves helping them come to accept such changes and limitations. The psychologist can introduce the following points for discussion:

- *Your value is not in what you do, but who you are.* In Western society, work and achievement often define an individual. To regain self-esteem, patients must often redefine themselves with a new set of accomplishments. To facilitate this process, the psychologist can have the patient make an inventory of his or her strengths and weaknesses and help the patient think of ways to build on the strengths.
- *You may have lost a great deal, but you can also gain from the loss.* Many patients have gone into blue collar work out of economic necessity, thereby limiting their intellectual or academic development. Job retraining, which may be available through the state vocational rehabilitation agency or the employer, may allow the patient to develop and use untapped cognitive and intellectual abilities. The psychologist can help the patient

explore areas that he or she previously considered but discarded because of time pressure or economic necessity.

- *Your family and friends love and appreciate you despite the injury.* Patients frequently report feeling "useless" because they cannot provide for their families or perform household tasks as they did prior to the injury, but most often this judgment is self-imposed. Family members usually are quite supportive, especially if the patient learns and remembers to reciprocate that support. The psychologist can invite family members or friends to sessions to discuss their feelings about the patient and how they can be mutually supportive. Family members can learn how to reinforce improvements in activity and avoid making invalidism a desirable state. When a marriage ends as a result of the injury, in most cases it was troubled before the injury, and the psychologist can help the patient see the end of the relationship as a chance to begin a better one.
- *You already have the ability to adapt.* Everyone experiences a lot of difficulty in life—difficulty that requires strength, flexibility, and resources to overcome. With the psychologist, the patient can explore past stresses and ways of coping with them and find ways to build on those coping strategies to deal with ongoing pain and limitations.

Termination

The long odyssey that began with the onset of pain and carried the patient through lengthy medical treatment, surgery, and rehabilitation must inevitably come to some sort of conclusion. Because the pain and limitations may continue indefinitely, albeit at a reduced and controllable level, how is one to decide when rehabilitation ends? And how does the health psychologist help the patient deal with what comes next?

Generally, interdisciplinary treatment is concluded when any or all of several events occur:

- The patient is declared at *maximum medical improvement* (MMI), defined as a state when the patient's condition is not expected to change by greater than 3%. In some states, such as Texas, a patient with a workers' compensation injury is declared at MMI on a statutory basis at 24 months after the injury regardless of the patient's current medical treatment or symptoms.
- The patient returns to work at full duty.
- The patient chooses not to undergo any further treatment.
- The health care team decides that no further treatment will be effective.

For the patient, the end of active treatment can be quite traumatic. Especially when pain and limitations persist, the patient often does not want treatment to end. Further, financial considerations may come into play. For example, many patients are uncertain whether the employer will allow them to return to work and wish to delay termination to get clearer resolution or explore job options. Patients involved in litigation may feel it will hurt their case if treatment is concluded. Family members, especially, may press for continuation of treatment in the desperate hope that the patient will continue to improve.

Just as the patient must accept limitations, the psychologist must accept that there are limitations to the help that he or she can provide. The psychologist must reach a point, normally coincident with the patient's medical discharge, where he or she is satisfied that the patient has learned necessary skills to deal with the pain and that little more can be gained by further treatment. The patient may seem desperate to hang on to the psychotherapy relationship, expressing fears and concerns about his or her ability to cope. In fact, it is not unusual to see an increase in emotional distress or in pain just before discharge. Except in extreme cases, the health psychologist must resist the temptation to respond to these behaviors by requesting additional treatment. Most often, further treatment is ineffective and expensive and furthers a dependency that both is difficult to break and denigrates the patient's self-esteem.

The rehabilitation team should consider termination a critical part of treatment from the very outset of intervention. Establishing the boundaries of the therapeutic relationship limits the patient's focus to pain management and recovery of function. Psychologists can refer patients with long-term issues, such as physical or sexual abuse or personality disorders, to a therapist who specializes in such intervention or to a local community mental health center.

Beginning about halfway through treatment, the psychologist should discuss termination directly with the patient. He or she should acknowledge the difficulty of ending both the psychological and medical treatment and ask the patient to discuss any concerns he or she may have. Together they should review all the gains the patient has made and how these were achieved, and the patient should be encouraged to take pride in these achievements.

The psychologist should resist the temptation to act as an advocate for the patient in the posttreatment period. This is a difficult but important issue. The patient will be facing many problems: with the employer, with attorneys, with social services, perhaps even with the law. Patients may implore the psychologist to contact these individuals or agencies and act on their behalf. It is important that the psychologist keep within his or her role as an agent of change and development for the patient and, if necessary, to refer the patient to a social worker or occupational therapist for posttreatment support.

In addition, the psychologist can refer the patient to resources that provide assistance after treatment has ended. Web sites, such as spineuniverse.com and spine-health.com, can provide important information and links to other important services. Referrals to community support groups, such as those under the aegis of the American Chronic Pain Association, can be beneficial, as can information about religious and faith-based organizations.

Finally, the psychologist should consider offering a support group for program graduates. Most patients will attend only a few times, if at all, but such a group provides a safety net that may give the patient a greater sense of support.

REIMBURSEMENT ISSUES FOR PSYCHOLOGISTS IN REHABILITATION PROGRAMS

In this era of managed care, there has been an erosion of reimbursement for comprehensive, interdisciplinary rehabilitation programs, and especially for psychological services within such programs. In most cases, psychological services need to be preauthorized by the insurance carrier. Unfortunately, pre-authorization issues can sometimes obligate psychologists working in a fee-for-service practice to limit their practice to treatment of primary or comorbid mental health disorders (e.g., major depression in a cardiac patient or adjustment disorders in a patient with newly diagnosed diabetes) to get reimbursed. Six new current procedural terminology (CPT) codes have recently become available for behavioral assessment and interventions with physical health patients. These codes eliminate the need for a mental health diagnoses for psychological services to be reimbursed (Smith, 2002). Unfortunately, these codes are usually reimbursed at a significantly lower level than medical CPT codes. Table 12.2 lists the behavior CPT codes.

Rather than a fee-for-service approach, it may be useful for psychologists to integrate into interdisciplinary private group practices; such practices may have an advantage over independent practitioners when contracting with third-party payers. Some health management companies may be more willing to contract with a relatively small number of group practices than with a large number of individual providers, thus making the integrated practice more attractive (American Psychological Association Practice Directorate, 1996). Of course, the laws are different in each state as to how psychologists and physicians can associate in practice (e.g., partnerships, professional corporations, limited liability companies). Psychologists interested in these arrangements are referred to the American Psychological Association Practice Directorate's (1996) publication *Models for Multidisciplinary Arrangements: A State-by-State Review of Options* and should also seek legal counsel.

CONCLUSION

So, at last, the patient's search for a cure is complete. If the patient has not come full circle to return to his or her preinjury level of functioning, at

TABLE 12.2
Health and Behavior Assessment and Intervention Codes

Code	Description
CPT 96150	Initial assessment of patients to determine the biological, psychological, and social factors affecting the patient's physical health and any treatment problems.
CPT 96151	Reassessment to evaluate the patient's condition and determine the need for further treatment. A clinician other than the one who conducted the patient's initial assessment period may perform it.
CPT 96152	Intervention to modify the psychological, behavioral, cognitive, and social factors affecting the patient's physical health and well-being. Examples include increasing the patient's awareness about his or her disease and using cognitive–behavioral approaches to initiate a physician-prescribed diet and exercise regimen.
CPT 96153	Intervention provided to a group. An example would be a smoking cessation program including educational information, cognitive–behavioral treatment, and social support. Group sessions typically last for 90 minutes and involve 8–10 patients.
CPT 96154	Intervention provided to a family with the patient present. For example, a psychologist may use relaxation techniques with both a patient and parent to reduce fear of reinjury when the patient returns to work.
CPT 96155	Intervention provided to the family without the patient present. An example would be working with a spouse to shape the active exercise of a patient, such as praising successful progression in the program and ignoring avoidance behavior.

Note. CPT = current procedure terminology. More information about these new health and behavior CPT codes can be found online at www.apa.org/practice/cpt.

least he or she has obtained the best possible outcome of surgery. Pain has been reduced, quality of life improved. Emotional stability has returned. Life has its imperfections and limitations, but these have for the most part become challenges rather than obstacles. The health psychologist has been instrumental throughout the process. In conducting PPS, the psychologist has identified risk factors that might have diminished surgical outcome and developed treatments that minimized these risk factors. With the assistance of the psychologist, the patient prepared thoroughly for the surgery, learning to minimize stress, control pain, and turn irrational thoughts into ones that augment recovery. After surgery, the psychologist participated as part of an interdisciplinary rehabilitation team in helping the patient to benefit most fully from the surgery and ultimately to reintegrate into the work and home environments. Thus, the psychologist has assisted the patient in learning that although surgery may not have produced the dramatic and immediate changes he or she once desired, it has improved life and created many gains to counteract the significant losses of spine injury.

GLOSSARY

arachnoiditis: scarring or adherence of the nerve roots to each other

autogenous bone graft: bone graft taken from the patient's own body to be used in a spinal fusion

bone scanning: diagnostic procedure in which radioactive technetium is injected into the patient's vein; calcium is tagged with this material and scanning identifies areas of high metabolic activity to help identify bone fractures, infection, or tumors

catecholamines: adrenaline and norepinephrine; responsible for the fight or flight response

cauda equina: as the spinal cord terminates, the nerve roots form this structure, having the appearance of a "horses's tail", in the lumbar portion of the spine

chemonucleolysis: the injection of an enzyme into the disc to remove a small amount of disc tissue; used in the treatment of disc herniation

circumferential fusion (also known as 360° fusion): spinal fusion procedure in which an anterior interbody fusion is performed as well as a posterior fusion

computed tomography (CT): radiographic imaging procedure that produces cross-sectional views of the body in multiple planes

cytotoxic T-cells: cells that circulate and destroy abnormal cells

deconditioning syndrome: progressive worsening of a patient's general fitness due to lack of activity associated with pain

dermatomal distribution (of pain): pain that radiates in the pattern of a specific nerve root

differential spinal: diagnostic injection study used to help assess the role of pain sensitivity by determining if the patient's pain is primarily central (i.e., psychological) or peripheral in origin

disc annulus: the outer section of an intervertebral disc; composed of multiple layers

disc bulge: condition generally related to degeneration; the disc space decreases in height resulting in a bulging of the outer annulus of the disc

disc disruption: tears in the layers of the disc annulus, generally representing the early stages of disc degeneration

disc herniation: condition in which disc tissue passes through (herniates) the outer wall of the annulus; may result in nerve root compression

disc nucleus: the inner part of an intervertebral disc; a normal disc has a high water content

discectomy: surgical procedure in which part of a disc is removed

discography: diagnostic procedure performed by injecting contrast into the disc nucleus; used to assess the condition of the disc and to aid in determining if the disc is related to the patient's pain

Distress and Risk Assessment Method (DRAM): a psychological screening tool combining elements of a modified version of the Zung Depression Inventory (Zung, 1965) and the Modified Somatic Perception Questionnaire (Main, 1983); a test of heightened autonomic or somatic awareness, or "somatic anxiety"

dural sac: the layer of tissue covering the spinal cord and cauda equina containing cerebrospinal fluid

edema: swelling

electromyogram: a nerve conduction study used to identify significant nerve root compression or irritation

empowerment: a process of enabling others to take control of their own lives

endplate: the part of the disc that interfaces with the bony vertebral bodies

epidural space: the open space just outside the dura

facet joints: bilateral structures formed by vertebral posterior elements at each spinal motion segment; responsible for load bearing and motion

facet rhizotomy: procedure in which the nerves associated with pain in the facet are ablated

failed back surgery syndrome: persistent or recurrent chronic pain after one or more surgical procedures on the lumbosacral spine

foramen (plural *foramiena*): opening formed by the posterior elements of adjacent vertebral bodies through which a nerve root passes from the cauda equina to distal locations

foraminotomy: surgical procedure in which the superior arch of the foramen is removed; typically done to reduce bony compression of the exiting nerve root

homeostasis: steady state or balance

hyperextension (of the spine): excessive backward bending motion

hypertrophy (of facet joints): related to degeneration of a spinal segment in which there is increased bony growth of the facets; may result in compression of neural structures

hypervigilance: heightened awareness of physical symptoms

hypochondriasis: preoccupation with the body and concomitant fears of illness and disease

hysteria: a psychoanalytic term describing patients who have physical symptoms that arise from emotional conflicts rather than an organic basis

iatrogenic: caused by medical intervention

internal fixation: metallic devices such as screws and rods that are implanted in a spine segment to help stabilize it; usually done in conjunction with spinal fusion

intradiscal electrothermal therapy (IDET): intervention in which a catheter with a heating element is placed in the invertebral disc for the treatments of early, painful disc degeneration

intrathecally: into the sheath covering the spinal cord

lamina: part of the vertebrae forming the posterior margin of the spinal canal

laminectomy/discectomy: a surgery in which part of the lamina is removed to gain access to the disc space (laminectomy) and then to remove disc tissue responsible for compressing neural tissue (discectomy)

learned helplessness: condition wherein people come to believe they have no ability to control or influence the outcome of events; based on research by Seligman (1975)

ligmentum flavum: band of fibrous tissue passing between the lamina of adjacent vertebrae

lymphocytes: white blood cells that modulate immune system response

lymphoid organs: bone marrow, thymus, lymph nodes, spleen, tonsils, appendix, and lymphoid tissue in the small intestine

magnetic resonance imaging (MRI): diagnostic imaging tool using a strong magnet to create images

malingering: the intentional production of false or grossly exaggerated physical or psychological symptoms motivated by external incentives

meninges: three membranes covering the brain and spinal cord, including dura mater, arachnoid, and pia mater

microdiscectomy: surgery to remove part of an intervertebral disc performed through a small incision and using a microscope for image magnification

myelography: diagnostic imaging procedure performed by injecting a water-soluble contrast into the dural sac and then taking radiographs; most commonly used to identify compression of neural elements

nerve roots: bundles of nerve tissue that exit the spinal cord or cauda equina

neuroablation: procedure designed to destroy nerve endings responsible for producing pain

nociception: painful stimulation of nerve endings

nociceptors: nerve endings that, when stimulated, are responsible for the sensation of pain

nonorganic signs (also called Waddell signs): patient behaviors identified during evaluation that indicate that a patient may have a strong "psychogenic" component to his or her pain complaints

osteoblasts: bone-producing cells

osteophytes: bone spurs; often form on the edges of vertebral bodies in a degenerated spinal segment

palpation: application of the fingers with light pressure to the surface of the body for the purpose of determining the conditions of the parts below; used for physical diagnosis

pars interarticularis: the bony structure that joins the upper and lower facet joint of a vertebra

pedicle: bony structure that forms a bridge between the vertebral body and the other posterior elements; forms the margins of the foramen

percutaneous discectomy: surgical procedure involving the removal of a small amount of intervertebral disc tissue through a cannula (tube through which instruments are passed)

pseudoarthrosis: failure to achieve bony union in an attempted spinal fusion

psychoneuroimmunology: the study of the influence of emotion and cognition on physiological response, including endocrine and immune function

sacroiliac joint: the joint between the sacrum and the pelvis

secondary gain: receipt of psychologically meaningful consequences as a result of engaging in a behavior; such consequences may include interpersonal attention, financial gain, or avoidance of undesirable activities

self-efficacy: the belief that one can effectively perform a given behavior and that the behavior will result in desired outcomes

self-regulation: cognitive and behavioral activity whereby the patient influences the course of surgical recovery

somatization disorder: a pattern of recurring, multiple, clinically significant physical complaints that cannot be adequately explained by a known medical condition

spinal cord stimulation: placement of a lead with multiple electrodes over the dura of the spinal cord to block, reduce, or alter ascending nociceptive input

spinal fusion: surgical procedure in which a bone graft or other material is placed onto or between vertebral bodies to stabilize the motion segment

spinal motion segment: consists of two adjacent vertebral bodies and the intervening intervertebral disc

spondylolisthesis: bilateral fracture of the pars that allows the vertebral body to slip forward and out of alignment with the adjacent vertebral bodies

spondylolysis: a unilateral stress fracture in the pars interarticularis

spondylosis: a condition related to degeneration that ultimately results in narrowing of the spinal canal

Stauffer and Coventry (1972) criteria: surgery outcome assessment method incorporating pain level, medication use, functional limitations, and return to work

stenosis: a narrowing of a passageway; in the spine, a degenerative narrowing of the spinal canal, possibly compressing the spinal cord or cauda equina, or of the foramena, possibly compressing the nerve roots

symptom magnification: expression or display of greater pain than can be explained by identified medical conditions

vertebrae: the large bony structures of the spine

Waddell signs: see *nonorganic signs*

REFERENCES

Agazzi, S., Reverdin, A., & May, D. (1999). Posterior lumbar interbody fusion with cages: an independent review of 71 cases. *Journal of Neurosurgery, 91(Suppl)*, 186–192.

Agency for Health Care Policy and Research (AHCPR). (1992). *Acute pain management: Operative or medical procedures and trauma* (Clinical Practice Guideline No. 1, AHCPR Publication No. 92-0032). Rockville, MD: U.S. Department of Health and Human Services. (Available from: AHCPR Clearinghouse, P.O. Box 8547, Silver Spring, MD, 20907, 800-358-9295)

Agency for Health Care Policy and Research (AHCPR). (February, 2000). *20 Tips to Help Prevent Medical Errors.* (AHCPR Publication No. 92-0032). Rockville, MD: U.S. Department of Health and Human Services. (Available from: AHCPR Clearinghouse, P.O. Box 8547, Silver Springs, MD 20907, 800-358-9295 or http:/www.ahrq.gov/consumer/20tips.htm).

Akeson, W., Amiel, D., & Woo, S. (1980). Immobility effects on synovial joints: The pathomechanics of joint contracture. *Biorheology, 17(1–2)*, 95–110.

Alberti, R. E., & Emmons, M. (1974). *Your perfect right* (rev. ed.). San Luis Obispo, CA: Impact Press.

American Academy of Pain Medicine, American Pain Society, & American Society of Addiction Medicine. (2001). *Definitions related to the use of opioids for the treatment of pain: A consensus document.* Glenview, IL: Authors.

American Pain Foundation. (2001a). *Pain action guide.* Baltimore, MD: Author. (Available at www.painfoundation.org or American Pain Foundation, 210 N. Charles Street, Suite 710, Baltimore, MD 21201)

American Pain Foundation. (2001b). *Pain care bill of rights*. Baltimore, MD: Author. (Available at www.painfoundation.org or American Pain Foundation, 210 N. Charles Street, Suite 710, Baltimore, MD 21201, 888-615-PAIN)

American Pain Society. (1992). *Principles of analgesic use in the treatment of acute pain and chronic cancer pain: A concise guide to medical practice* (3rd ed.). Glenview, IL: Author. (Available at www.ampainsoc.org, or American Pain Society, 4700 W. Lake Ave., Glenview, IL 60025, 847-375-4715)

American Pain Society. (2001). *Promoting pain relief and preventing abuse of pain medications: A critical balancing act. A joint statement from 21 health organizations and the Drug Enforcement Administration.* (Available at www.ampainsoc.org or American Pain Society, 4700 W. Lake Ave., Glenview, IL 60025, 847-375-4715)

American Psychiatric Association. (1987). *Diagnostic and Statistical Manual of Mental Disorders* (3rd edition, revised). Washington, DC: American Psychiatric Association.

American Psychiatric Association. (1994). *Diagnostic and statistical manual of mental disorders* (4th ed.). Washington, DC: American Psychiatric Association.

American Psychological Association Practice Directorate. (1996). *Models for multidisciplinary arrangements: A state-by-state review of options.* Washington, DC: American Psychological Association.

An, H. S., Silveri, C. P., Simpson, M., File, P., Simmons, C., Simeone, A., et al. (1994). Comparison of smoking habits between patients with surgically confirmed herniated lumbar and cervical disc disease and controls. *Journal of Spinal Disorders, 7*, 369–373.

Anand, K. J. S., Sippel, W. G., & Aynsley-Green, A. (1987). Randomised trial of fentanyl anaesthesia in preterm babies undergoing surgery: Effects on the stress response. *Lancet, 1*, 243–247.

Anderson, R. (1991). Learning to empower patients: Results of professional education program for diabetes. *Diabetes Care, 14*, 584–590.

Atkinson, J. H., Slater, M. A., Patterson, T. L., Grant, I., & Garfin, S. R. (1991). Prevalence, onset and risk of psychiatric disorders in chronic pain patients: A controlled study. *Pain, 45*, 111–121.

Atlas, S. J., Keller, R. B., Robson, D., Deyo, R. A., & Singer, D. E. (2000). Surgical and non-surgical management of lumbar spinal stenosis. *Spine, 25*, 556–562.

Bandura, A. (1977). Self-efficacy: Toward a unifying theory of behavioral change. *Psychological Review, 84*, 191–215.

Bandura, A. (1991). Self-efficacy mechanism in physiological activation and health-promoting behavior. In I. V. Madden (Ed.), *Neurobiology of learning, emotion, and affect* (pp. 229–269). New York: Raven Press.

Barber, J. P., Connolly, M. B., Crits-Christoph, P., Gladis, L., & Siqueland, L. (2000). Alliance predicts patient's outcome beyond in-treatment change in symptoms. *Journal of Consulting and Clinical Psychology, 68,* 1027–1032.

Barron, M., & Zazandijan, V. A. (1993). Geographic variation in lumbar diskectomy: A protocol for evaluation. *QBR, 18,* 98–107.

Bastone, E. C., & Kerns, R. D. (1995). Effects of self-efficacy and perceived social support on recovery-related behaviors after coronary artery bypass graft surgery. *Annals of Behavioral Medicine, 17,* 324–330.

Battie, M. C., & Bigos, S. J. (1991). Industrial back pain complaints: A broader perspective. *Orthopedic Clinics of North America, 22,* 273–283.

Baum, A., Gatchel, R. J., & Krantz, D. (Eds.). (1997). *An introduction to health psychology* (3rd ed.). New York: McGraw-Hill.

Baumstark, K. F., Buckelew, S. P., Sher, K. J., Beck, N., Buescher, K. L., Hewett, J., et al. (1993). Pain behavior predictors among fibromyalgia patients. *Pain, 55,* 339–346.

Beck, A. T. (1979). *Cognitive therapy and the emotional disorders.* New York: Meridian.

Beck, A. T., Ward, C. H., Mendelsohn, M., Mock, J., & Erbaugh, J. (1961). An inventory for measuring depression. *Archives of General Psychiatry, 4,* 561–571.

Beckman, H. B., & Frankel, R. M. (1984). The effect of physician behavior on the collection of data. *Annals of Internal Medicine, 101,* 692–696.

Beecher, H. K. (1956). Relationship of significance of the wound to the pain experienced. *Journal of the American Medical Association, 161,* 1609–1613.

Benjamini, E., Sunshine, G., & Leskowitz, S. (1996). *Immunology: A short course.* New York: Wiley-Liss.

Benson, H. (1975). *The relaxation response.* New York: Morrow.

Benson, H. (1996). *Timeless healing: The power and biology of belief.* New York: Scribner.

Benton, P. G. (2001, May/June). Informed consent: Legal review. *SpineLine,* pp. 35–39.

Benveniste, K., & Thut, P. (1981). The effect of chronic alcoholism on wound healing. *Proceedings of the Society for Experimental Biology and Medicine, 166,* 568–575.

Benzel, E. C., & Benton, P. G. (2001, May/June). Informed consent. *SpineLine,* pp. 33–34.

Bhandari, M., Louw, D., & Reddy, K. (1999). Predictors of return to work after anterior cervical discectomy. *Journal of Spinal Disorders*, *12*, 94–98.

Bigos, S. J., Battie, M. C., Spengler, D. M., Fisher, L. D., Fordyce, W. E., Hansson, T., et al. (1991). A prospective study of work perceptions and psychosocial factors affecting the report of back injury. *Spine*, *16*, 1–6.

Blankfield, R. (1991). Suggestion, relaxation, and hypnosis as adjuncts in the care of surgery patients: A review of the literature. *American Journal of Clinical Hypnosis*, *33*, 172–187.

Block, A. R. (1981). An investigation of the response of the spouse to chronic pain behavior. *Psychosomatic Medicine*, *43*, 415–422.

Block, A. R. (1992). Psychological screening of spine surgery candidates. In S. H. Hochschuler, H. B. Cotler, & R. D. Guyer (Eds.), *Rehabilitation of the spine: Science and practice* (pp. 617–625). St. Louis: Mosby.

Block, A. R. (1996). *Presurgical psychological screening in chronic pain syndromes: A guide for the behavioral health practitioner*. Mahwah, NJ: Erlbaum.

Block, A. R., & Boyer, S. L. (1984). The spouse's adjustment to chronic pain: Cognitive and emotional factors. *Social Science and Medicine*, *19*, 1313–1317.

Block, A. R., Boyer, S. L., & Silbert, R. V. (1985). Spouse's perception of the chronic pain patient: Estimates of exercise tolerance. In H. L. Fields, R. Dubner, & F. Cervero (Eds.), *Advances in pain research and therapy* (Vol. 9., pp. 897–904). New York: Raven Press.

Block, A. R., Kremer, E. F., & Fernandez, E. (Eds.). (1999). *Handbook of pain syndromes*. Mahwah, NJ: Erlbaum.

Block, A. R., Kremer, E. F., & Gaylor, M. (1980). Behavioral treatment of chronic pain: The spouse as a discriminative cue for pain behavior. *Pain*, *9*, 243–252.

Block, A. R. & Ohnmeiss, D. (2000). *MMPI Profiles predict the outcome of spinal surgery*. Presented at North American Spine Society, 15th Annual Meeting, New Orleans.

Block, A. R., Ohnmeiss, D. D., Guyer, R. D., Rashbaum, R. F., & Hochschuler, S. H. (2001). The use of presurgical psychological screening to predict the outcome of spine surgery. *Spine Journal*, *1*, 274–282.

Block, A. R., Vanharanta, H., Ohnmeiss, D., & Guyer, R. D. (1996). Discographic pain report: Influence of psychological factors. *Spine*, *21*, 334–338.

Blumenthal, S. L., Ohnmeiss, D. D., Rashbaum, R. F., Zigler, J. E., Guyer, R. D., & Chang, Y. (2001). *Results of intradiscal electrothermal therapy (IDET)*. Unpublished data.

Boden, S. D., Davis, D. O., Dina, T. S., Patronas, N. J., & Wiesel, S. W. (1990). Abnormal magnetic-resonance scans of the lumbar spine in asymptomatic subjects. *Journal of Bone and Joint Surgery* (American ed.), *72*, 403–408.

Boos, N., Reider, R., Schnade, V., Spratt, K., Semmer, N., & Aebi, M. (1995). The diagnostic accuracy of MRI, work perception and psychological factors in identifying symptomatic disc herniation. *Spine, 20*, 2613–2625.

Boos, N., Semmer, N., Elfering, A., Schade, V., Gel, I., Zanetti, M., et al. (2000). Natural history of individuals with asymptomatic disc abnormalities in magnetic resonance imaging: Predictors of low back pain-related medical consultation and work incapacity. *Spine, 25*, 1484–1492.

Boothby, J. L., Thorn, B. E., Stroud, M. W., & Jensen, M. P. (1999). Coping with pain. In R. J. Gatchel & D. C. Turk (Eds.), *Psychosocial factors in pain: Critical perspectives*. New York: Guilford Press.

Bortz, W. (1984). The disuse syndrome [Commentary]. *Western Journal of Medicine, 141*, 691–694.

Bourne, E. J. (1995). *The anxiety and phobia workbook* (2nd ed.). Oakland, CA: New Harbinger Publications.

Bower, S. A., & Bower, G. H. (1991). *Asserting yourself*. Reading, MA: Addison-Wesley.

Bradley, L. A., Prokop, C. K., Gentry, W. D., Van der Heide, L. H., & Prieto, E. J. (1981). Assessment of chronic pain. In C. K. Prokop & L. A. Bradley (Eds.), *Medical psychology: Contributions to behavioral medicine* (pp. 91–117). New York: Academic Press.

Breuer, J., & Freud, S. (1895). *Studies in hysteria*. New York: Basic Books.

Brown, C. W., Orme, T. J., & Richardson, H. D. (1986). The rate of pseudoarthrosis (surgical nonunion) in patients who are smokers and patients who are nonsmokers: A comparison study. *Spine, 11*, 942–943.

Brown, G. K., & Nicassio, P. M. (1987). Development of a questionnaire for the assessment of active and passive coping strategies in chronic pain patients. *Pain, 31*, 53–64.

Buchbinder, R., Jolley, D., & Wyatt, M. (2001, June). *Effect of a mass media campaign on back pain beliefs and its potential influence on management of low back pain in general practice*. Paper presented at the meeting of the International Society for the Study of the Lumbar Spine, Edinburgh, Scotland.

Buckelew, S. P., Parker, J. C., Keefe, J. F., Deuser, W. E., Crews, T. M., Conway, R., et al. (1994). Self-efficacy and pain behavior among subjects with fibromyalgia. *Pain, 59*, 377–384.

Butler, R. W., Damarin, F. L., Bealieu, C. L., Schewebel, A. I., & Thorn, B. E. (1989). Assessing cognitive coping strategies for acute pain. *Psychological Assessment: A Journal of Consulting and Clinical Psychology, 1*, 41–45.

Cairns, D., & Pasino, J. A. (1977). Comparison of verbal reinforcement and feedback in the operant treatment of disability due to chronic low back pain. *Behavior Therapy, 8,* 621–630.

Calderone, R. R., Garland, D. E., Capen, D. A., & Oster, H. (1996). Cost of medical care for postoperative spinal infections. *Orthopedic Clinics of North America, 27,* 171–182.

Campanile, G., Hautmann, G., & Lotti, T. (1998). Cigarette smoking, wound healing, and face-lift. *Clinical Dermatology, 16,* 575–578.

Capen, D. A., Calderone, R. R., & Green, A. (1996). Perioperative risk factors for wound infections after lower back fusions. *Orthopedic Clinics of North America, 27,* 83–86.

Carpenter, C. T., Dietz, J. W., Leung, K. Y. K., Hanscom, D. A., & Wagner, T. A. (1996). Repair of a pseudoarthrosis of the lumbar spine: A functional outcome study. *Journal of Bone and Joint Surgery, 78,* 712–720.

Carragee, E. J., Khurana, S., Alamin, T., & Chen, Y. (2001, June). *Outcomes of intradiscal electrothermal therapy as a treatment for low back pain: A prospective comparison of IDET versus two control groups.* Paper presented at the meeting of the International Society for the Study of the Lumbar Spine, Edinburgh, Scotland.

Carragee, E. J., Tanner, C. M., Khurana, S., Hayward, C., Welsh, J., Date, E., et al. (2000). The rates of false-positive lumbar discography in select patients without low back pain. *Spine, 25,* 1373–1381.

Carragee, E. J., Tanner, C. M., Yang, B., Brito, J. L., & Truong, T. (1999). False-positive findings on lumbar discography: Reliability of subjective concordance assessment during provocative disc injection. *Spine, 24,* 2542–2547.

Carron, H. (1989). Extension of pain relief beyond the operating room. *Clinical Journal of Pain, 5,* S1–S4.

Cavanaugh, S., Clark, D. C., & Gibbons, R. D. (1983). Diagnosing depression in the hospitalized medically ill. *Psychosomatics, 24,* 809–815.

Cashion, E. L., & Lynch, W. J. (1979). Personality factors and results of lumbar disc surgery. *Neurosurgery 4,* 141–145.

Chan, C. W., Goldman, S., Ilstrup, D. M., Kunselman, A. R., & O'Neill, P. I. (1993). The pain drawing and Waddell's nonorganic physical signs in chronic low-back pain. *Spine, 18,* 1717–1722.

Chapman, C. R. (1978). Pain: The perception of noxious events. In R. A. Sternbach (Ed.), *The psychology of pain* (pp. 169–202). New York: Raven Press.

Chapman, C. R. (2000, July/August). New JCAHO standards for pain management: Carpe diem! *APS Bulletin,* pp. 2–3.

Chapman, C. R., Nakamura, Y., & Flores, L. Y. (1999). Chronic pain and consciousness: A constructivist perspective. In R. J. Gatchel & D. C. Turk (Eds.), *Psychosocial factors in pain: Critical perspectives* (pp. 35–55). New York: Guilford Press.

Ciol, M. A., Deyo, R. A., Kreuter, W., & Bigos, S. J. (1994). Characteristics in medicare beneficiaries associated with reoperation after lumbar spine surgery. *Spine, 19*(12), 1329–1334.

Cleary, J., & Backonja, M. (1996, March/April). Translating opioid tolerance research. *APS Bulletin*, pp. 4–7.

Cohen, M. (1995, May 17). Never mind the ebola, we have defiant bugs. *San Diego Union-Tribune*, p. A-18.

Cohen, S. (1988). Psychosocial models of the role of social support in the etiology of physical disease. *Health Psychology, 7*, 269–297.

Cohen, S., & Herbert, T. B. (1996). Health psychology: Psychological factors and physical disease from the perspective of human psychoneuroimmunology. *Annual Review of Psychology, 47*, 113–142.

Contrada, R. J., Leventhal, E. A., & Anderson, J. R. (1994). Psychological preparation for surgery: Marshaling individual and social resources to optimize self-regulation. In S. Maes, H. Leventhal, & M. Johnston (Eds.), *International review of health psychology* (Vol. 3, pp. 219–266). New York: Wiley.

Coyne, J. C., & DeLongis, A. (1986). Going beyond social support: The role of social relationships in adaptation. *Journal of Consulting and Clinical Psychology, 54*, 454–460.

Craig, K. D., Hill, M. I., & McMurtry, B. (1999). Detecting deception and malingering. In A. R. Block, E. F. Kremer, & E. Fernandez (Eds.), *Handbook of pain syndromes: Biopsychosocial perspectives* (pp. 41–58). Mahwah, NJ: Erlbaum.

Croft, P. R., Papageorgiou, A. C., Thomas, E., MacFarlane, G. J., & Silman, A. J. (1999). Short-term physical risk factors for new episodes of low back pain. *Spine, 24*, 1556–1561.

Crowell, M. D., & Barofsky, I. (1999). Functional gastrointestinal pain syndromes. In A. R. Block, E. F. Kremer, & E. Fernandez (Eds.), *Handbook of pain syndromes: Biopsychosocial perspectives* (pp. 475–498). Mahwah, NJ: Erlbaum.

Curran, S. L., Sherman, J. J., Cunningham, L. C., Okeson, J. P., Reid, K. K., & Carlson, C. R. (1995). Physical and sexual abuse among orofacial pain patients: Linkages with pain and psychologic distress. *Journal of Orofacial Pain, 9*, 340–345.

Cuschieri, R. J., Morran, C. G., Howie, J. C., & McArdle, C. S. (1985). Postoperative pain and pulmonary complications: Comparison of three analgesic regimens. *British Journal of Surgery, 72*, 495–498.

Cutrona, C. E., & Russell, P. (1987). The provisions of social relationships and adaptation to stress. In W. Jones & D. Perlman (Eds.), *Advances in personal relationships* (pp. 37–67). Greenwich, CT: JAI Press.

Davis, M., Eshelman, E. R., & McKay, M. (1995). *The relaxation and stress reduction workbook* (4th ed.). Oakland, CA: New Harbinger Publications.

Davis, R. A. (1994). A long-term outcome analysis of 984 surgically treated herniated lumbar discs. *Journal of Neurosurgery, 80,* 514–521.

Deardorff, W. W. (1986). Computerized health education: A comparison with traditional formats. *Health Education Quarterly, 13,* 61–73.

Deardorff, W. W. (2000). Psychological interventions for surgery patients. In L. VandeCreek & T. L. Jackson (Eds.), *Innovations in clinical practice: A source book* (Vol. 18, pp. 323–334). Sarasota, FL: Professional Resource Press.

Deardorff, W. W., & Reeves, J. L. (1997). *Preparing for surgery: A mind-body approach to enhance healing and recovery.* Oakland, CA: New Harbinger Publications. (Available from William W. Deardorff, PhD, P.O. Box 9061, Calabasas, CA 91372, 310-860-3416, Deardorff1@aol.com, www.surgeryprep.com)

DeGood, D. E., & Kiernan, B. (1996). Perception of fault in patients with chronic pain. *Pain, 64,* 153–159.

Dennis, M. D., Rocchio, P. O. & Wiltse, L. L (1981). The topographical pain representation and its correlation with MMPI scores. *Orthopedics, 5,* 432–434.

De La Porte, C., & Van de Kelft, E. (1993). Spinal cord stimulation in failed back surgery syndrome. *Pain, 52,* 55–61.

Derby, R., Eek, B., & Ryan, D. (1999, June). *Intradiscal electrothermal annuloplasty: 12 month follow-up pilot study.* Paper presented at the meeting of the International Society for the Study of the Lumbar Spine, Kona, HI.

de Vernejoul, M. C., Bielakoff, J., & Herve, M. (1983). Evidence for defective osteoblastic function: A role for alcohol and tobacco consumption in osteoporosis in middle-aged men. *Clinical Orthopedics, 179,* 107–115.

Devine, E. C. (1992). Effects of psychoeducation care for adult surgical patients: A meta-analysis of 191 studies. *Patient Education and Counseling, 19,* 129–142.

Devine, E. C., & Cook, T. D. (1983). A meta-analytic analysis of effects of psychoeducational interventions on length of postsurgical hospital stay. *Nursing Research, 32,* 267–273.

Devine, E. C., & Cook, T. D. (1986). Clinical and cost saving effects of psychoeducational interventions with surgical patients: A meta-analysis. *Research in Nursing and Health, 9,* 89–105.

Deyo, R. A., Cherkin, D., Loeser, J., Bigos, S., & Cociol, M. (1992). Morbidity and mortality in association with operations on the lumbar spine: The influence of age, diagnosis, and procedure. *Journal of Bone and Joint Surgery, 74,* 536–543.

Deyo, R. A., & Diehl, A. K. (1988). Psychosocial predictors of disability in patients with low back pain. *Journal of Rheumatology, 15,* 1557–1564.

Deyo, R. A., Diehl, A. K., & Rosenthal, M. (1986). How many days of bed rest for acute low back pain? A randomized clinical trial. *New England Journal of Medicine, 315,* 1064–1070.

Deyo, R. A., & Tsui-Wu, J. (1987). Descriptive epidemiology of low back pain and its related medical care in the United States. *Spine, 12,* 264–268.

Dolan, P., Greenfield, K., Nelson, R. J., & Nelson, I. W. (2000). Can therapy improve the outcome of microdiscectomy? *Spine, 25,* 1523–1532.

Doxey, N. C., Dzioba, R. B., & Mitson, G. L. (1988). Predictors of outcome in back surgery candidates. *Journal of Clinical Psychology, 44,* 611–622.

Dreyer, S. J., & Dreyfuss, P. H. (1996). Low back pain and the zygapophyseal (facet) joint. *Archives of Physical Medicine and Rehabilitation, 77,* 290–300.

Dvorak, J., Valach, L., Fuhrimann, P., & Heim, E. (1988). The outcome of surgery for lumbar disc herniation: II. A 4–17 years' follow-up with emphasis on psychosocial aspects. *Spine, 13,* 1423–1427.

Dworkin, R. H., Handlin, D. S., Richlin, D. M., Brand, L., & Vannucci, C. (1985). Unraveling the effects of compensation, litigation and employment on treatment response in chronic pain. *Pain, 23,* 49–59.

Dzioba, R. B., & Doxey, N. C. (1984). A prospective investigation in the orthopedic and psychologic predictors of outcome of first lumbar surgery following industrial injury. *Spine, 9,* 614–623.

Eddy, M. E., & Coslow, B. I. (1991). Preparation for ambulatory surgery: A patient education program. *Journal of Post Anesthesia Nursing, 6,* 5–12.

Ellis, A. (1975). *A new guide to rational living.* North Hollywood, CA: Wilshire Books.

Engel, G. L. (1959). "Psychogenic" pain and the pain-prone patient. *American Journal of Medicine, 26,* 899–918.

Engel, G. L. (1977). The need for new medical model: A challenge for biomedicine. *Science, 196,* 129–136.

Ernst, E. (1993). Smoking: A cause of back trouble? *British Journal of Rheumatology, 32,* 239–242.

Fairbank, J. C. T., Couper, J., Davies, J., & O'Brien, J. P. (1980). The Oswestry low back pain disability questionnaire. *Physiotherapy, 66,* 271–273.

Fanuele, J. C., Birkmeyer, N., Abdu, W. A., Tosteson, T. D., & Weinstein, J. N. (2000). The impact of spinal problems on the health status of patients: Have we underestimated the effect? *Spine, 25,* 1509–1514.

Fardon, D. F. and Whitesides, T. E. (2002). The smoking patient: To fuse or not to fuse. *SpineLine,* Sept/Oct, 10–12.

Feldman, D. E., Rossignol, M., Shrier, I., & Abenhaim, L. (1999). Smoking: A risk factor for development of low back pain in adolescents. *Spine, 24,* 2492–2496.

Ferguson, T. (1993). Working with your doctor. In D. Coleman & J. Gurin (Eds.), *Mind-body medicine* (pp. 429–450). Yonkers, NY: Consumer Reports Books.

Fernandez, E., Clark, T. S. & Ruddick-Davis, D. (1999). A Framework for conceptualization and assessment of affective disturbance in pain. In A. R. Block, E. F. Kremer & E. Fernandez (Eds.), *Handbook of Pain Syndromes: Biopsychosocial Perspectives.* Mahwah, NJ: Lawrence Erlbaum Associates.

Fernandez, E. & Turk, D. C. (1995). The scope and significance of anger in the experience of chronic pain. *Pain, 61,* 165–175.

Ferrante, F. M., Ostheimer, G. W., & Covino, B. G. (Eds.). (1990). *Patient-controlled analgesia.* Cambridge, MA: Blackwell Scientific.

Festinger, L. (1954). A theory of social comparison processes. *Human Relations, 7,* 117–140.

Finneson, B. E., & Cooper, V. R. (1979). A lumbar disc surgery predictive score card: A retrospective evaluation. *Spine, 4,* 141–144.

Fishbain, D. A., Cutler, R. B., Rosomoff, H. L., Khalil, T., & Steele-Rosomoff, R. (1997). Impact of chronic pain patients' job perceptions variables on actual return to work. *Spine, 13,* 197–206.

Fishbain, D. A., Goldberg, M., Meagher, B. R., Steele, R., & Rosomoff, H. L. (1986). Male and female chronic pain patients categorized by DSM-III psychiatric diagnostic criteria. *Pain, 26,* 181–197.

Folkman, S., & Lazarus, R. S. (1985). An analysis of coping in a middle aged community sample. *Journal of Health and Social Behavior, 21,* 219–239.

Fordyce, W. E. (1976). *Behavioral methods for chronic pain and illness.* St. Louis: Mosby.

Franklin, G. M., Haug, J., Heyer, N. J., McKeefrey, S. P., & Picciano, J. F. (1994). Outcome of lumbar fusion in Washington State workers' compensation. *Spine, 19,* 1897–1904.

Freeman, C., Calsyn, D., & Loucks, J. (1976). The use of the Minnesota Multiphasic Personality Inventory with low back pain patients. *Journal of Clinical Psychology, 32,* 294–298.

Fritzell, P., Hagg, O., Wessberg, P., & Nordwall, A. (2002). Chronic low back pain and fusion: a comparison of three surgical techniques: A prospective multicenter randomized study from the Swedish lumbar spine study group. *Spine, 27,* 1131–1141.

Frymoyer, J. W., & Cats-Baril, W. L. (1987). An overview of the incidences and cost of low back pain. *Orthopedic Clinics of America, 22,* 263–271.

Frymoyer, J. W., Pope, M. H., Clements, J. H., Wilder, D. G., MacPherson, B., & Ashikaga, T. (1983). Risk factors in low-back pain: An epidemiological survey. *Journal of Bone and Joint Surgery* (American ed.), *65,* 213–218.

Gaines, W. G., & Hegman, K. T. (1999). Effectiveness of Waddell's nonorganic signs in predicting a delayed return to regular work in patients experiencing acute occupational low back pain. *Spine, 24,* 396–401.

Gallup, G. H., Jr. (1990). *Religion in America.* Princeton, NJ: Princeton Religion.

Gamsa, A. (1994). The role of psychological factors in chronic pain. II. A critical appraisal. *Pain, 57,* 17–29.

Gatchel, R. J. (1991a). Early development of physical and mental deconditioning in painful spinal disorders. In T. G. Mayer, V. Mooney, & R. J. Gatchel (Eds.), *Contemporary conservative care for painful spinal disorders* (pp. 278–289). Philadelphia: Lea & Febiger.

Gatchel, R. J. (1991b). Psychosocial assessment and disability management in the rehabilitation of painful spinal disorders. In T. Mayer, V. Mooney, & R. Gatchel (Eds.), *Contemporary conservative care for painful spinal disorders* (pp. 441–454). Philadelphia: Lea & Febiger.

Gatchel, R. J. (1996). Psychological disorders and chronic pain: Cause and effect relationships. In R. J. Gatchel & D. C. Turk (Eds.), *Psychological approaches to pain management: A practitioner's handbook* (pp. 33–52). New York: Guilford Publications.

Gatchel, R. J. (2000). How practitioners should evaluate personality to help manage chronic pain patients. In R. J. Gatchel & J. N. Weisberg (Eds.), *Personality characteristics of patients with pain* (pp. 241–258). Washington, DC: American Psychological Association.

Gatchel, R. J., Garofalo, J. P., Ellis, E., & Holt, C. (1996). Major psychological disorders in acute and chronic TMD: An initial examination. *Journal of the American Dental Association, 127,* 1365–1374.

Gatchel, R. J., Polatin, P. B., & Kinney, R. K. (1995). Predicting outcome of chronic back pain using clinical predictors of psychopathology: A prospective analysis. *Health Psychology, 14,* 415–420.

Gatchel, R. J., Polatin, P., Mayer, T., & Garcy, P. (1994). Psychopathology and the rehabilitation of patients with chronic low back pain. *Archives of Physical Medicine and Rehabilitation, 75,* 666–670.

Gatchel, R. J., & Turk, D. C. (Eds.). (1996). *Psychological approaches to pain management: A practitioner's handbook.* New York: Guilford Publications.

Gatchel, R. J., & Turk, D. C. (Eds.). (1999). *Psychosocial factors in pain: Critical perspectives.* New York: Guilford Press.

Gatchel, R. J. & Weisberg, J. N. (2000). *Personality Characteristics of Patients with Pain.* Washington, DC: American Psychological Association.

Geisser, M., & Colwell, M. (1999). Chronic back pain: Conservative approaches. In A. R. Block, E. F. Kremer, & E. Fernandez (Eds.), *Handbook of pain syndromes* (pp. 169–190). Mahwah, NJ: Erlbaum.

Gelberman, R. H., Manske, P. R., Akeson, W. H., Woo, S. L., Lundborg, G., & Amiel, D. (1986). Flexor tendon repair. *Journal of Orthopaedic Research, 4*(1), 119–128.

Gil, K. M., Ginsberg, B., Muir, M., Sykes, D., & Williams, D. A. (1990). Patient controlled analgesia in postoperative pain: The relation of psychological factors to pain and narcotic use. *Clinical Journal of Pain, 8,* 215–221.

Gil, K. M., Ross, S., & Keefe, F. (1988). Behavioral treatment of chronic pain: Four pain management protocols. In R. D. France & K. R. R. Krishnan (Eds.), *Chronic pain* (pp. 376–414). Washington, DC: American Psychiatric Press.

Glaser, R., & Kiecolt-Glaser, J. K. (Eds.). (1994). *Handbook of human stress and immunity.* San Diego, CA: Academic Press.

Glassman, S. D., Minkow, R. E., Dimar, J. R., Puno, R. M., Raque, G. H., & Johnson, J. R. (1998). Effect of prior lumbar discectomy on outcome of lumbar fusion: A prospective analysis using the SF-36 measure. *Journal of Spinal Disorders, 11,* 383–388.

Goleman, D., & Gurin, J. (Eds.). (1993). *Mind-body medicine: How to use your mind for better health.* Yonkers, NY: Consumer Reports Books.

Goliszek, A. G. (1987). *Breaking the stress habit.* Winston-Salem, NC: Carolina Press.

Graham, J. R. (1990). *The MMPI-2: Assessing personality and psychopathology.* New York: Oxford University Press.

Greenough, C. G., & Fraser, R. D. (1989). The effects of compensation on recovery from low-back injury. *Spine, 14,* 947–955.

Grevitt, M., Pande, K., O'Dowd, J., & Webb, J. (1998). Do first impressions count? A comparison of subjective and psychological assessment of spinal patients. *European Spine Journal, 7,* 218–223.

Griffin, K. (1996, November/December). They should have washed their hands: Medicine's dirty little secret. *Health*, pp. 82–89.

Gross, A. R. (1986). The effect of coping strategies on the relief of pain following surgical intervention for lower back pain. *Psychosomatic Medicine*, 48, 229–238.

Gross, R. J., Doerr, H., Caldirola, D., Guzinski, G., & Ripley, H. S. (1980). Borderline syndrome and incest in chronic pain patients. *International Journal of Psychiatry in Medicine*, 10, 70–86.

Guo, H. R., Tanaka, S., Halperis, W. E., & Cameron, L. L. (1999). Back pain prevalence in US industry and estimates of lost work days. *American Journal of Public Health*, 8, 1029–1035.

Haber, J., & Roos, C. (1985). Effects of spouse abuse and/or sexual abuse in the development and maintenance of chronic pain in women. *Advances in Pain and Research Therapy*, 9, 889–895.

Haddad, G. H. (1987). Analysis of 2932 workers' compensation back injury cases: The impact of the cost to the system. *Spine*, 12, 765–769.

Hafen, B. Q., Karren, K. J., Frandsen, K. J., & Smith, N. L. (1996). *Mindbody health: The effects of attitudes, emotions, and relationships*. Needham, MA: Allyn & Bacon.

Haider, T. T., Kishino, N. D., Gray, T. P., Tomlin, M. A., & Daubert, H. B. (1998). Functional restoration: Comparison of surgical and nonsurgical spine patients. *Journal of Occupational Rehabilitation*, 8, 247–253.

Halmosh, A. F., & Israeli, R. (1984). Family interactions as modulator in the post-traumatic process. *Medicine and Law*, 1, 125–134.

Hanley, E. N., & Shapiro, D. E. (1989). The development of low back pain after excision of a lumbar disc. *Journal of Bone and Joint Surgery*, 71, 719–721.

Hansen, F. R., Biering-Sorenson, R., & Schroll. M. (1995) Minnesota Mutiphasic Personality Inventory profiles in persons with or without low back pain: A 20-year follow-up study. *Spine*, 20, 2716–2720.

Hanvik, L. J. (1950). MMPI profiles in patients with low-back pain. *Journal of Consulting Psychology*, 15, 350–353.

Hashemi, L., Webster, B. S., Clancy, E. A., & Volinn, E. (1997). Length of disability and cost of worker's compensation low back pain claims. *Journal of Occupational and Environmental Medicine*, 39, 937–945.

Hathaway, D. (1986). Effect of preoperative instruction on postoperative outcomes: A meta-analysis of studies. *Nursing Research*, 35, 269–275.

Haythornthwaite, J., Seiber, W. J., & Kerns, R. (1991). Depression in the chronic pain experience. *Pain*, 46, 177–184.

Hellsing, A., & Bryngelsson, I. (2000). Predictors of musculoskeletal pain in men: A twenty-year follow-up from examination at enlistment. *Spine*, 25, 3080–3086.

Herbert, T. B., & Cohen, S. (1993). Stress and immunity in humans: A meta-analytic review. *Psychosomatic Medicine*, 55, 364–379.

Herron, L.D., & Pheasant, H.C. (1982). Changes in MMPI profiles after low-back surgery. *Spine*, 7, 591–597.

Herron, L., Turner, J. A., Ersek, M., & Weiner, P. (1992). Does the Millon Behavioral Health Inventory (MBHI) predict lumbar laminectomy outcome? A comparison with the Minnesota Multiphasic Personality Inventory (MMPI). *Journal of Spinal Disorders*, 5,188–192.

Hilgard, E. R., & Hilgard, J. R. (1975). *Hypnosis in the relief of pain*. Los Altos, CA: William Kaufman.

Hobby, J. L., Lutchman, J. M., Powell, D. J., & Sharp, R. E. (2001). The distress and risk assessment method (DRAM): Failure to predict the outcome of lumbar discectomy. *Journal of Bone and Joint Surgery*, 83-b, 19–21.

Hoffman, R. M., Deyo, R. A., & Wheeler, K. J. (1993). Surgery for herniated lumbar discs: A literature synthesis. *Journal of General Internal Medicine*, 8, 487–496.

Horne, D. J., Vatmanidis, P., & Careri, A. (1994). Preparing patients for invasive medical and surgical procedures: 1. Adding behavioral and cognitive interventions. *Behavioral Medicine*, 20, 5–13.

Hubner, G., Brauchle, M., Smola, H., Madlener, M., Fassler, R., & Werner, S. (1996). Differential regulation of pro-inflammatory cytokines during wound healing in normal and glucocorticoid-treated mice. *Cytokine*, 8, 548–556.

Hudgins, W. R. (1976). Laminectomy for treatment of lumbar disc disease. *Texas Medicine*, 72, 65–69.

Hueppe, M., Uhlig, T., Vogelsang, H., & Schmucker, P. (2000). Personality traits, coping style, and mood in patients awaiting lumbar-disc surgery. *Journal of Clinical Psychology*, 56, 119–130.

Indahl, A., Velund, L., & Reikeraas, O. (1995). Good prognosis for low back pain when left untampered: A randomized clinical trial. *Spine*, 20, 473–477.

Janis, I. L. (1958). *Psychological stress*. New York: Wiley.

Janis, I. L. (1971). *Stress and frustration*. New York: Harcourt Brace Jovanovich.

Jarrett, P. E. M. (1995). Day case surgery. *Surgery*, 13, 5–7.

Jensen, M. C., Brantz-Zawadzki, M. N., Obuchowski, N., Modic, M. T., Malkasian, D., & Ross, J. S. (1994). Magnetic resonance imaging of the lumbar spine in people without back pain. *New England Journal of Medicine*, *331*, 69–73.

Jensen, M. P., Turner, J. A., Romano, J. M., & Karoly, P. (1991). Coping with chronic pain: A critical review of the literature. *Pain*, *47*, 249–283.

Johnston, M. (1988). Impending surgery. In S. Fisher & J. Reason (Eds.), *Handbook of life stress, cognition and health* (pp. 79–100). New York: Wiley.

Johnston, M., & Vogele, C. (1993). Benefits of psychological preparation for surgery: A meta-analysis. *Annals of Behavioral Medicine*, *15*(4), 245–256.

Johnston, M., & Wallace, L. (Eds.). (1990). *Stress and medical procedures*. Oxford, England: Oxford University Press.

Joint Commission on Accreditation of Healthcare Organizations. (2000). *Pain assessment and management: An organizational approach*. Washington, DC: Author.

Jorgensen, L. N., Kallehave, F., Christensen, E., Siana, J. E., & Gottrup, F. (1998). Less collagen production in smokers. *Surgery*, *123*, 450–455.

Junge, A., Dvorak, J., & Ahrens, S. (1995). Predictors of bad and good outcomes of lumbar disc surgery: A prospective clinical study with recommendations for screening to avoid bad outcomes. *Spine*, *20*, 460–468.

Junge, A., Frohlich, M., Ahrens, S., Hasenbring, M., Sandler, M., Grob, D., et al. (1996). Predictors of bad and good outcome of lumbar spine surgery: A prospective clinical study with 2 years follow-up. *Spine*, *21*, 1056–1065.

Kaplan, S. H., Greenfield, S. S., & Ware, J. E. (1989). Assessing the effects of physician-patient interactions on the outcomes of chronic disease. *Medical Care*, *27*(Suppl. 3), S110–S127.

Karasek, M., & Bogduk, N. (2000). Twelve-month follow-up of a controlled trial of intradiscal thermal anuloplasty for back pain due to internal disc disruption. *Spine*, *25*, 2601–2607.

Katz, J., Stucki, G., Lipson, S., Fossel, A., Grobler, L., & Weinstein, J. (1999). Predictors of surgical outcome in degenerative lumbar spinal stenosis. *Spine*, *24*, 2229–2233.

Keefe, F. J., & Block, A. R. (1982). Development of an observation method for assessing pain behavior in chronic low back pain patients. *Behavioral Therapy*, *13*, 363–375.

Keefe, F. J., & Van Horn, Y. V. (1993). Cognitive-behavioral treatment of rheumatoid arthritis pain: Maintaining treatment gains. *Arthritis Care and Research*, *6*, 213–222.

Keel, P. J. (1984). Psychosocial criteria for patient selection: Review of studies and concepts for understanding chronic back pain. *Neurosurgery*, *15*, 935–941.

Kehlet, H. (1984). The stress response to anaesthesia and surgery: Release mechanisms and modifying factors. *Clinical Anaesthesiology, 2,* 315–339.

Kehlet, H. (1997). Multimodal approach to control postoperative pathophysiology and rehabilitation. *British Journal of Anaesthesia, 78,* 606–617.

Keller, L. S., & Butcher, J. N. (1991). *Assessment of chronic pain patients with the MMPI-2* (MMPI-2 Monographs, Vol. 2.) Minneapolis: University of Minnesota Press.

Kennedy, F. (1946). The mind of the injured worker: Its affect on disability periods. *Compensation Medicine, 1,* 19–24.

Kerns, R. D., Southwick, S., Giller, E., Haythornthwaite, J. A., Jacob, M. C., & Rosenberg, R. (1991). The relationship between reports of pain-related social interactions and expressions of pain and affective distress. *Behavior Therapy, 22,* 101–111.

Kerns, R. D., Turk, D. C., & Rudy, E. E. (1985). The West Haven-Yale Multidimensional Pain Inventory (WHYMPI). *Pain, 23,* 345–356.

Kessler, R., & Dane, J. R. (1996). Psychological and hypnotic preparation for anesthesia and surgery: An individual differences perspective. *International Journal of Clinical Hypnosis, 44,* 189–207.

Kettelkamp, D. B., & Wright, D. G. (1971). Spondylolysis in the Alaskan Eskimo. *Journal of Bone and Joint Surgery* (American ed.), *53,* 563–566.

Kiecolt-Glaser, J. K., Dura, J. R., Speicher, C. E., Trask, O. J., & Glaser, R. (1991). Spousal caregivers of dementia victims: Longitudinal changes in immunity and health. *Psychosomatic Medicine, 53,* 345–362.

Kiecolt-Glaser, J. K., & Glaser, R. (1992). Psychoneuroimmunology: Can psychological interventions modulate immunity? *Journal of Consulting and Clinical Psychology, 60,* 569–575.

Kiecolt-Glaser, J. K., & Glaser, R. (1995). Measurement of immune response. In S. Cohen, R. C. Kessler, & L. G. Underwood (Eds.), *Measuring stress: A guide for health and social scientists* (pp. 213–230). New York: Oxford University Press.

Kiecolt-Glaser, J. K., Glaser, R., Gravenstein, S., Malarkey, W. B., & Sheridan, J. (1996). Chronic stress alters the immune response to influenza virus vaccine in older adults. *Proceedings of the National Academy of Sciences, 93,* 3043–3047.

Kiecolt-Glaser, J. K., Malarkey, W. B., Cacioppo, J. T., & Glaser, R. (1994). Stressful personal relationships: Endocrine and immune function. In R. Glaser & J. K. Kiecolt-Glaser (Eds), *Handbook of human stress and immunity* (pp. 321–339). San Diego, CA: Academic Press.

Kiecolt-Glaser, J. K., Marucha, P. T., Malarkey, W. B., Mercado, A. M., & Glaser, R. (1995). Slowing of wound healing by psychological stress. *Lancet, 346,* 1194–1196.

Kiecolt-Glaser, J. K., Page, G. G., Marucha, P. T., MacCallum, R. C., & Glaser, R. (1998). Psychological influences on surgical recovery: Perspectives from psychoneuroimmunology. *American Psychologist, 53*, 1209–1218.

Kim, S. S., & Michelsen, C. B. (1992). Revision surgery for failed back surgery syndrome. *Spine, 17*, 957–959.

Kinney, R. K., Gatchel, R. J., Polatin, P. B., Fogarty, W. T., & Mayer, T. G. (1993). Prevalence of psychopathology in acute and chronic low back pain patients. *Journal of Occupational Rehabilitation, 3*(2), 95–103.

Kishino, N. D., Polatin, P. B., Brewer, S., & Hoffman, K. (2000). Long-term effectiveness of combined spine surgery and functional restoration: A prospective study. *Journal of Occupational Rehabilitation, 10*, 235–240.

Kjelby-Wendt, G., Styf, J. R., & Carlsson, S. G. (1999). The predictive value of psychometric analysis in patients treated by extirpation of lumbar intervertebral disc herniation. *Journal of Spinal Disorders, 12*, 375–379.

Klekamp, J., McCarty, E., & Spengler, D. (1998). Results of elective lumbar discectomy for patients involved in the workers' compensation system. *Journal of Spinal Disorders, 11*, 277–282.

Knox, B. D., & Chapman, T. M. (1993). Anterior lumbar interbody fusion for discogram concordant pain. *Journal of Spinal Disorders, 6*, 242–244.

Koltun, W. A., Bloomer, M. M., Tilberg, A. F., Seaton, J. F., Ilahi, O., Rung, G., et al. (1996). Awake epidural anesthesia is associated with improved natural killer cell cytotoxicity and a reduced stress response. *American Journal of Surgery, 171*, 68–73.

Kondraske, G. (1986, June). *Towards a standard clinical measure of postural stability*. Paper presented at the Proceedings of the 8th Annual Conference of the IEEE Engineering in Medicine and Biology Society. Chicago, IL.

Kondraske, G. (in press). Human performance: Measurement, science, concepts and computerized methodology. *Neurology*.

Kremer, E. F., Block, A. R., & Atkinson, J. J. (1983). Assessment of pain behavior: Factors that distort self-report. In R. Melzack (Ed.), *Pain management and assessment* (pp. 165–171). New York: Raven Press.

Kuperman, S. K., Osmon, D., Golden, C. J., & Blume, H. G. (1979). Prediction of neurosurgical results by psychological evaluation. *Perceptual and Motor Skills, 48*, 311–315.

Lacoumenta, S., Yeo, T. H., Burrin, J. M., Bloom, S. R., Paterson, S. L., & Hall, G. M. (1987). Fentanyl and the beta-endorphin, ACTH, and glucoregulatory hormonal response to surgery. *British Journal of Anaesthesia, 59*, 713–720.

Lancourt, J., & Kettelhut, M. (1992). Predicting return to work for lower back pain patients. *Spine, 17,* 629–640.

Larson, D. B. (1993). *The faith factor: An annotated bibliography of systematic reviews and clinical research on spiritual subjects* (Vol. 2). Boston: John Templeton Foundation.

Lautenbacher, S., & Rollman, G. B. (1999). Somatization, hypochondriasis and related conditions. In A. R. Block, E. F. Kremer, & E. Fernandez (Eds.), *Handbook of pain syndromes* (pp. 613–632). Mahwah, NJ: Erlbaum.

Lawlis, G. F., Cuencas, R., & Selby, D. (1989). The development of the Dallas Pain Questionnaire: An assessment of the impact of spinal pain on behavior. *Spine, 14,* 511–514.

Lazarus, R. S. (1966). *Psychological stress and the coping process.* New York: McGraw-Hill.

Lazarus, R. S., & Folkman, S. (1984). *Stress, appraisal, and coping.* New York: Springer.

Leape, L. L. (1994). Error in medicine. *Journal of the American Medical Association, 272,* 1851–1857.

Leape, L. L., Bates, D. W., Cullen, D. J., Cooper, J., Demonaco, H. J., Gallivan, T., et al. (1995). Systems analysis of adverse drug events. *Journal of the American Medical Association, 274,* 35–43.

Leavitt, F., & Sweet, J. J. (1986). Characteristics and frequency of malingering among patients with low back pain. *Pain, 25,* 357–364.

Leavitt, S. S., Johnston, T. L., & Beyer, R. D.(1971). The process of recovery: patterns in industrial back injury. 2. Predicting outcomes from early case data. *Industrial Medicine and Surgery, 40,* 7–15.

Leboeuf-Yde, C. (1999). Smoking and low back pain: A systematic literature review of 41 journal articles reporting 47 epidemiologic studies. *Spine, 24,* 1463–1470.

Leboeuf-Yde, C. (2000). Body weight and low back pain: A systematic literature review of 56 journal articles reporting on 65 epidemiologic studies. *Spine, 25,* 226–237.

Lehmann, T. R., & Rocca, H. S. (1981). Repeat lumbar surgery: A review of patients with failure from previous lumbar surgery treated with spinal canal exploration and lumbar spinal fusion. *Spine, 6,* 615–619.

Lehmann, T. R., Russell, D. W., & Spratt, K. F. (1983). The impact of patients with nonorganic physical findings on a controlled trial of transcutaneous electrical nerve stimulation and electroaccupuncture. *Spine, 8,* 625–634.

Leow, Y. H., & Maibach, H. I. (1998). Cigarette smoking, cutaneous vasculature, and tissue oxygen. *Clinical Dermatology, 16,* 579–584.

Leventhal, H., Diefenbach, M., & Leventhal, E. (1992). Illness cognition: Using common sense to understand treatment adherence and affect-cognition interactions. *Cognitive Therapy and Research, 16,* 143–163.

Leventhal, H., & Johnson, J. (1983). Laboratory and field experimentation: Development of a theory of self-regulation. In P. J. Wooldridge, M. H. Schmitt, J. K. Skipper, & R. C. Leonard (Eds.), *Behavioral science and nursing theory* (pp. 189–262). St. Louis, MO: Mosby.

Levin, J. S. (1994). Religion and health: Is there an association, is it valid, and is it causal? *Social Science and Medicine, 38,* 1475–1482.

Levinson, W., & Chaumeton, N. (1999). Communication between surgeons and patients in routine office visits. *Surgery, 125,* 127–134.

Liebeskind, J. C. (1991). Pain can kill. *Pain, 44,* 3–4.

Lindsay, P., & Wyckoff, M. (1981). The depression-pain cycle and its response to antidepressants. *Psychosomatics, 22,* 571–577.

Linn, B. S., & Jensen, J. (1983). Age and immune response to a surgical stress. *Archives of Surgery, 118,* 405–409.

Linton, S. J. (1997). A population-based study of the relationship between sexual abuse and back pain: Establishing a link. *Pain, 73,* 47–53.

Linton, S. J. (2000). A review of psychological risk factors in back and neck pain. *Spine, 25,* 1148–1156.

Loeser, J. D., Butler, S. H., Chapman, C. R., & Turk, D. C. (Eds.). (2001). *Bonica's management of pain* (3rd ed.). Philadelphia: Lippincott, Williams & Wilkins.

Long, C. (1981). The relationship between surgical outcome and MMPI profiles in chronic pain patients. *Journal of Clinical Psychology, 37,* 744–749.

Loranger, A., Lehmann-Susman, V., Oldham, J., & Russakof, L. (1985). *Personality Disorder Examination (PDE): A structured interview for DSM-III-R personality disorders.* White Plains, NY: New York Hospital-Cornell Medical Center.

Lousberg, R., Schmidt, A. J., & Groenman, N. H. (1992). The relationship between spouse solicitousness and pain behavior: Searching for more evidence. *Pain, 51,* 75–79.

Lowry, S. F. (1993). Cytokine mediators of immunity and inflammation. *Archives of Surgery, 28,* 1235–1241.

Lynch, D. F. (1999). Empowering the patient: Hypnosis in the management of cancer, surgical disease and chronic pain. *American Journal of Clinical Hypnosis, 42,* 122–130.

Magni, G., Andreoli, C., de Leo, D., Martinotti, G., & Rossi, C. (1986). Psychological profile of women with chronic pelvic pain. *Archives of Gynecology and Obstetrics, 237,* 165.

Mahler, H. I. M., & Kulik, J. A. (1998). Effects of preparatory videotapes on self-efficacy beliefs and recovery from coronary bypass surgery. *Annals of Behavioral Medicine, 20,* 39–46.

Main, C. J. (1983). The modified somatic perception questionnaire (MSPQ). *Journal of Psychosomatic Research, 27,* 503–514.

Main, C. J., & Waddell, G. (1998). Behavioral responses to examination: A reappraisal of the interpretation of "nonorganic signs." *Spine, 23,* 2367–2371.

Main, C. J., Wood, P. L. R., Hollis, S., Spanswick, C. C., & Waddell, G. (1992). The Distress and Risk Assessment Method: A simple patient classification to identify distress and evaluate the risk of poor outcome. *Spine, 17,* 42–52.

Malmivaara, A., Hakkinen, U., Aro, T., Heinrichs, M. L., Koskenniemi, L., Kuosma, E., et al. (1995). The treatment of acute low back pain—Bed rest, exercises, or ordinary activity? *New England Journal of Medicine, 332,* 351–355.

Malter, A. D., Larson, E. B., Urban, N., & Deyo, R. A. (1996). Cost-effectiveness of lumbar discectomy for the treatment of herniated intervertebral disc. *Spine, 21,* 1048–1055.

Mann, N. H., & Brown, M. D. (1991). Artificial intelligence in the diagnosis of low back pain. *Orthopedic Clinics of North America, 22,* 303–314.

Manniche, C., Asmussen, K. H., Lauritsen, B., Vinterberg, H., Karbo, H., Abildstrup, S., et al. (1993). Intensive dynamic back exercises with or without hyper extension in chronic back pain after surgery for lumbar disc protrusion: A clinical trial. *Spine, 18,* 560–567.

Manniche, C., Asmussen, K. H., Vinterberg, H., Rose-Hansen, E. B. R., Kramhoft, J., & Jordan, A. (1994). Analysis of preoperative prognostic factors in first-time surgery for lumbar disc herniation, including Finneson's and modified Spengler's score systems. *Danish Medical Bulletin, 41,* 110–115.

Manniche, C., Skall, H. F., Braundholt, L., Christensen, B. H., Christophersen, L., Ellegaard, B., et al. (1993). Clinical trial of postoperative dynamic back exercises after first lumber discectomy. *Spine, 18,* 92–97.

Margolis, R. B., Tait, R. C., & Krause, S. J. (1986). A rating system for use with patient pain drawings. *Pain, 24,* 57–65.

Marlatt, G. A., & Gordon, J. R. (1985). *Relapse prevention.* New York: Guilford Press.

Marras, W. S., Davis, K. G., Heaney, C. A., Maronitis, A. B. & Allread, W. G. (2000). The influence of psychosocial stress, gender and personality on mechanical loading of the lumbar spine. *Spine, 25,* 3045–3054.

Marras, W. S., Granata, K.P. and Davis, K.G. (1999). Variability in spine loading model performance. *Clinical Biomechanics, 14*, 505–514.

Marucha, P. T., Kiecolt-Glaser, J. K., & Favagehi, M. (1998). Muscosal wound healing is impaired by examination stress. *Psychosomatic Medicine, 60*, 362–365.

Maruta, T., & Osborne, D. (1976). Sexual activity in chronic pain patients. *Psychosomatics, 19*, 531–537.

Matthews, D. A., Larson, D. B., & Barry, C. P. (1994). *The faith factor: An annotated bibliography of systematic reviews and clinical research on spiritual subjects* (Vol. 1). Boston: John Templeton Foundation.

Mayer, T. G. (1991). Rationale for modern spine care. In T. G. Mayer, V. Mooney, & R. J. Gatchel (Eds.), *Contemporary conservative care for painful spinal disorders: Concepts, diagnosis, and treatment* (pp. 3–9). Philadelphia: Lea & Febiger.

Mayer, T. G., & Gatchel, R. J. (1988). *Functional restoration for spinal disorders: The sports medicine approach.* Philadelphia: Lea & Febiger.

Mayer, T. G., Gatchel, R. J., & Evans, T. H. (2001). Chronic low back pain. In R. Fitzgerald, H. Kauffer, & A. Malkani (Eds.), *Orthopaedics* (pp. 1192–1197). Chicago: Mosby.

Mayer, T. G., Gatchel, R. J., Mayer, H., Kishino, N. D., Keeley, J., & Mooney, V. (1987). A prospective two-year study of functional restoration in industrial low back injury. *Journal of the American Medical Association, 258*, 1763–1768.

Mayer, T. G., McMahon, M. J., Gatchel, R. J., Sparks, B., Wright, A., & Pegues, P. (1998). Socioeconomic outcomes of combined spine surgery and functional restoration in workers' compensation spinal disorders with matched controls. *Spine, 23*, 598–605; discussion 606.

Mayfield, M. (1993). Nutrition and obesity. In S. H. Hochschuler, H. B. Cotler, & R. D. Guyer (Eds.), *Rehabilitation of the spine: Science and practice* (pp. 677–684). St. Louis, MO: Mosby.

McCracken, L. M., Gross, R. T., Aikens, J., & Carnrike, C. L. M. (1996). The assessment of anxiety and fear in persons with chronic pain: A comparison of instruments. *Behavior Research and Therapy, 31*, 647–652.

McCreary, C. P., Turner, J., & Dawson, E. (1979). The MMPI as a predictor of response to conservative treatment for low back pain. *Journal of Clinical Psychology, 3*, 278–284.

McDaniel, L. K., Anderson, K. O., Bradley, L. A., Young, L. D., Turner, R. A., Agudelo, C. A., et al. (1986). Development of an observation method for assessing pain behavior in rheumatoid arthritis patients. *Pain, 24*, 165–184.

McDermid, A. J., Rollman, G. R., & McCain, G. A. (1996). Generalized hypervigilance in fibromyalgia: Evidence of perceptual amplification. *Pain, 66,* 133–144.

McEwen, B. S. (1990). Hormones and the nervous system. *Advances, 7,* 50–54.

McKay, M., Davis, M., & Fanning, P. (1983). *Messages: The communication book.* Oakland, CA: New Harbinger Publications.

McKay, M., & Fanning, P. (1991). *Prisoners of belief: Exposing and changing beliefs that control your life.* Oakland, CA: New Harbinger Publications.

Meichenbaum, D. H. (1977). *Cognitive behavior modification: An integrative approach.* New York: Plenum Press.

Melzack, R., & Casey, K. L. (1968). Sensory, motivational, and central control determinants of pain: A new conceptual model. In D. Kenshalo (Ed.), *The skin senses* (pp. 423–443). Springfield, IL: Thomas.

Melzack, R., & Wall, P. D. (1965). Pain mechanisms: A new theory. *Science, 150,* 971–979.

Melzack, R., & Wall, P. D. (1982). *The challenge of pain.* New York: Basic Books.

Merskey, H. (1965). The effect of chronic pain upon the response to noxious stimuli by psychiatric patients. *Journal of Psychosomatic Research, 9,* 291–298.

Merskey, H., & Moulin, D. (1999). Pharmacological treatment in chronic pain. In A. R. Block, E. F. Kremer, & E. Fernandez (Eds.), *Handbook of Pain Syndromes* (pp. 149–162). Mahwah, NJ: Erlbaum.

Meyer, G. J., Finn, S. E., Eyde, L. D., Kay, G. G., Moreland, K. L., Dies, R. R., et al. (2001). Psychological testing and psychological assessment: A review of evidence and issues. *American Psychologist, 56,* 128–165.

Miller, G. E., Dopp, J. M., Myers, H. F., Stevens, S. Y., & Fahey, J. L. (1999). Psychosocial predictors of natural killer cell mobilization during marital conflict. *Health Psychology, 18,* 262–271.

Miller, S. M. (1987). Monitoring and blunting: Validation of a questionnaire to assess styles of information seeking under threat. *Journal of Personality and Social Psychology, 52,* 345–353.

Miller, S. M. (1992). Individual differences in the coping process: What to know and when to know it. In B. Carpenter (Ed.), *Personal coping: Theory, research and application* (pp. 77–91). Westport, NJ: Erlbaum.

Miro, J., & Raich, R. M. (1999). Effects of a brief and economical intervention in preparing patients for surgery: Does coping matter? *Pain, 83,* 471–475.

Mitchell, M. (1997). Patients' perceptions of pre-operative preparation for day surgery. *Journal of Advanced Nursing, 26,* 356–363.

Moller, I. W., Dinesen, K., Sondergard, S., Knigge, U., & Kehlet, H. (1988). Effect of patient-controlled analgesia on plasma catecholamine, cortisol and glucose concentrations after cholecystectomy. *British Journal of Anaesthesia, 61*, 160–164.

Mooney, V. (1990). A randomized double-blind prospective study of the efficacy of pulsed electromagnetic fields for interbody lumbar fusions. *Spine, 15*, 708–712.

Morris, D. B. (1999). Sociocultural and religious meaning of pain. In R. J. Gatchel & D. C. Turk (Eds.), *Psychosocial factors in pain: Critical perspectives* (pp. 118–131). New York: Guilford Press.

Mosely, L. H., & Finseth, F. (1977). Cigarette smoking: Impairment of digital flow and wound healing in the hand. *Hand, 9*, 97–101.

Moulin, D. E., Iezzi, A., Amireah, R., & Merskey, H. (1996). Randomized trial of oral morphine for chronic non-cancer pain. *Lancet, 347*, 143–147.

Mumford, E., Schlesinger, H. J., & Glass, G. V. (1982). The effect of psychological intervention on recovery from surgery and heart attacks: An analysis of the literature. *American Journal of Public Health, 72*, 141–151.

Mutran, E. J., Reitzes, D. C., Mossey, J., & Fernandez, M. E. (1995). Social support, depression and recovery of walking ability following hip fracture surgery. *Journal of Gerontology, 50B*, 5354–5361.

Niehoff, D. (1999). *The biology of violence*. New York: Free Press.

North, R. B., Campbell, J. N., James, C. S., Conover-Walker, M. K., Wang, H., Piantadosi, S., et al. (1993). Failed back surgery syndrome: 5-year follow up in 102 patients undergoing repeated operation. *Neurosurgery, 28*, 685–691.

Oaklander, A. L., & North, R. B. (2001). Failed back surgery syndrome. In J. D. Loeser, S. H. Butler, C. R. Chapman, & D. C. Turk (Eds.), *Bonica's management of pain* (3rd ed.; pp. 1540–1549). Philadelphia: Lippincott, Williams & Wilkins.

O'Brien, M. E. (1980). Effective social environment and hemodialysis adaptation: A panel analysis. *Journal of Health and Social Behavior, 21*, 360–370.

Oetker-Black, S. L., & Taunton, R. L. (1994). Evaluation of a self-efficacy scale for preoperative patients. *Association of Orthopaedic and Rehabilitation Nursing Journal, 60*, 43–50.

Ohnmeiss, D. D. (2000). *Pain drawings in the evaluation of lumbar disc-related pain*. Stockholm: Karolinska Institute.

Ohnmeiss, D. D., Vanharanta, H., & Guyer, R. D. (1995). The association between pain drawings and CT/discographic pain responses. *Spine, 20*, 729–733.

O'Leary, A. (1990). Stress, emotion, and human immune function. *Psychological Bulletin, 108*, 363–382.

Oman, R. F., & King, A. C. (2000). The effect of life events and exercise program format on the adoption and maintenance of exercise behavior. *Health Psychology, 19*, 605–612.

Oxman, T. E., Freeman, D. H., & Manheimer, E. D. (1995). Lack of social participation or religious strength and comfort as risk factors for death after cardiac surgery in the elderly. *Psychosomatic Medicine, 57*, 5–15.

Padgett, D. A., Marucha, P. T., & Sheridan, J. F. (1998). Restraint stress slows cutaneous wound healing in mice. *Brain, Behavior, and Immunity, 12*, 64–73.

Page, G. G. (1996). The medical necessity of adequate pain management. *Pain Forum, 5*, 227–233.

Pasqualucci, A., Contardo, R., Da Broi, U., Colo, F., Terrosu, G., Donini, A., et al. (1994). The effects of intraperitoneal local anesthetic requirements and endocrine response after laparoscopic cholecystectomy: A randomized double-blind controlled study. *Journal of Laparoendoscopic Surgery, 4*, 405–412.

Paulsen, J. S., & Altmaier, E. M. (1995). The effect of perceived versus enacted social support of the discriminative cue function of spouses for pain behavior. *Pain, 60*, 103–110.

Pearlin, L. I., Mullan, J. T., Semple, S. J., & Skaff, M. M. (1990). Caregiving and the stress process: An overview of concepts and their measures. *Gerontologist, 51*, 583–591.

Peebles, R. J., & Schneiderman, D. S. (1991). *Socio-economic factbook for surgery, 1991–1992.* Chicago: American College of Surgeons.

Pellino, T., Tluczek, A., Collins, M., Trimborn, S., Norwick, H., Engelke, Z. K., et al. (1998, July/August). Increasing self-efficacy through empowerment: Preoperative education for orthopaedic patients. *Orthopaedic Nursing*, pp. 48–59.

Pellino, T. A., & Ward, S. E. (1998). Perceived control mediates the relationship between pain severity and patient satisfaction. *Journal of Pain and Symptom Management, 15*, 110–116.

Penta, M., & Fraser, R. D. (1997). Anterior lumbar interbody fusion. A minimum 10-year follow-up. *Spine, 22*, 2429–2434.

Perry, F., Parker, R. K., White, P. F., & Clifford, A. (1994). Role of psychological factors in post-operative pain control and recovery with patient-controlled analgesia. *Clinical Journal of Pain, 10*, 57–63.

Pezzone, M. A., Dohanics, J., & Rabin, B. S. (1994). Effects of footshock stress upon spleen and peripheral blood lymphocyte mitogenic responses in rats with lesions of the paraventricular nucleus. *Journal of Neuroimmunology, 53*, 39–46.

Pfohl, B., Blum, N., & Simmerman, M. (1995). *Structured interview for DSM-IV personality disorders*. Iowa City: University of Iowa.

Pheasant, H. C., Gelbert, D., Goldfarb, J., & Herron, L. (1979). The MMPI as predictor of outcome in low-back surgery. *Spine, 4*, 78–84.

Pilowsky, I. (1978). A general classification of abnormal illness behavior. *British Journal of Medical Psychiatry, 51*(2), 131–137.

Polatin, P. B., & Gajraj, N. M. (2002). Integration of pharmacotherapy with psychological treatment of chronic pain. In D. C. Turk & R. J. Gatchel (Eds.), *Psychological approaches to pain management* (2nd ed.; pp. 276–299). New York: Guilford Press.

Polatin, P. B., Kinney, R. K., Gatchel, R. J., Lillo, E., & Mayer, T. G. (1993). Psychiatric illness and chronic low-back pain: The mind and the spine—which goes first? *Spine, 18*, 66–71.

Polatin, P. B., Rainville, J., Haider, T. T., & Kishino, N. D. (2000). Postoperative treatment: Outpatient medical rehabilitation. In T. G. Mayer, R. J. Gatchel, & P. B. Polatin (Eds.), *Occupational musculoskeletal disorders* (pp. 535–546). Philadelphia: Lippincott, Williams & Wilkins.

Pollock, R. E., Lotzova, E., & Stanford, S. D. (1991). Mechanism of surgical stress impairment of human perioperative natural killer cell cytotoxicity. *Archives of Surgery, 126*, 338–342.

Portenoy, R. K. (1994). Opioid therapy for chronic non-malignant pain: Current status. In H. L. Fields & J. C. Liebeskind (Eds.), *Progress in pain research and therapy* (Vol. 1; pp. 247–287). Seattle, WA: International Association for the Study of Pain Press.

Porter, J., & Jick, H. (1980). Addiction is rare in patients treated with narcotics. *New England Journal of Medicine, 302*, 123.

Porter, S. E., & Hanley, E. N. (2001). The musculoskeletal effects of smoking. *Journal of the American Academy of Orthopaedic Surgeons, 9*, 9–17.

Pressman, P., Lyons, J. S., Larson, D. B., & Strain, J. J. (1990). Religious belief, depression, and ambulation status in elderly women with broken hips. *American Journal of Psychiatry, 147*, 758–760.

Prokop, C. K., Bradley, L. A., Burish, T. G., Anderson, K. O., & Fox, J. E. (1991). Psychological preparation for stressful medical and dental procedures. In C. K. Prokop & L. A. Bradley (Eds.), *Health psychology: Clinical methods and research* (pp. 159–196). New York: Macmillan.

Rabin, B. S. (1999). *Stress, immune function, and health: The connection*. New York: Wiley.

Raleigh, E. H., Lepczyk, M., & Rowley, C. (1990). Significant others benefit from preoperative information. *Journal of Advanced Nursing, 15,* 941–945.

Ransford, A. O., Cairns, D., & Mooney, V. (1976). The pain drawing as an aid to the psychologic evaluation of patients with low-back pain. *Spine, 20,* 127–136.

Ready, L. B., & Edwards, W. T. (Eds). (1992). *Management of acute pain: A practical guide.* Seattle, WA: International Association for the Study of Pain Press.

Redd, W. H., & Jacobsen, P. (2001). Behavioral intervention in comprehensive cancer care. In A. Baum, T. A. Revenson, & J. E. Singer (Eds.), *Handbook of health psychology* (pp. 757–776). Mahwah, NJ: Erlbaum.

Reesor, K. A., & Craig, K. D. (1998). Medically incongruent back pain: Physical limitations, suffering and ineffective coping. *Pain, 32,* 35–45.

Reich, J., Tupen, J. P. & Abramowitz, S. I. (1987). Psychiatric diagnosis of chronic pain patients. *American Journal of Psychiatry, 150,* 471–475.

Reiter, R. C., & Gambone, J. C. (1990). Demographic and historic variables in women with idiopathic chronic pelvic pain. *Obstetrics and Gynecology, 75,* 428–432.

Riley, J. L., Robinson, M. E., Geisser, M. E., Wittmer, V. T., & Smith, A. G. (1995). Relationship between MMPI-2 cluster profiles and surgical outcome in low-back pain patients. *Journal of Spinal Disorders, 8,* 213–219.

Rizzo, J. A., Abbott, T. A., III, & Berger, M. (1998). The labor productivity effects of chronic backache in the United States. *Medical Care, 36,* 1471–1488.

Robinson, M. E., & Riley, J. L. (1999). Models of pain. In A. R. Block, E. F. Kremer, & E. Fernandez (Eds.), *Handbook of pain syndromes: Biopsychosocial perspectives* (pp. 23–40). Mahwah, NJ: Erlbaum.

Rodriguez, J. E. (1993). Clinical examination and documentation. In S. H. Hochschuler, H. B. Cotler, & R. D. Guyer (Eds.), *Rehabilitation of the spine: Science and practice* (pp. 27–44). St. Louis, MO: Mosby.

Romano, J. M., Turner, J. A., & Clancy, S. L. (1989). Sex differences in the relationship of pain patient dysfunction to spouse adjustment. *Pain, 39,* 289–296.

Romano, J. M., Turner, J. A., Jensen, M. P., Friedman, L. S., Bulcroft, R. A., Hops, H., et al. (1995). Chronic pain patient–spouse interactions predict patient disability. *Pain, 63,* 353–360.

Rosenstiel, A. K., & Keefe, F. J. (1983). The use of coping strategies in chronic low back pain patients: Relationship to patient characteristics and current adjustment. *Pain, 17,* 33–44.

Saal, J. A., & Saal, J. S. (2000). Intradiscal electrothermal treatment for chronic discogenic low back pain: A prospective outcome study with minimum 1-year follow-up. *Spine, 25*, 2622–2627.

Saal, J. S., & Saal, J. A. (2000). Management of chronic discogenic low back pain with a thermal intradiscal catheter: A preliminary report. *Spine, 25*, 382–388.

Sacerdote, P., Manfredi, B., Bianchi, M., & Panerai, A. E. (1994). Intermittent but not continuous inescapable footshock stress affects immune responses and immunocyte beta-endorphin concentrations in the rat. *Brain, Behavior, and Immunity, 8*, 251–260.

Salomaki, T. E., Leppaluoto, J., Laitinen, J. O., Vuolteenaho, O., & Nuutinen, L. S. (1993). Epidural versus intravenous fentanyl for reducing hormonal, metabolic, and physiologic responses after thoracotomy. *Anesthesiology, 79*, 672–679.

Schade, V., Semmer, N., Main, C. J., Hora, J., & Boos, N. (1999). The impact of clinical, morphological, psychosocial and work-related factors on the outcome of lumbar discectomy. *Pain, 80*, 239–249.

Schiaffino, K. M., & Revenson, T. A. (1995). Relative contributions of spousal support and illness appraisals to depressed mood in arthritis patients. *Arthritis Care and Research, 8*, 80–87.

Schmidt, A. J. M. (1987). The behavioral management of pain: A criticism of a response. *Pain, 30*, 285–291.

Schmidt, A. J. M., & Brands, A. E. F. (1986). Persistence behavior of chronic low back pain patients in an acute pain situation. *Journal of Psychosomatic Research, 30*, 339–346.

Schofferman, J., Anderson, D., Hinds, R., Smith, G., & White, A. (1992). Childhood psychological trauma correlates with unsuccessful lumbar spine surgery. *Spine, 17*(6, Suppl.), S1380–S1384.

Schwartz, L., Slater, M. A., Birchler, G. R., & Atkinson, J. H. (1991). Depression in spouses of chronic pain patients: The role of patient pain and anger, and marital satisfaction. *Pain, 44*, 61–68.

Schwarzer, A. C., Aprill, C. N., & Bogduk, N. (1995). The sacroiliac joint in chronic low back pain. *Spine, 20*, 31–37.

Schwarzer, A. C., Aprill, C. N., Derby, R., Fortin, J., Kine, G., & Bogduk, N. (1994). The relative contributions of the disc and zygapophyseal joint in chronic low back pain. *Spine, 19*, 801–806.

Schweizer, A., Feige, U., Fontana, A., Muller, K., & Dinarello, C. A. (1988). Interleukin-1 enhances pain reflexes: Mediation through increased prostaglandin E2 levels. *Agents and Action, 25*, 246–251.

Scott, S. C., Goldberg, M. S., Mayo, N. E., Stock, S. R., & Poîtras, B. (1999). The association between cigarette smoking and back pain in adults. *Spine*, *24*, 1090–1098.

Scudds, R. A., Rollman, G. B., Harth, M., & McCain, G. A. (1987). Pain perception and personality measures as discriminators in the classification of fibrositis. *Journal of Rheumatology*, *14*, 563–569.

Seligman, M. E. P. (1975). *Helplessness: On depression, development, and death*. San Francisco: W. H. Freeman.

Sherwin, M. A., & Gastwirth, C. M. (1990). Detrimental effects of cigarette smoking on lower extremity wound healing. *Journal of Foot Surgery*, *29*, 84–87.

Shuldman, C. (1999). A review of the impact of pre-operative education on recovery from surgery. *International Journal of Nursing Studies*, *36*, 171–177.

Silverstein, P. (1992). Smoking and wound healing. *American Journal of Medicine*, *93*, 22S–24S.

Sinel, M., & Deardorff, W. (1999). *Back pain remedies for dummies*. Foster City, CA: IDG.

Skinner, B. F. (1974). *About Behaviorism*. New York: Alfred A. Knopf.

Slosar, P. J., Perkins, R. B., & Snook, D. (2002). Effects of cigarette smoking on the spine: A focused review. *SpineLine*, Sept/Oct, 6–9.

Slosar, P. J., Reynolds, J. B., Schofferman, J., Goldthwaite, N., White, A. H., & Keaney, D. (2000). Patient satisfaction after circumferential lumbar fusion. *Spine*, *25*, 722–726.

Smith, D. (2002, January). Psychologists now eligible for reimbursement under six new health and behavior codes. *Monitor on Psychology*, *33*, 19.

Smith, W. L., & Duerksen, D. L. (1979). Personality and the relief of chronic pain: Predicting surgical outcome. *Clinical Neuropsychology*, *1*, 35–38.

Sorenson, L. V. (1992). Preoperative psychological testing with the MMPI at first operation for prolapsed lumbar disc. *Danish Medical Bulletin*, *39*, 186–190.

SpineLine. (Mar/Apr, 2001). *Preventing medical errors: AHRQ tips for patients*. Chicago, IL: North American Spine Society.

Spence, A. P. (1982). *Basic human anatomy*. Menlo Park, CA: Benjamin/Cummings Publishing.

Spengler, D. M., Bigos, S. J., Martin, N. A., Zeh, J., Fisher, L., & Nachemson, A. (1986). Back injuries in industry: A retrospective study. I. Overview and cost analysis. *Spine*, *11*, 241–245.

Spengler, D. M., Freeman, C., Westbrook, R., & Miller, J. W. (1980). Low-back pain following multiple lumbar spine procedures: Failure of initial selection? *Spine*, *5*, 356–360.

Spengler, D. M., Ouelette, E. A., Battie, M., & Zeh, J. (1990). Elective discectomy for herniation of a lumbar disc. *Journal of Bone and Joint Surgery* (American ed.), *12*, 230–237.

Spielberger, C. D., Gorusch, R. I., & Lushene, R. (1983). *Manual for the State-Trait Anxiety Inventory*. Palo Alto, CA: Consulting Psychology Press.

Spitzer, W. O., Leblanc, F. E., Dupuis, M., & LeBlanc, P. (1987). Scientific approach to the assessment and management of activity-related spinal disorders. *Spine, 12*(Suppl.), S1.

Spitzer, W. O., Williams, J. B., Gibbon, M., & First, M. (1988). *Structured Clinical Interview for DSM-III-R*. New York: New York State Psychiatric Institute.

Stauffer, R. N., & Coventry, M. B. (1972). Anterior interbody lumbar spine fusion: Analysis of Mayo Clinic series. *Journal of Bone and Joint Surgery* (American ed.), *54*, 756–789.

Steptoe, A., Wardle, J., Pollard, T. M., Canaan, L., & Davies, G. J. (1996). Stress, social support and health-related behavior: A study of smoking, alcohol consumption and physical exercise. *Journal of Psychosomatic Research, 41*, 171–180.

Stewart, M. A. (1995). Effective physician–patient communication and health outcomes: A review. *Canadian Medical Association Journal, 152*, 1423–1433.

Suls, J., & Wan, C. K. (1989). Effects of sensory and procedural information on coping with stressful medical procedures and pain: A meta-analysis. *Journal of Consulting and Clinical Psychology, 57*, 372–379.

Szasz, T. S. (1968). The painful person. *Lancet, 88*, 18–22.

Takata, K., & Hirotani, H. (1995). Pain drawings in the evaluation of low back pain. *International Orthopedics, 19*, 361–366.

Tandon, V., Campbell, F., & Ross, E. R. S. (1999). Posterior lumbar interbody fusion: Association between disability and psychological disturbance in noncompensation patients. *Spine, 24*, 1833–1838.

Taylor, H., & Curren, H. M. (1985). *The Nuprin pain report*. New York: Louis Harris.

Taylor, S. E. (1983). Adjustment to threatening events: A theory of cognitive adaptation. *American Psychologist, 38*, 1161–1173.

Taylor, V. M., Deyo, R. A., Ciol, M., Farrar, E. L., Lawrence, M. S., Shonnard, N. H., et al. (2000). Patient-oriented outcomes from low back surgery: A community-based study. *Spine, 25*, 2445–2452.

Temple, W., Toews, J., Fidler, H., Lockyer, J. M., Taenzer, P., & Parboosingh, J. (1998). Concordance in communication between surgeon and patient. *Canadian Journal of Surgery, 41*, 439–445.

Thalgott, J. S., Chin, A. K., Ameriks, J. A., Jordan, F. T., Daubs, M. D., Giuffre, J. M., et al. (2000). Gasless endoscopic anterior lumbar interbody fusion utilizing the B.E.R.G. approach. *Surgical Endoscapy, 14,* 546–552.

Thalgott, J. S., Cotler, H. B., Sasso, R. C., LaRocca, H., & Gardner, V. (1991). Postoperative infections in spinal implants: Classifications and analysis—A multicenter study. *Spine, 16,* 981–984.

Thomas, D. R., & Ritchie, C. S. (1995). Preoperative assessment of older adults. *Journal of the American Geriatrics Society, 43,* 811–821.

Tonnessen, E., Brinklov, M. M., Christensen, N. J., Olesen, A. S., & Madsen, T. (1987). Natural killer cell activity and lymphocyte function during and after coronary artery bypass grafting in relation to the endocrine stress response. *Anesthesiology, 67,* 526–533.

Tonnessen, E., & Wahlgreen, C. (1988). Influence of extradural and general anaesthesia on natural killer cell activity and lymphocyte subpopulations in patients undergoing hysterectomy. *British Journal of Anesthaesia, 60,* 500–507.

Trief, P. M., Grant, W., & Fredrickson, B. (2000). A prospective study of psychological predictors of lumbar surgery outcome. *Spine, 25,* 2616–2621.

Trousdale, R. T., McGrory, B. J., Berry, D. J., Becker, M. W., & Harmsen, W. S. (1999). Patients' concerns prior to undergoing total hip and total knee arthroplasty. *Mayo Clinic Proceedings, 74,* 978–982.

Turk, D. C., & Fernandez, E. (1995). Personality assessment and the Minnesota Multiphasic Personality Inventory in chronic pain: Underdeveloped and overexposed. *Pain Forum, 4*(2), 104–107.

Turner, J. A., Ersek, M., Herron, L., Haselkorn, J., Kent, D., Ciol, M. A., et al. (1992). Patient outcomes after lumbar spinal fusions. *Journal of the American Medical Association, 268*(7), 907–911.

Turner, J. A., Herron, L. & Weiner, P. (1986). Utility of the MMPI pain assessment index in predicting outcome after lumbar surgery. *Journal of Clinical Psychology, 42,* 764–769.

Uchino, B. N., Cacioppo, J. T., & Kiecolt-Glaser, J. K. (1996). The relationship between social support and physiological processes: A review with emphasis on underlying mechanisms and implications for health. *Psychological Bulletin, 119,* 488–531.

Uden, A., Astrom, M., & Bergenudd, H. (1988). Pain drawings in chronic back pain. *Spine, 13,* 389–392.

Uden, A., & Landin, L. A. (1987). Pain drawing and myelography in sciatic pain. *Clinical Orthopedics, 216,* 124–130.

Ulrich, R. E., & Azrin, N. H. (1962). Reflexive fighting in response to aversive stimulation. *Journal of the Experimental Analysis of Behavior, 5,* 511–520.

Uomoto, J. M., Turner, J. A., & Herron, L. D. (1988). Use of the MMPI and MCMI in predicting outcome of lumbar laminectomy. *Journal of Clinical Psychology, 44,* 191–197.

Van De Kerkhof, P. C. M., Van Bergen, B., Spruijt, K., & Kuiper, J. P. (1994). Age-related changes in wound healing. *Clinical and Experimental Dermatology, 19,* 369–374.

Vanharanta, H., Sachs, B. L., Ohnmeiss, D. D., April, C., Spivey, M., Guyer, R.D., et al. (1989). Pain provocation and disc deterioration by age: A CT/discography study in low back pain population. *Spine, 14,* 420–423.

Vanharanta, H., Sachs, B. L., Spivey, M. A., Guyer, R. D., Hochschuler, S. H., Rashbaum, R. F., et al. (1987). The relationship of pain provocation to lumbar disc deterioration as seen by CT/discography. *Spine, 12,* 295–298.

Veldhuis, J. D., & Iranmanesh, A. (1996). Physiological regulation of the human growth hormone (GH)-insulin-like growth factor type I (IGF-I) axis: Predominant impact of age, obesity, gonadal function, and sleep. *Sleep, 19,* S221–S224.

Verhoef, J. (1990). Transient immunodepression. *Journal of Antimicrobial Chemotherapy, 26,* 23–29.

Vingard, E., Alfredsson, L., Hagberg, M., Kilbom, A., Theorell, T., Waldenstrom, M., et al. (2000). To what extent do current and past physical and psychosocial occupational factors explain care-seeking for low back pain in a working population? *Spine, 25,* 493–500.

Von Korff, M., Dworkin, S. F., & Le Resche, L. (1990). Graded chronic pain status: An epidemiologic evaluation. *Pain, 40,* 279–291.

Wacholz, E. H., & Block, A. R. (2000, November). *The influence of spousal response on early outcome after spine surgery.* Paper presented at the North American Spine Society Annual Convention, New Orleans.

Waddell, G. (1987). A new clinical model for the treatment of low-back pain. *Spine, 12,* 632–644.

Waddell, G. (1998). *The back pain revolution.* London: Churchill Livingstone.

Waddell, G., McCulloch, J. A., Kummel, E., & Venner, R. M. (1980). Nonorganic physical signs in low-back pain. *Spine, 5,* 117–125.

Walker, E., Katon, W., Harrop-Griffiths, J., Holm, L., Russo, J., & Hickok, L. R. (1988). Relationship of chronic pelvic pain to psychiatric diagnoses and childhood sexual abuse. *American Journal of Psychiatry, 145,* 75–80.

Warfield, C. A., & Kahn, C. H. (1995). Acute pain management: Programs in U.S. hospitals and experiences and attitudes among U.S. adults. *Anesthesiology, 38,* 19–25.

Watkins, L. R., Goehler, L. E., Relton, J. K., Tartaglia, N., Silbert, L., Martin, D., et al. (1994). Characterization of cytokine-induced hyperalgesia. *Brain Research, 654,* 15–26.

Watkins, L. R., Goehler, L. E., Relton, J. K., Tartaglia, N., Silbert, L., Martin, D., et al. (1995). Blockade of interleukin-1 induced hyperthermia by subdiaphragmatic vagotomy: Evidence for vagal mediation of immune-brain communication. *Neuroscience Letters, 183,* 27–31.

Webber, G. C. (1990). Patient education: A review of the issues. *Medical Care, 28,* 1089–1103.

Weisberg, J. N., Gallagher, R. M., & Gorin, A. (1996, October). *Personality disorder in chronic pain: A longitudinal approach to validation of diagnosis.* Paper presented at the 15th meeting of the American Pain Society, Washington, DC.

Weisberg, J. N., & Keefe, F. J. (1997). Personality disorders in the chronic pain population: Basic concepts, empirical findings and clinical implications. *Pain Forum, 6,* 1–9.

Wernecke, M. W., Harris, D. F., & Lichter, R. L. (1993). Clinical effectiveness of behavioral signs for screening chronic low back pain patients in a work-oriented physical rehabilitation program. *Spine, 18,* 2412–2418.

Wetzel, F. T., Brustein, M., Phillips, F. M., & Trott, S. (1999). Hardware failure in an unconstrained lumbar pedicle screw system. A 2-year follow-up study. *Spine, 24,* 1138–1143.

White, B., & Sanders, S. (1985). Differential effects on pain and mood in chronic pain patients with time- versus pain-contingent medication delivery. *Behavior Therapy, 16,* 28–38.

Whitecloud, T. S., III, Castro, F. P. Jr., Brinker, M. R., Hartzog, C. W. Jr., Ricciardi, J. E., & Hill, C. (1998). Degenerative conditions of the lumbar spine treated with intervertebral titanium cages and posterior instrumentation for circumferential fusion. *Journal of Spinal Disorders, 11,* 479–486.

Whitesides, T. E., Hanley, E. N., & Fellrath, R. F. (1994). Smoking abstinence: Is it necessary before spinal fusion? *Spine, 19,* 2012–2014.

Wilder-Smith, C. H., & Schuler, L. (1992). Postoperative analgesia: Pain by choice? The influence of patient attitudes and patient education. *Pain, 50,* 257–262.

Williams, D. A. (1996). Acute pain management. In R. J. Gatchel & D. C. Turk (Eds.), *Psychological approaches to pain management: A practitioner's handbook* (pp. 55–77). New York: Guilford Press.

Williams, D. A. (1997). Acute procedural and postoperative pain: Patient-related factors in its undermanagement. *APS Bulletin, 7,* 4–7.

Wiltse, L. L., & Rocchio, P. D. (1975). Preoperative psychological tests as predictors of success of chemonucleolysis in the treatment of low-back syndrome. *Journal of Bone and Joint Surgery* (American ed.), *75,* 478–483.

Woo, S., & Buckwalter, J. (1988). *Injury and repair of the musculoskeletal soft tissues.* Park Ridge, IL: AAOS Symposium.

Wood, D. P., & Hirschberg, B. C. (1994). Hypnosis with the surgical patient. *Military Medicine, 159,* 353–357.

Woolf, C. J. (1994). A new strategy for treatment of inflammatory pain: Prevention or elimination of central sensitization. *Drugs, 47,* 1–9.

Yeager, M. P., Glass, D. D., Neff, R. K., & Brinck-Johnsen, T. (1987). Epidural anesthesia and analgesia in high-risk surgical patients. *Anesthesiology, 66,* 729–736.

Zenz, M., Strumpf, M., & Tryba, M. (1992). Long-term opioid therapy in patients with chronic nonmalignant pain. *Journal of Pain and Symptom Management, 7,* 69–77.

Zung, W. (1965). A self-rating depression scale. *Archives of General Psychiatry, 12,* 63–70.

Zwilling, B. S. (1994). Neuroimmunomodulation of macrophage function. In R. Glaser & J. K. Kiecolt-Glaser (Eds.), *Handbook of human stress and immunity* (pp. 53–76). San Diego, CA: Academic Press.

ADDITIONAL RESOURCES

Commercial Web Sites

Spine-health.com
www.spine-health.com
   Excellent information source for patients.

SpineUniverse.com
www.spineuniverse.com
   Excellent information for patients. Also contains practitioner information and research.

Texas Back Institute
www.texasback.com
   Excellent general information source.

Professional Society Web Sites

American Academy of Pain Management
www.painmed.org
   Primarily practitioner information. Also has links and a job board.

American Pain Society
www.ampainsoc.org
   Primarily practitioner information.

International Association for the Study of Pain
www.iasp-pain.org
   Primarily professional information.

North American Spine Society
www.spine.org
   An excellent source for practitioners, with patient information also.

Society for Pain Practice Management
www.sppm.org

Private Organization Web Sites

American Chronic Pain Association
www.theacpa.org
   Information for patients having various chronic pain syndromes, including support group information.

American Pain Foundation
www.painfoundation.org
   Excellent patient information.

Dannemiller Memorial Education Foundation
www.pain.com
   Primarily for professionals, including CME and CE credits.

National Foundation for the Treatment of Pain
www.paincare.org
   Excellent links and email answered by physicians.

AUTHOR INDEX

Green, A., 128
Greenfield, K., 56
Greenfield, S. S., 172
Greenough, C. G., 65
Grevitt, M., 32, 34
Griffin, K., 174
Groenman, N. H., 69
Gross, A. R., 96, 97
Gross, R. J., 71
Gross, R. T., 90
Guo, H. R., 4
Gurin, J., 163
Guyer, R. D., 21, 40
Guzinski, G., 71

Haber, J., 71
Haddad, G. H., 65
Hafen, B. Q., 118, 122, 124
Haag, O., 24
Haider, T. T., 199, 200, 202, 210n
Halmosh, A. F., 179
Halperis, W. E., 4
Handlin, D. S., 66
Hanley, E. N., 127, 128, 129
Hanscom, D. A., 128
Hansen, F. R., 82
Hanvik, L. J., 83
Harmsen, W. S., 150
Harris, D. F., 48
Harth, M., 53
Hartzog, C. W., Jr., 24
Hashemi, L., 4
Hathaway, D., 137
Haug, J., 30
Hautmann, G., 128
Haythornthwaite, J., 85
Heaney, C. A., 63
Hegman, K. T., 48
Hellsing, A., 54, 55
Herbert, T. B., 120, 123, 129
Herron, L. D., 31, 51, 73, 81, 87, 106
Herve, M., 128
Heyer, N. J., 30
Hilgard, E. R., 78
Hilgard, J. R., 78
Hill, C., 24
Hill, M. I., 67
Hinds, R., 39
Hirotani, H., 51, 107
Hirschberg, B. C., 167, 168
Hobby, J. L., 34, 85, 86
Hochschuler, S. H., 40

Hoffman, K., 200
Hoffman, R. M., 30, 51, 53, 107
Hollis, S., 33
Holt, C., 92
Hora, J., 64
Horne, D. J., 132, 134, 137, 150, 152
Howie, J. C., 126
Hubner, G., 123
Hudgins, W. R., 65
Hueppe, M., 148

Iezzi, A., 73
Ilstrup, D. M., 51
Indahl, A., 22
Iranmanesh, A., 124
Israeli, R., 179

Jacobsen, P., 78
Janis, I. L., 136
Jarrett, P. E. M., 133
Jensen, J., 130
Jensen, M. C., 19
Jensen, M. P., 96
Jick, H., 188
Jorgensen, L. N., 128
Johnson, J., 139
Johnston, M., 132, 137, 142, 150, 151n, 187
Johnston, T. L., 4
Joint Commission on Accreditation of
        Healthcare Organizations
        (JCAHO), 183
Jolley, D., 26
Junge, A., 39, 44, 64, 66, 84, 102, 106, 107

Kahn, C. H., 182, 186
Kallehave, F., 128
Kaplan, S. H., 172
Karasek, M., 23
Karoly, P., 96
Karren, K. J., 118
Katz, J., 56, 85
Keaney, 24
Keefe, F. J., 48, 61, 92, 96, 204, 212
Keel, P. J., 75, 83
Kehlet, H., 126, 127
Keller, L. S., 80, 82, 89, 93
Keller, R. B., 30
Kelsey, J. L., 62
Kennedy, F., 66
Kerns, R. D., 69, 85, 138
Kessler, R., 167
Kettelkamp, D. B., 16

McCulloch, J. A., 38
McDaniel, L. K., 61
McDermid, A. J., 53
McEwen, B. S., 122
McFarlane, G. J., 55
McGrory, B. J., 150
McKay, M., 156, 163, 177
McKeefrey, S. P., 30
McMurtry, B., 67
Meagher, B. R., 74
Meichenbaum, D. H., 137, 155, 156
Melzack, R., 146
Mendelsohn, M., 84–85
Mercado, A. M., 125
Mersky, H., 73, 74, 86, 216
Meyer, G. J., 78
Michelsen, C. B., 52
Miller, G. E., 6
Miller, J. W., 73, 127
Miller, S. M., 136, 152
Miro, J., 136
Mitchell, M., 133
Moller, I. W., 126
Mooney, V., 48, 55
Morran, C. G., 126
Morris, D. B., 73
Mosely, L. H., 128
Mossey, J., 69
Moulin, D. E., 73, 74, 216
Muir, M., 186
Mullan, J. T., 145
Muller, K., 123
Mumford, E., 132
Mutran, E. V., 69
Myers, H. F., 6

Nakamura, Y., 146, 147
Neff, R. K., 126
Nelson, I. W., 56
Nelson, R. J., 56
Nicassio, P. M., 78, 95, 96
Niehoff, D., 87
Nordwall, 24
North, R. B., 17, 31, 51, 52, 107
Nuutinen, L. S., 126

Oaklander, A. L., 17, 31, 51
O'Brien, J. P., 80
O'Brien, M. E., 6
O'Dowd, J., 32
Oetker-Black, S. L., 137, 138, 139

Ohnmeiss, D. D., 21, 40, 49, 94, 106
Oldham, J., 91
O'Leary, A., 120
Olesen, A. S., 124
Oman, R. F., 6
O'Neill, P. I., 51
Orme, T. J., 54–55, 128
Osborne, D., 70
Oster, H., 128
Ostheimer, G. W., 186
Ouelette, E. A., 38
Oxman, T. E., 180

Padgett, D. A., 125
Page, G. G., 90, 119, 120, 123, 124, 126
Pande, K., 32
Panerai, A. E., 126
Papageorgiou, A. C., 55
Parker, R. K., 186
Pasino, J. A., 62
Pasqualucci, A., 126
Patronas, N. J., 19
Patterson, T. L., 86
Paulsen, J. S., 70
Pearlin, L. I., 145
Peebles, R. J., 182
Pellino, T., 137, 138, 139
Penta, M., 24
Perkins, R. B., 127
Perry, F., 186
Pezzone, M. A., 126
Pfohl, B., 91
Pheasant, H. C., 31, 51, 81, 107
Phillips, F. M., 24
Picciano, J. F., 30
Poîtras, B., 54
Polatin, P. B., 74, 80, 82, 86, 92, 93, 200, 202, 208, 210n, 216
Pollard, T. M., 127
Pollock, R. E., 124, 126
Portenoy, R. K., 73, 188
Porter, J., 188
Porter, S. E., 127, 129
Powell, D. J., 34
Pressman, P., 180
Prieto, E. J., 80
Prokop, C. K., 80, 132, 134, 136, 137, 152

Rabin, B. S., 120, 126
Raich, R. M., 136
Rainville, J., 202, 210n
Raleigh, E. H., 179

SUBJECT INDEX

and pain drawings, 51
Discectomy, lumbar, 30
  intensive rehabilitation from, 198–199
  success and failures of, 30
Disc endplate, 12, 224
Disc herniation, 14, 15, 224
  and failed back surgery syndrome, 17
  procedures for, 25
  and surgical results, 52
Disc nucleus, 12, 13, 224
Discography, 20–21, 224
Discordant pain reproduction, 84
Disc replacement, 24–25
Discriminative stimuli, 68
Disc space narrowing, and plain radiographs,
  18
Distress and Risk Assessment Method
  (DRAM), 33–34, 85, 86–87, 224
Doctor-patient communication gap, 172–
  174
Doctor visits
  bringing companion to, 174
  developing questions for, 173
DRAM (Distress and Risk Assessment
  Method), 33–34, 85, 86–87, 224
Drawings, pain, 48, 49–51
DSM-IV (*Diagnostic and Statistical Manual of
  Mental Disorders*, fourth edition)
  on malingering, 67
  on personality disorders, 91
  on substance abuse, 74
Dural sac, 224
Duration of injury, as medical risk factor, 43

Edema, 195, 224
Education campaign, public, 26
Education of patient
  on barrier-to-recovery issues, 203
  on pain control, 187
  on postoperative pain, 215–216
  preoperative, 136–137
  on progression procedures, 205
  as treatment option, 22
Electromyography, 20, 224
Emotional disturbance, surgeons' ability to
  identify, 32
Emotional support, 144
Emotion-focused coping, 141
Emotions
  of chronic pain patients, 5
  and healing, 6
Employers

and patients' state of mind, 171
  skepticism of, 5
  and workers' compensation, 64
Empowerment, 224
  and surgery preparation, 139
Endplate, 12, 224
Environments, psychosocial, 179–180
Epictetus, 155
Epidural space, 224
Errors, medical, 174–175
Eskimos, American, 16
Ethnicity, in spondylolisthesis, 16
Expectations of patient, and rehabilitation,
  213–215
Expected recovery time after spine surgery,
  201–202

Fact sheet, medical, 175
Facet joint, 12, 224
Facet joint injections, 21
Facet rhizotomy, 23, 45, 224
Failed back surgery syndrome, 17, 32, 51,
  224
  avoidance of 31–32
  procedures to alleviate, 25
  and psychosocial profile, 113
Family
  in acceptance of limitations, 219
  in surgery preparation, 179
Fears, assessing of, 150, 151
Feelings and thoughts, 156
Fibromyalgia, 53
Fight or flight response, 122
Filtering, 156, 161–162
Financial stress, 65
Foramen, 12, 224
Foraminal stenosis, 24
Foraminotomy, 24, 224
Freud, Sigmund, on psychogenic pain, 82–
  83
Functional restoration approach, 207–213
Fusion, spinal. *See* Spinal fusion

Gender differences, in spondylolisthesis, 16
Guidance, and patient's spirituality, 181

Handout to patient. *See* Patient handout
Health and behavior assessment and intervention codes, 222
Health care professionals, communication
  with. *See* Communication with
  health care professionals

Maximum medical improvement (MMI), 219

MDMP (multimodal disability management program), 211–212

Meaning, and patient's spirituality, 181

Medical chart, 43
    and medical risk factors, 43 (*see also* Medical risk factors)

Medical errors, avoiding of, 174–175

Medical fact sheet, 175

Medical history, 57

Medical information, ability to understand and remember, 152–153. *See also* Information

Medically incongruent pain, 48

Medical risk factors, 106–107
    duration of injury, 43–44
    lifestyle issues, 54–56
    nonorganic signs, 46–49
    on PPS scorecard, 106–107
    previous surgeries, 51–52
    prior medical utilization, 52–53
    type of surgery, 45–46

Medical utilization, prior, as risk factor, 52–53

Medications
    antidepressant, 110, 217
    hospital errors in, 174
    for pain, 72, 133–134, 216–218

Medication seeking, in PPS scorecard, 109

Medico-legal system, 5

Meninges, 225

Mental deconditioning, 196–198

Mental reconditioning program, 204

Microdiscectomy, 23, 45, 225

Mind reading, as negative self-talk, 158, 162

Minnesota Multiphasic Personality Inventory (MMPI), 79, 80, 98
    Hypochondriasis and Hysteria scores on, 104
    multiple scale elevations for, 93–94
    scale D (depression) of, 84
    scale Pd (Psychopathic Deviate) of, 87
    scale Pt (Psychesthenia) of, 89

Minnesota Multiphasic Personality Inventory—2 (MMPI-2), 79, 79–80, 98
    and cluster analysis of spine surgery candidates, 94
    Cook-Medley Hostility subscale of, 88
    Hysteria and Hypochondriasis scales of, 21, 39, 47, 75, 80, 82, 83, 84

MMI (maximum medical improvement), 219

Modeling, self-efficacy from, 138

Models for Multidisciplinary Arrangements: A State-by-State Review of Options (APA Practice Directorate), 221

Modified Somatic Perception Questionnaire (MSPQ), 32, 34
    and DRAM, 224

Morphine pump, 25

Motivation
    assessment of in PPS interview, 59
    and timely attendance, 110
    and vocational factors, 64

Motivation and compliance measures, 40, 109–114

MRI (magnetic resonance imaging), 18–19, 225

Multidimensional Pain Inventory, 69

Multimodal disability management program (MDMP), 211–212

Myelography, 19, 225
    and CT scanning, 18, 19

Myers-Briggs Type Indicator, 63

Narcissistic personality disorder, 91

National Institutes of Health, as information source, 153

National Spine Network's Health Survey Questionnaire, 88

Natural killer (NK) cells, 121

Negative self-talk
    challenging of, 160–163
    styles of, 156–160

Nerve roots, 225

Neuroablation, 23, 225

Neuroendocrine system, 121–122
    and pain, 125–126
    and wound healing, 123–124

Nociception, 225

Nociceptors, 225

Noncompliance
    and PPS interview, 59
    in PPS scorecard, 109

Noninvasive treatments, 13, 22, 113

Nonorganic signs, 226
    as medical risk factors, 46–49

Nonsteroidal anti-inflammatory (NSAID), 217

Nonverbal behavior, assertive, 177

North American Spine Society, 153

NSAID (nonsteroidal anti-inflammatory), 217

Physical reconditioning, 203–206
Physical therapist, 201
Physicians, communication with. *See* Communication with health care professionals
Physiological states, and self-efficacy, 138
PNI (psychoneuroimmunology), 118, 130, 226
Postdischarge instructions for spinal fusion patients, 135
Postoperative pain control, 182–189
Postsurgical preprogram, 209
Postsurgical rehabilitation. *See* Rehabilitation after spine surgery
PPS. *See* Presurgical psychological screening
PPS algorithm, 104–109
PPS interview, 75–76
    behavioral factors in, 61–62
    interpersonal, 67–70
    and litigation, 66–67
    vocational, 62–64
    workers' compensation, 64–66
    goals of, 58–59
    historical factors in, 71
    abuse and abandonment, 71–72
    substance abuse, 72–74
    techniques for, 59–61
Practice Guidelines for Acute Pain Management, 183
Preoperative education, 136–137
Preparation of patient for surgery, 7, 117, 131–132, 147–148, 189–190
    cognitive–behavioral interventions in, 137, 150, 169
    and assessing of beliefs and fears, 150, 151
    cognitive restructuring, 155–163
    deep relaxation training, 163–167
    fostering informed patients, 150–155, 169
    hypnosis, 167–169
    compliance and motivation measures in, 110
    conceptual models of, 134–136, 148
    biopsychosocial model, 146–147, 150
    cognitive–behavioral model, 137 (*see also* Cognitive–behavioral interventions or approach)
    individual and social self-regulation, 139–146
    informative preparations, 136
    preoperative education, 136–137

    self-efficacy and empowerment, 137–139
    in overall surgery process, 222
    programs for, 149–150
    improving communication with health care professionals, 172–178
    nurturing patients' spirituality, 180–182
    for postoperative pain control, 182–189
    strengthening patients' psychosocial environments, 179–180
    and trend toward outpatient surgery, 132–134
    and two phases of recovery process, 118
Preprogram, postsurgical, 209
Presurgical psychological screening (PPS), 7, 36–37
    and compliance or motivation measures, 109–111
    evaluation of destructiveness in, 46
    formulations of recommendations, 40
    and hysteria or hypochondriasis, 83
    identifying appropriate candidates for, 33–34
    information gathering for, 37–38
    in overall surgery process, 222
    for pain-sensitive patients, 94
    in preparation of patient for surgery, 190
    psychometric testing in, 78–79, 98 (*see also* Psychometric testing)
    rationale for, 29–32
    recommendations from
        to patient, 111–113
        to surgeon, 111, 112
    referring patients for, 34–36
    scorecard approach to, 38–40, 102–104
    and PPS algorithm, 104–109
    and surgry preparation, 150
Presurgical Psychological Screening Summary Form, 112
Previous surgeries, as medical risk factor, 51–52
Priorities, and patient's spirituality, 181
Prior medical utilization, as medical risk factor, 52–53
Prior psychological problems, and PPS interview, 74–75
Problem-focused coping, 140–141
Problem representation, 140
Procedural information, 136
Pseudoaddiction, 189
Pseudoarthrosis, 25, 226
    and failed back surgery syndrome, 17

in smokers, 55
and surgical results, 52
Pseudotolerance, 188
Psychological assessment, of spine surgery
candidates, 6
Psychological dependence, definition of, 73–74
Psychological examination, 57–58
Psychological preparation for surgery. *See*
Preparation of patient for surgery
Psychological problems, prior (and PPS interview), 74–75
Psychological testing, in PPS, 38
Psychometric testing, 78–79, 98
and anger, 87–89
and anxiety, 89–91
and coping strategies, 94–98
Dallas Pain Questionnaire, 80
and depression, 84–87
and insurers, 98–99
MMPI-2, 79–80 (*see also* Minnesota
Multiphasic Personality Inventory—2)
and multiple MMPI scale elevations,
93–94
Oswestry Disability Index, 80, 87, 103
and pain sensitivity, 80, 82–84
and personality disorders, 91–93
and PPS, 78–79, 98
on PPS scorecard, 104
Psychoneuroimmunology (PNI), 118, 130,
226
Psychosocial factors
and chronic pain, 6
and failure of spine surgery, 31–32
in pain reduction, 101
as risk factors, 105–107
in PPS scorecard, 102
and surgical outcome, 104, 105, 109,
114
vocational, 63, 64
Psychosocial interventions
improving communication with health
care professionals, 172–178
nurturing patients' spirituality, 180–182
for postoperative pain control, 182–189
strengthening patients' psychosocial
environments, 179–180
Psychosocial problems
from pain after surgery, 196–198
surgeon's ability to identify, 32
Public education, 26

Purpose, and patient's spirituality, 181

Questions asked about surgery, 153, 154, 173

Radiographs, plain, 18
Rand Health Insurance study, 85
Ransford Pain Drawing, 48, 49–51
Reconditioning process, 203–206
Recovery from spine surgery, 207
Recovery time, 201–202
Rehabilitation after spine surgery, 193–194
barriers to recovery in, 208, 209, 211
expected recovery time in, 201–202
functional restoration approach to, 207–213
intensive program of, 198–200
interdisciplinary team for, 200–201
mental deconditioning, 196–198
in overall surgery process, 222
pain during, 207, 215–216
and intensity of rehabilitation, 193–194
in reconditioning, 205
and pain medication, 216–218
and patients' expectations, 213–215
for patients who fail to progress, 202–203
and physical deconditioning, 194–196,
198
reconditioning process, 203–206
reimbursement issues in, 221, 222
termination of, 219–221
Reimbursement issues, for psychologists in
rehabilitation programs, 221, 222
Relapse-prevention model, 212
Relaxation, cue-controlled, 166
Relaxation response, 163–164
Relaxation training, 137, 163–167
as coping strategy, 97
Religion. *See* Spirituality of patient, nurturing of
Replacement, disc, 24–25
Road rage, 88
Role-focused social self-regulation, 144

Sacroiliac joint, 226
Sacroiliac joint injections, 22
Schizoid personality disorder, 91
Schizotypal personality disorder, 91
SCL-90, 98
Scoliosis, and plain radiographs, 18
Scorecard approach, to PPS, 38–40, 102–104
and PPS algorithm, 104–109

on PPS scorecard, 106
Staff splitting, in PPS scorecard, 109
State-Trait Anxiety Inventory (STAI), 90
Stauffer and Coventry criteria, 227
Stenosis, 14, 227
Stimulation, spinal cord, 25, 52, 217–218, 226
Stress
    and coping, 95
    financial, 65
    and low back pain, 63
    physical effects of, 90
    and relaxation response, 163
    and surgery, 127
    and wound healing, 123, 124–125
Structured Clinical Interview for DSM-III-R, 91
Subjective problem representation, 140
Substance abuse
    and PPS interview, 72–74
    on PPS scorecard, 106
    as surgical risk factor, 58
Support group, chronic pain, 113
Support person, 143–146, 179
Suppressor T-cells, 121
Surgeon-patient communication
    at referral, 35–36
    See also Communication with health care professionals
Surgery, 117–118
    change in meaning of pain after, 194
    outpatient, 132–134
Surgery experience, 117
    phases of, 141–143
Surgery patients
    information for, 150–155
    questions asked by, 153, 154
    spirituality of, 180–182
    worries of, 151
Surgery preparation. See Preparation of patient for surgery
Surgical failure
    and measures of psychosocial distress, 39–40
    See also Failed back surgery syndrome
Surgical intervention. See Spine surgery; Surgery
Surgical technology, and outpatient care, 133
Symptomatic pseudoarthrosis
    and failed back surgery syndrome, 17
    See also Pseudoarthrosis
Symptom magnification, 227

patient's overstatement, 5

Tangible assistance, 144
Task-focused social self-regulation, 144
T-cells, 120–121
TENS (transcutaneous electrical nerve stimulation), 187
    vs. spinal cord stimulation, 25
Termination, of rehabilitation treatment, 219–221
Testing in PPS, 38
Texas Back Institute, 23
Therapeutic alliance, 38
Thoughts and feelings diary, 156
Threatening behavior, in PPS scorecard, 109
Time-contingent scheduling, of pain medication, 185–186
Tolerance, of narcotics, 188, 189
Transcutaneous electrical nerve stimulation (TENS), 187
    vs. spinal cord stimulation, 25
Treatment of patients with back pain, 26
    and anger, 89
    noninvasive, 13, 22, 113
Tunnel vision, 156
Type of surgery, as medical risk factor, 45–46

Vanderbilt Pain Management Inventory, 96
Verbal persuasion, self-efficacy from, 138
Vertebra, 227
Vicarious experience, self-efficacy from, 138
Vocational factors
    and PPS interview, 62–64
    See also Work

Waddell signs, 47–49, 226
    and pain drawings, 51
Ways of Coping Checklist, 95–96
Web sites
    on pain control issues, 182
        of American Pain Foundation, 183
    spine surgery information on, 153, 155
West Coast Spine Restoration Center (WCSRC), 208–209, 210
Wiltse, Leon, 6
Work
    and acceptance of limitations, 218–219
    and surgery preparation, 179–180
    See also Employers; Vocational factors
Workers' compensation
    back-pain filings for, 4

and passive-aggressive type, 92
and PPS interview, 64–66
on PPS scorecard, 106
Worksheet for patient outcome projections,
    213–214
Wound healing, 123
    and age, 129–130
    anxiety and stress as slowing, 90
    and immune system, 123–124
    and neuroendocrine system, 123–124

and physical deconditioning syndrome,
    129
and preoperative alcohol abuse, 127
and smoking, 127–129
and stress, 123, 124–125
See also Spine surgery outcome

Zung Depression Inventory, 32, 34, 85
    and DRAM, 224

ABOUT THE AUTHORS

Andrew R. Block received his PhD from Dartmouth College and was a National Institutes of Health postdoctoral fellow in neurobehavioral sciences at Duke University Medical Center. He is the founder and director of The WellBeing Group, specializing in the evaluation and treatment of patients with spinal pain. He has served as director of psychological services for the Indiana Center for Rehabilitation Medicine and director of behavioral medicine at the Texas Back Institute. He also served as an assistant professor of psychology at Purdue University. Dr. Block has written numerous books and peer-reviewed articles. He is the author of *Presurgical Psychological Screening in Chronic Pain Syndromes* and the editor-in-chief of *Handbook of Pain Syndromes*. He is also currently a clinical assistant professor of psychiatry at Southwestern Medical Center and an adjunct associate professor of psychology at the University of Texas at Dallas. He also serves on the Conservative Care Committee of the North American Spine Society.

Robert J. Gatchel received his PhD from the University of Wisconsin. His initial interest in the area of spinal pain disorders began with the development of a close collaboration between his institution (the University of Texas Southwestern Medical Center at Dallas) and the Productive Rehabilitation Institute of Dallas for Ergonomics (PRIDE). At PRIDE, he helped develop a successful functional restoration treatment program for dealing with back pain disability problems. He received the Volvo Award on low back pain research in 1986. He is currently the director of the research council for the North American Spine Society (NASS) and was the first psychologist to be awarded NASS's Henry Farfan Award for his outstanding contribution to the field of spine care. He has authored and edited a number of academic and clinical texts, including *Psychosocial Factors in Pain* (with Dennis Turk) and *Personality Characteristics of Patients with Pain* (with James Weisberg). He has

287

served as program director at the Eugene McDermott Center for Pain Management at the University of Texas Southwestern Medical Center at Dallas, where he is also the Elizabeth H. Penn Professor of Clinical Psychology and a professor in the departments of psychiatry and rehabilitation counseling.

William W. Deardorff received his PhD in clinical psychology from Washington State University, did an internship at the University of Washington Medical School, and then completed a postdoctoral fellowship in behavioral medicine at Kaiser Permanente Medical Center in Los Angeles. Dr. Deardorff is a fellow of the American Psychological Association in two divisions, founding president of the American Academy of Clinical Health Psychology, and assistant clinical professor at the UCLA School of Medicine. Dr. Deardorff has many peer-reviewed research publications and is the co-author of six previous books, including *Back Pain Remedies for Dummies*, *Preparing for Surgery*, and *Win the Battle Against Back Pain*. *Preparing for Surgery* was the winner of the Small Press Book Award in Health in 1998. Dr. Deardorff is in a multidisciplinary practice in Beverly Hills specializing in the treatment of spinal conditions.

Richard D. Guyer is a board certified orthopedic spine surgeon. He received his MD and completed his orthopedic residency at the University of Pennsylvania School of Medicine. He then completed two spine fellowships, under the supervision of Henry Bohlman, MD, and Leon Wiltse, MD. He practices at the Texas Back Institute in Plano, TX. He is the founder and chairman of the board of the Texas Back Institute Research Foundation. He is an associate clinical professor of orthopedics at the University of Texas Southwestern Medical Center. An editorial board member of several professional journals, Dr. Guyer is the author of numerous peer-reviewed articles and an editor of two books, *Lumbar Disc Disease* and *Rehabilitation of the Spine*. In 1996 he received the Volvo Award for basic research in low back pain.